POSTCARD HISTORY SERIES

Wappinger

On the Front Cover: Annual Parade. This view shows the Johnson Fire Company during the annual Firemen's Parade on Main Street in the village around 1908. (Author's collection.)

On the Back Cover: New Hamburgh Railroad Station. Located in the heart of New Hamburgh, the railroad station became the lifeblood to the small hamlet and the town of Wappinger. (Author's collection.)

POSTCARD HISTORY SERIES

Wappinger

David Turner

ARCADIA
PUBLISHING

ISBN 978-0-7385-7559-9

Published by Arcadia Publishing
Charleston, South Carolina

Printed in the United States of America

Library of Congress Control Number: 2010943013

For all general information contact Arcadia Publishing at:
Telephone 843-853-2070
Fax 843-853-0044
E-mail sales@arcadiapublishing.com
For customer service and orders:
Toll-Free 1-888-313-2665

Visit us on the Internet at www.arcadiapublishing.com

I would like to dedicate this book to my mother, Susanne Laszlo Turner and my father, M. Thomas Turner, for the continued love and support.

Contents

ACKNOWLEDGMENTS

This book would not be possible without the help of the Wappingers Historical Society. I would like to thank all those who have inspired me to write this book within the organization and those that have given me insight into the town's history. I would also like to thank Sandra Vacchio, president of the historical society, for allowing me access to their archives and her continued support.

A special thanks to Lawson and Barbara Edgar who have so generously allowed me to intrude on their lives to learn more about the hamlet of New Hamburgh. Barbara's photographic collection and Lawson's vast knowledge of the hamlet's history was an invaluable asset! Thank you again.

I would also like to thank Timothy Holls, Ed Hogan, Ted and Jen Turner, Christina Gugliada, and George Lucas for their contributions to the book through the photographs they supplied and Judge Vincent Francese, Mary Shmaltz, Steve Q. Marshall, and Beth Divine for their insight into the history of the town.

Thank you also to Rachel DiGrazia and her husband for their hours of work trying to scan glass slides. Their help made the factory chapter possible. Thank you to Artcraft Photography in the Poughkeepsie Plaza for their work with my antique glass slides.

Finally, a special thank you to Edgar A. Popper (1895–1980) for writing the book *The Birth and Growth of an Old Village—Wappingers Falls NY 1707–1977,* which proved vital for the creation of this book. Thank you to Timothy Holls who created the index for that book, which saved me hours of searching. Lastly, I would like to thank all those who have worked so hard in the past to preserve the history of town, including Janice Hildebrand, former president of the historical society, and Frances S. Reese (1917–2003), a local resident who still inspires us all to continue working towards the preservation of our history and environment.

All unaccredited photographs are from the author's personal photograph collection. All other photographs have been credited to their respective owner.

Introduction

The town of Wappinger has always been a place of opportunity. Its waterways were stocked with fish for the early natives, while its flat fertile land to the east proved perfect for farming. Early European settlers saw the deep waters of the Hudson River and the gentle slopes along its shore as an optimal place for docks to access the resource rich interior. The biggest opportunity for these early pioneers was the Wappingers Falls, a 75-foot waterfall that would power the town's factories.

The earliest inhabitants of the region were the Wappani people, a Native American tribe that lived along the eastern portion of the Hudson River. Small fishing communities consisting of one or two families lined the river for hundreds of years before any European explorer would set foot in the area. The land that they controlled stretched from Manhattan Island north to Albany, consisting of old growth forests, fertile farmland, and fully stocked streams and rivers. Although, Henry Hudson would later speak of a demonic ritual he witnessed on Danskammer Point, the Wappani were known as a peaceful tribe.

In 1683, Guilian Verplank purchased 85,000 acres from the Wappani called the Rombout Patent. In the area just south of New Hamburgh, he would construct a large wharf for his flour mill in Fishkill Plains. The Brewer brothers, who would construct their homes and mill along the Wappingers Falls in the mid-1700s, followed Verplank. After the death of the Brewers, Peter Mesier purchased their old homestead and mill in 1777 and established the first store in Wappinger on the corner of East Main and Market Streets.

By the mid-1800s, Wappinger had changed into an industrial center with one of its most prominent residents, Henry Clapp. He constructed two large factories along the falls called the Clinton Mill and the Franklindale Mill. As the area grew in population, the town of Wappinger was split from the town of Fishkill in 1875. Although the youngest and smallest town in Dutchess County, Wappinger's large factories along the creek made it one of the most populous in the region.

Wappinger focuses on the birth and growth of this new town. The earliest photographs are of the village of Wappingers Falls, which was established in 1871. Incorporated from a number of small hamlets along the Wappingers Creek, the village would grow dramatically during the turn of the 20th century. The interior of the town was mostly agricultural with the small hamlets of New Hackensack, Diddell, Swartoutville, Myers Corners, and Red Oaks supplying much of the produce being sent south to New York City from the docks at Chelsea and New Hamburgh.

The first chapter will focus on the early inhabitants of the town. Since most of the Wappani tribe would leave the area by the mid-1800s, the chapter will many focus on the first Europeans to settle in the area. The second chapter shows the small farming communities along the easternmost border of the town called New Hackensack, Red Oaks, and Swartoutville. The flatland of New

Hackensack and the rolling hills farther south proved to be fertile enough to sustain large farms that would dominate the landscape until the 1960s. Most of what was New Hackensack is now the Dutchess County Airport, which would prove to be the downfall of the once quaint hamlet. The third chapter focuses on the small riverfront hamlet of Chelsea-on-Hudson. First called Low Point and Carthage Landing, the hamlet was once an important dock for farmers in the interior of the county.

The third and fourth chapters depict the hamlets of Hughsonville and New Hamburgh. Hughsonville, a small crossroads between the village of Wappingers Falls and the city of Beacon, is lined by many small colonial homes. The community's main industry was the Faulkner Mill near Middlebush Road. About a mile west of Hughsonville is the hamlet of New Hamburgh. One of the earliest settled areas along the Hudson River, New Hamburgh has long been a transportation hub. Although in the town of Poughkeepsie, New Hamburgh was vital to the nearby village of Wappingers Falls, which had no railroad or river access of its own. By the early 1800s, Verplank's wharf was replaced by two larger docks, one of which was next to the large lime quarry near Division Street. In the 1850s, the railroad reached the hamlet from New York City, allowing local residents to send their goods to the booming population centers to the south. As the river traffic slowed, New Hamburgh became a bedroom community, almost unknown to those living outside of it.

The fifth chapter focuses on the factories that once dominated the village of Wappingers Falls. From the stone factories on Mill and Market Streets to the large Dutchess Print Works on Lower Creek, Wappingers Falls owes most of its growth and prosperity to these early industries. One of its most famous factories was the Sweet Orr & Company that sold denim jeans across the country and remained successful into the 1970s.

The last two chapters show the village of Wappingers Falls during its heyday from 1860 to 1930. The east side of Wappingers Creek, first known as Franklindale, was where many of the earliest settlers constructed their homes. Main, Market and Mill Streets became the industrial and commercial center for the village. The top of the hill on East Main Street is where many of the village's most prominent homes were constructed alongside the village's Protestant Churches. Factory homes were constructed along Spring Street and the area between South Avenue and Market Street, just south of the village center. Also incorporated into the village was the west side of the creek known as Ednamville and Channingville. Here, predominantly Irish factory workers settled along West Main Street and its many side streets near the large brick St Mary's Catholic Church.

One

Early Settlement
Colonial Life

For thousands of years before any European would settle in the area, the land along the east side of the Hudson River was inhabited by the Wappani tribe, a division of the Mohican people. When Henry Hudson first sailed up the river that bears his name, he described a group of natives dancing around a bonfire on Danskammer Point across from New Hamburgh in what he called a satanic display. The Wappani were actually a peaceful people. In 1683, the land was granted for settlement under the Rombout Patent, where the Wappani were given a small consideration for their land.

Most of the early settlers were of Dutch origin with names like Mesier, Verplank, Brewer, Von Vorhiss, and Van Alden. Small Dutch houses still dot the landscape in the region from these early pioneers. Two miles up the Wappingers Creek from the river is a 75-foot waterfall that would house the first mill in the town, run by the Brewer brothers and later Peter Mesier. Along the river, New Hamburgh was established as an important river dock for flour and crops grown in the interior hamlets of New Hackensack, Diddell, and Fishkill Plains.

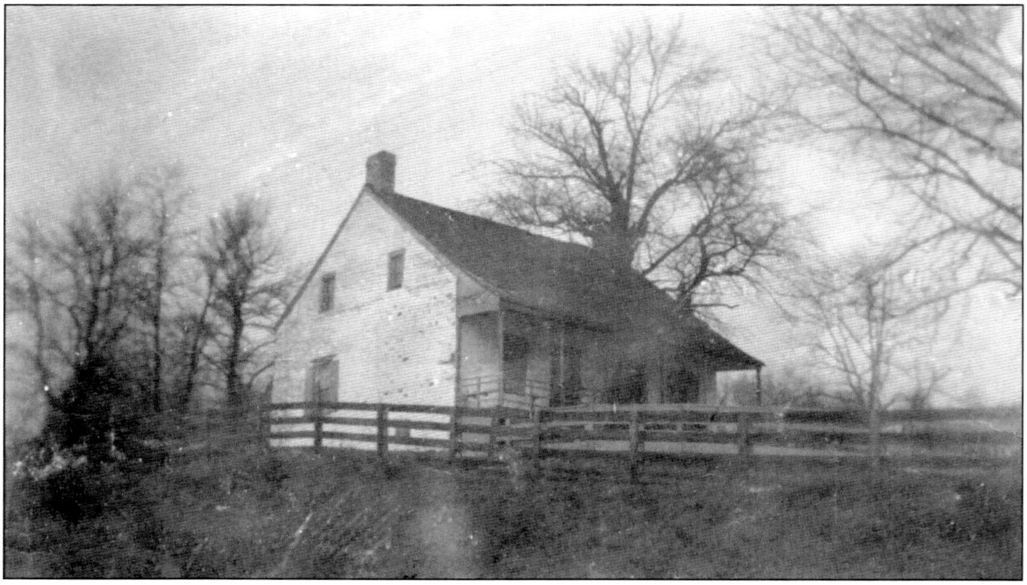

Farmers Landing, 1902. Once part of a larger wharf with several buildings, this small Dutch house is the last relic of Farmers Landing located just south of New Hamburgh. Owned by the Verplank family during the late 1700s, the wharf was used to ship flour produced at their Sprout Creek mill in Fishkill Plains. This small stone house was occupied by the wharf foreman who managed Verplank's shipments down to New York City. (Courtesy of Lawson Edgar.)

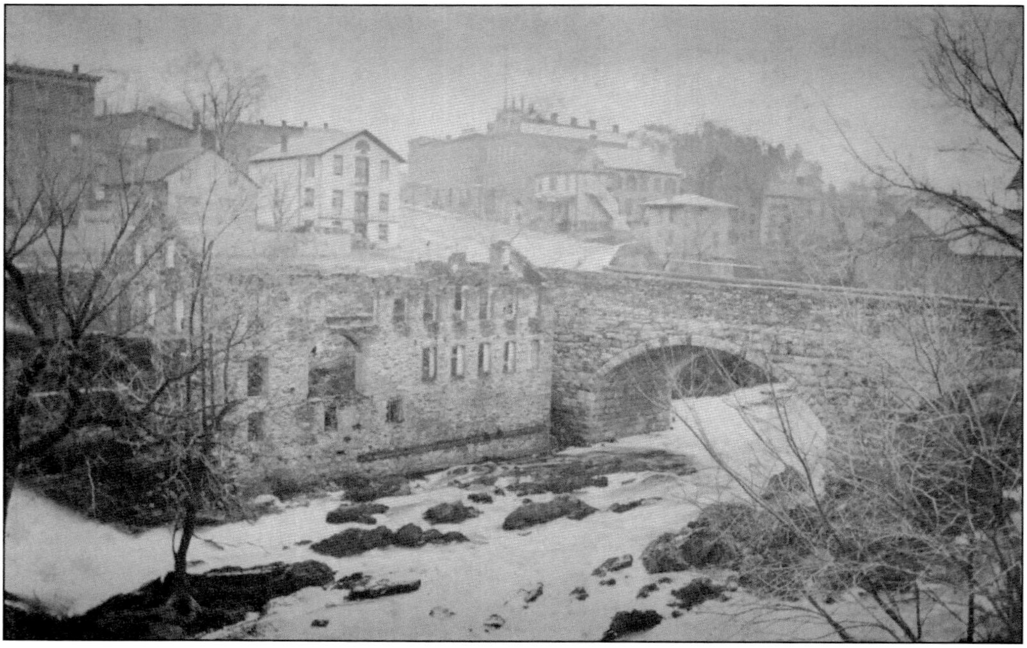

Colonial Buildings along the Creek, 1862. This early photograph shows many of the original buildings in the hamlet. In the foreground are the ruins of the Clinton Mill and the original stone bridge before it was widened. Behind the ruins are the Brewer Homestead and the Manning Building. Across the street one can see the two-story Brewer House built in the 1780s, whose second story was occupied by the original Grinnell Library. (Courtesy of the Wappingers Historical Society.)

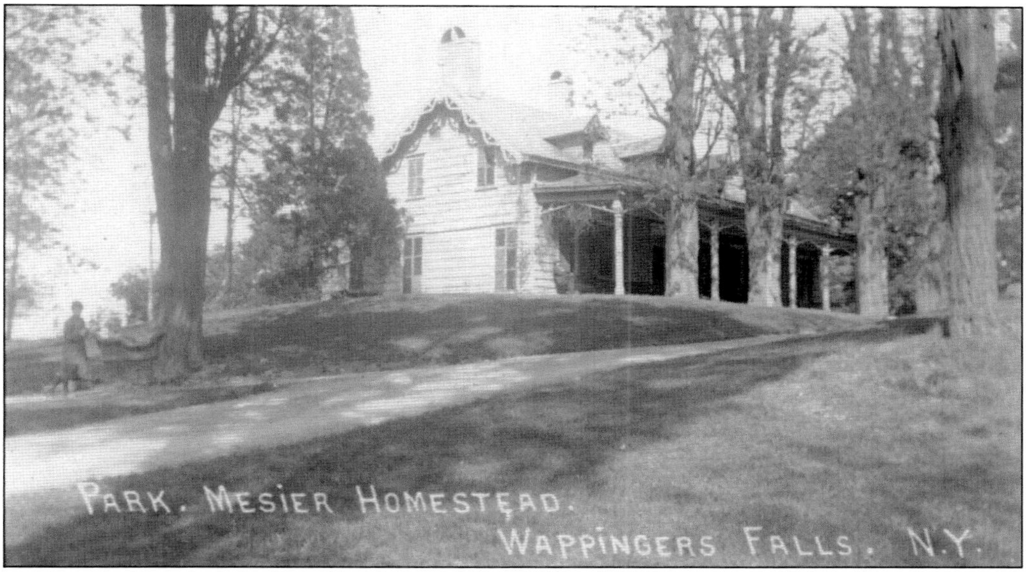

MESIER HOMESTEAD, C. 1906. Peter Mesier moved to Wappingers Falls to escape the crowds of New York City in the 1770s. Operating a small store out of his home, his peace was soon broken in May 1777. Mesier, a loyalist, had angered local residents for charging the English Crown's tax on tea. When he refused to lower the price, a large crowd gathered outside the homestead. The mob soon overtook Mesier, beating him and raiding both the store and cellar. (Courtesy of the Wappingers Historical Society.)

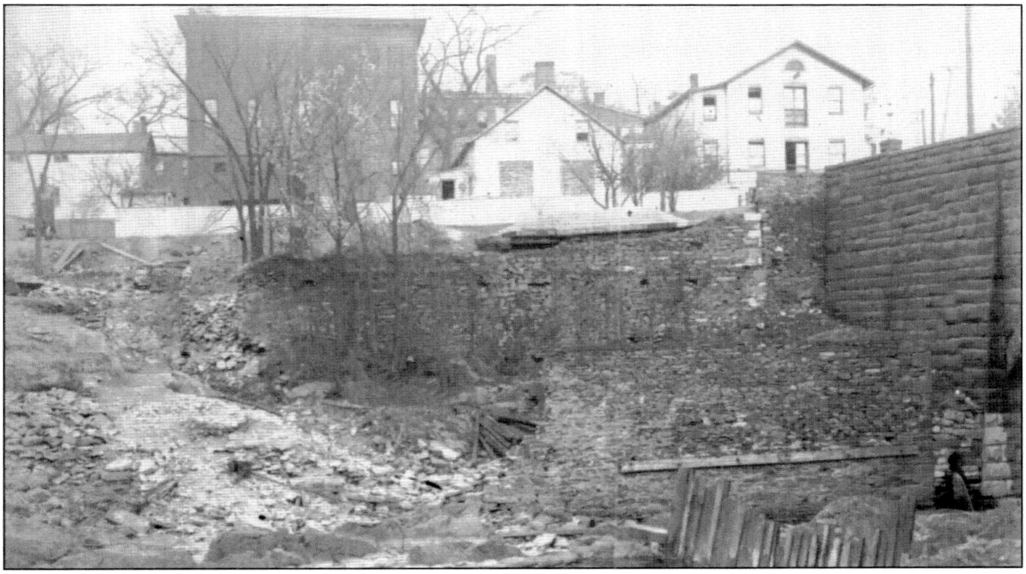

BREWER HOMESTEAD, C. 1908. Also built in the late 1700s, the Brewer Homestead was constructed in the same Dutch colonial style as other period homes in the area. Owned by Aldolphus Brewer, he lived in the small house until his death from a lightning strike in 1742. Seen here from the creek, the home was pinned in between the Garner Print Works building to the left and the Manning Building on the right. Over the decades, the small residential house was closed in by Wappingers Business district. In 1953, the Marine Midland Bank purchased the house to be demolished for the bank's expansion and a parking lot. (Courtesy of the Wappingers Historical Society.)

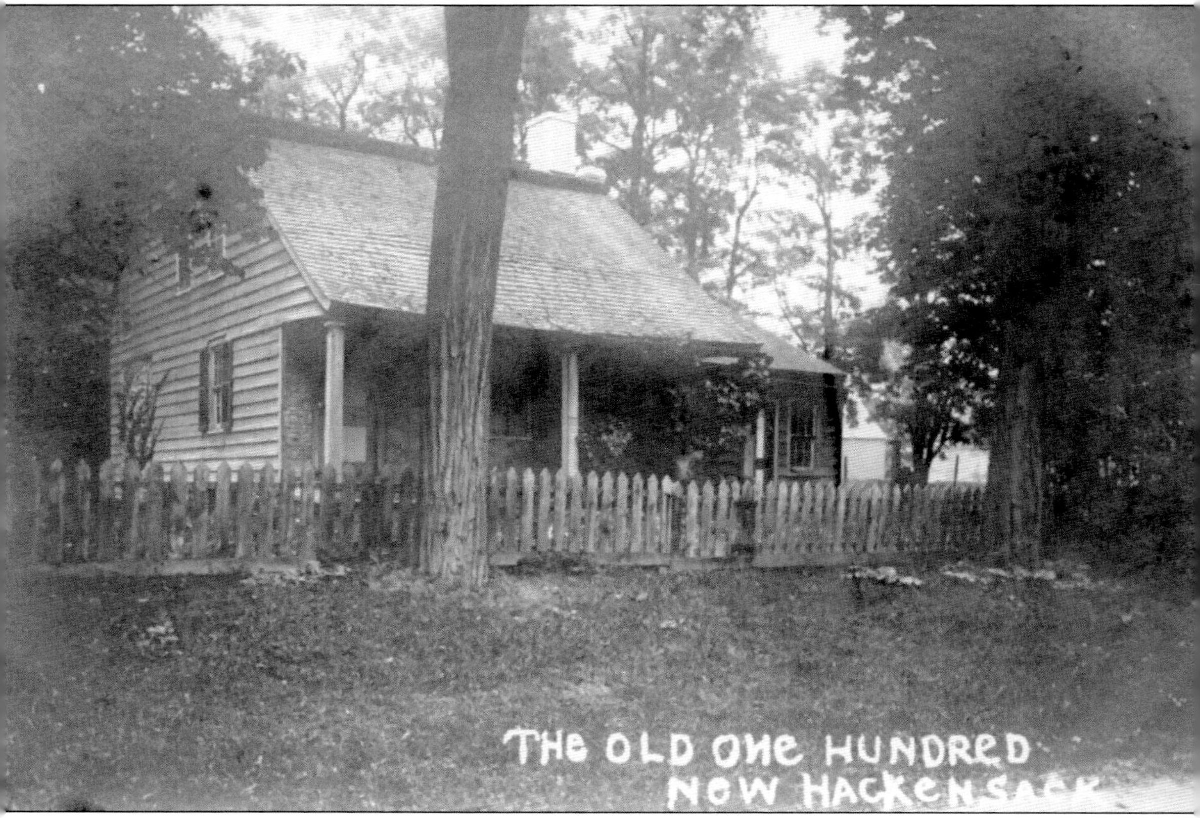

The Old One Hundred, c. 1909. Built in New Hackensack in 1754, the Old One Hundred was one of the first structures constructed in the town of Wappinger. Sitting on a curve on Route 376, the Dutch home once sat on a large tract of land that covered much of the hamlet. By the time this photograph was taken, the property had shrunk to about 100 acres, which gave it its nickname. Today, the house is one of the last in Dutchess County to retain its original features, including a gabled roof, a Dutch door, and a double chimney.

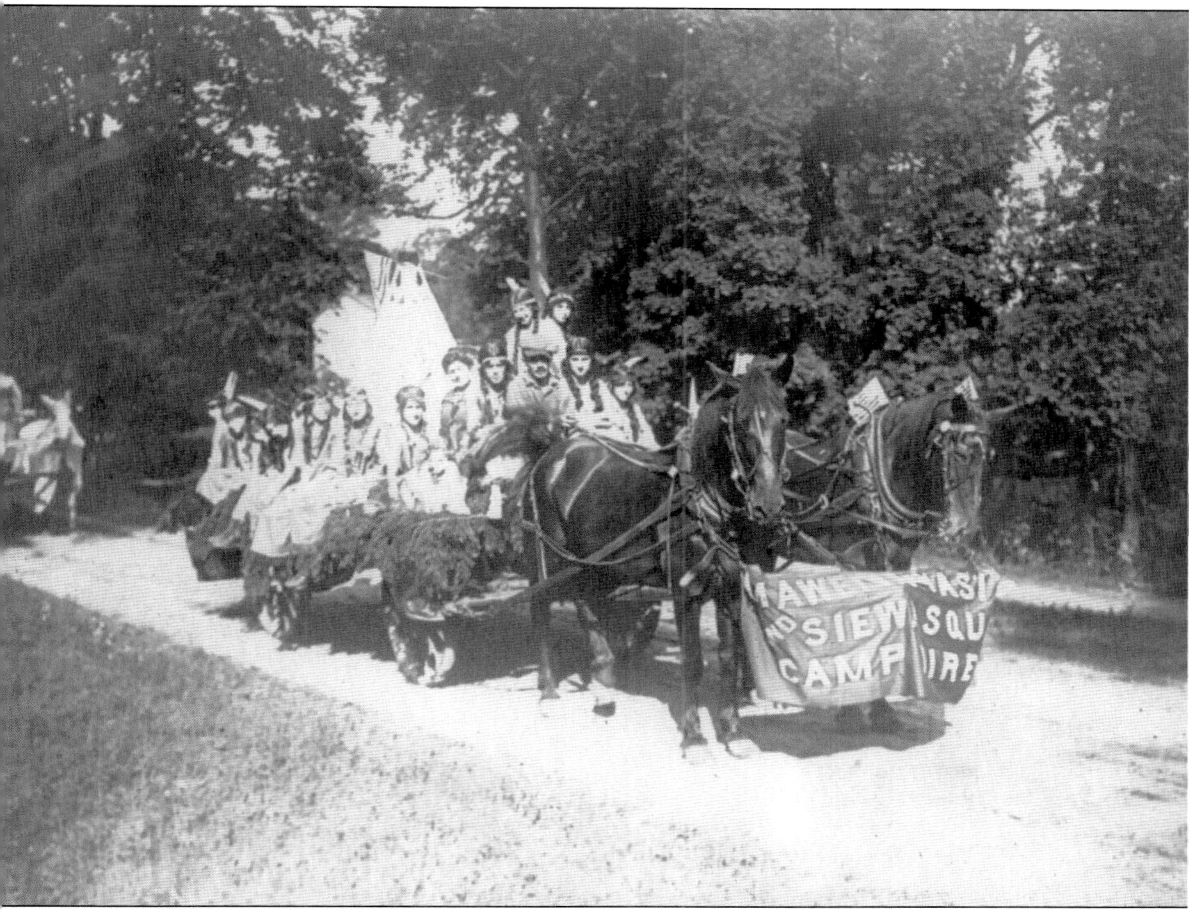

Campfire Girls, c. 1908. During the 1909 Firemen's Parade, the Wappinger branch of the Campfire Girls dressed in Native American costumes for their float. The town of Wappinger has a long history of Native American settlement that spans thousands of years. Most of the Wappani tribe was located on the banks of the Hudson River with the Wappingers Creek being a major route into the interior. The Wappani people would leave the area by the early 1800s, settling in Connecticut; Shekomeko, New York; and Wyoming. (Courtesy of the Wappingers Historical Society.)

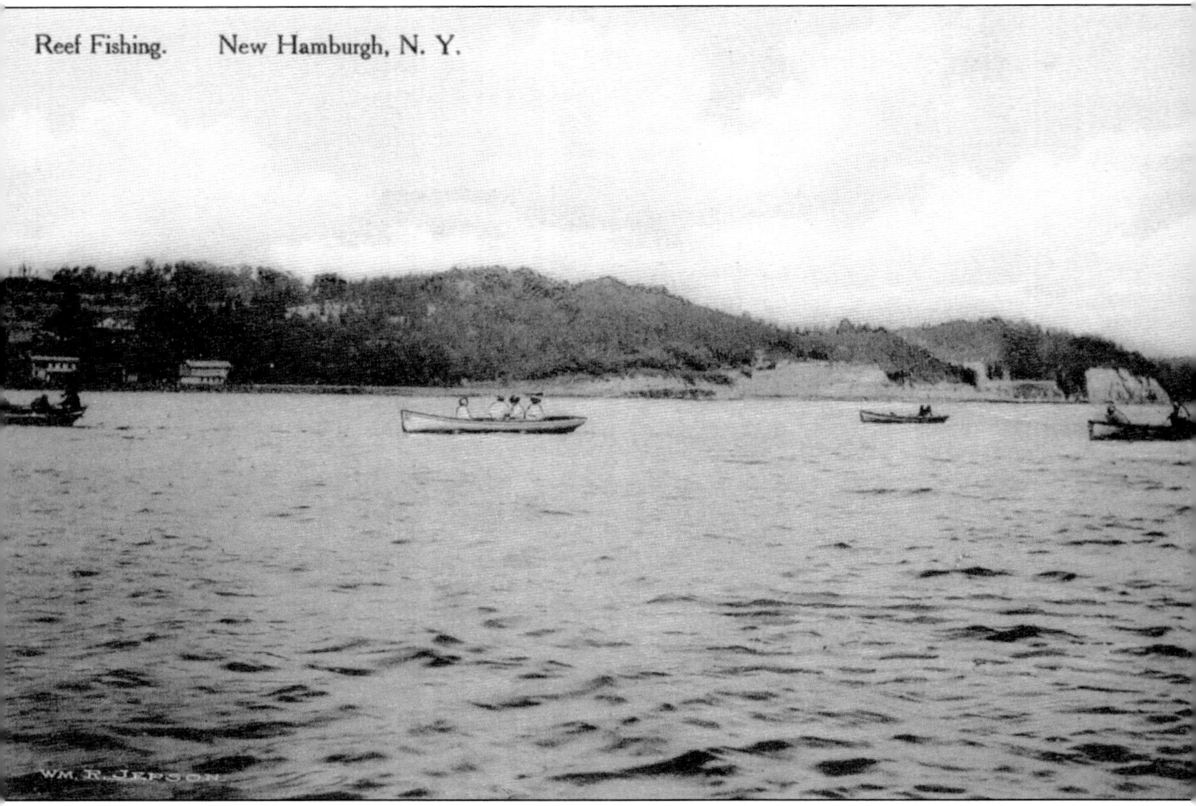

REEF FISHING, C. 1910. The Hudson River was the major food source for the native Wappani people. Early settlers would trade gun powder, lead, and brandy for canoes full of fish from these waters off New Hamburgh. During the spring months, American shad migrate up the river to spawn north of Albany. This large migration of fish enabled settlers to restock their food stores after the long winter. Local resident Lawson Edgar recalls the importance of fishing on the Hudson River during the Great Depression, where many had no other option to find food.

Two

New Hackensack and Red Oaks
The Rural Communities

The small hamlet of New Hackensack is one of Dutchess County's oldest communities. Named after Hackensack, New Jersey, and settled in the early 1700s, most of the early residents were of Dutch and German descent. Situated along the Wappingers Creek, the area was seen as ideal for its flat land and good soil. To the north of New Hackensack was the small community of Red Oaks Mill. The title came from a local nickname for the red oak trees that surrounded the flour and lumber mill operated by a Mr. Wodell.

At the turn of the 20th century, New Hackensack was a quiet farming community. The hamlet boasted a store, a schoolhouse, a small Dutch church, and a large hotel. During the 1930s, a small airfield was established in the flat land surrounding the hamlet to the west. Later named the Dutchess County Airport, it soon dominated the once rural landscape.

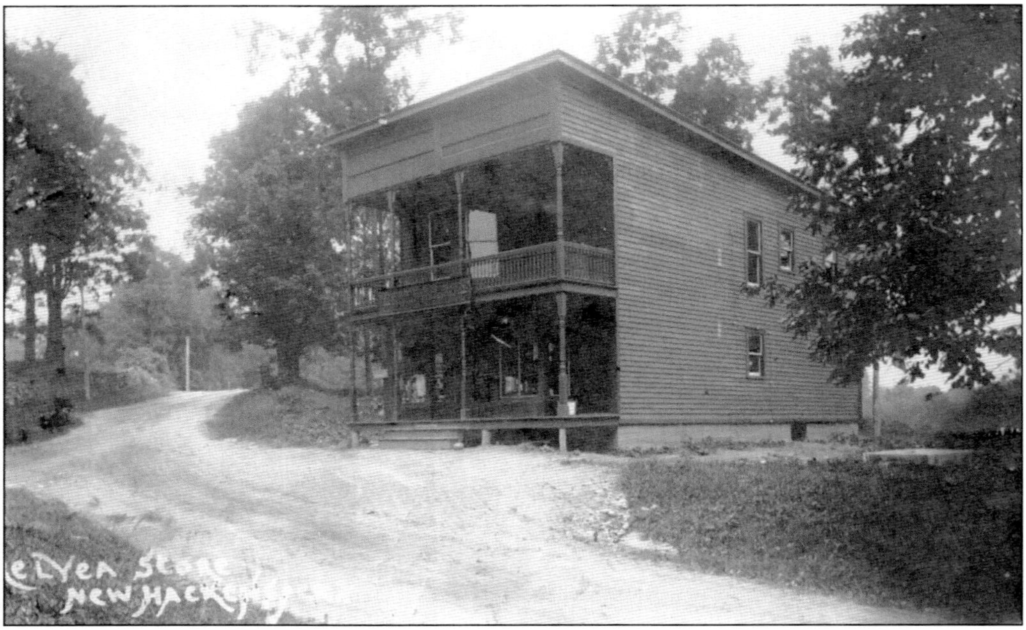

New Hackensack Store, 1910. Sitting at the intersection of four roads leading to Wappingers Falls, Fishkill Plains, Red Oaks Mill, and Swartoutville, the New Hackensack Store was in the center of the town of Wappinger. The store was opened in the mid-1800s by F.E. Hopkins, and it originally housed the community's post office. Today, the original building was removed and a modern structure now stands in its place along the busy intersection.

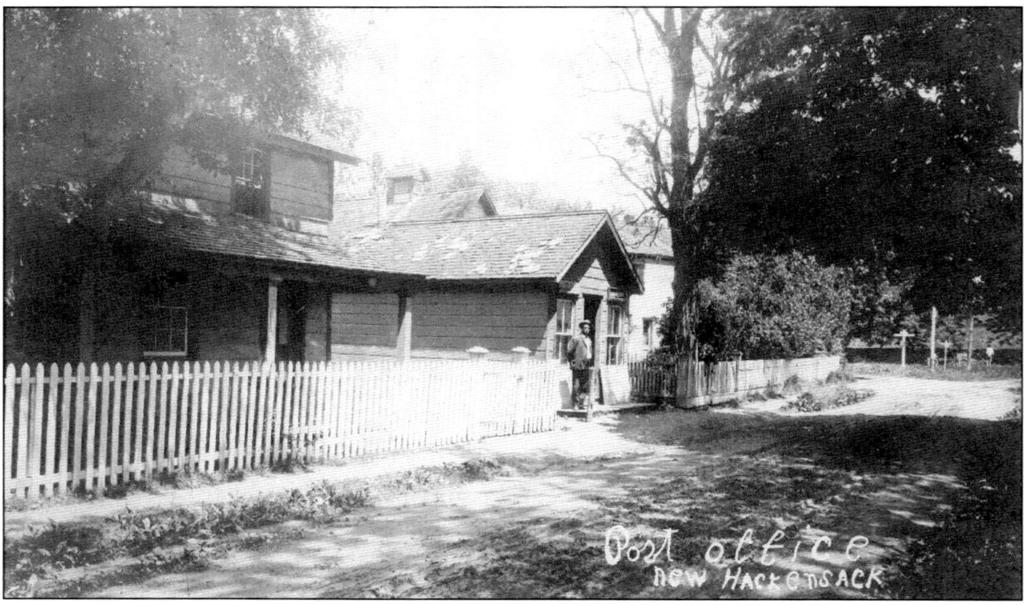

Post Office, 1910. As the small hamlet grew, the post office moved out of the New Hackensack Store and into this small building down the street. During most of the 1800s, mail was delivered by horse and wagon from the docks and railroad station at New Hamburgh. Standing on the porch here is the postmaster Edd, who lived with his wife, Sarah, in a small house attached to the back of the building. By the 1950s, the post office branch was closed and the entire block was torn down for the expansion of the Dutchess County Airport.

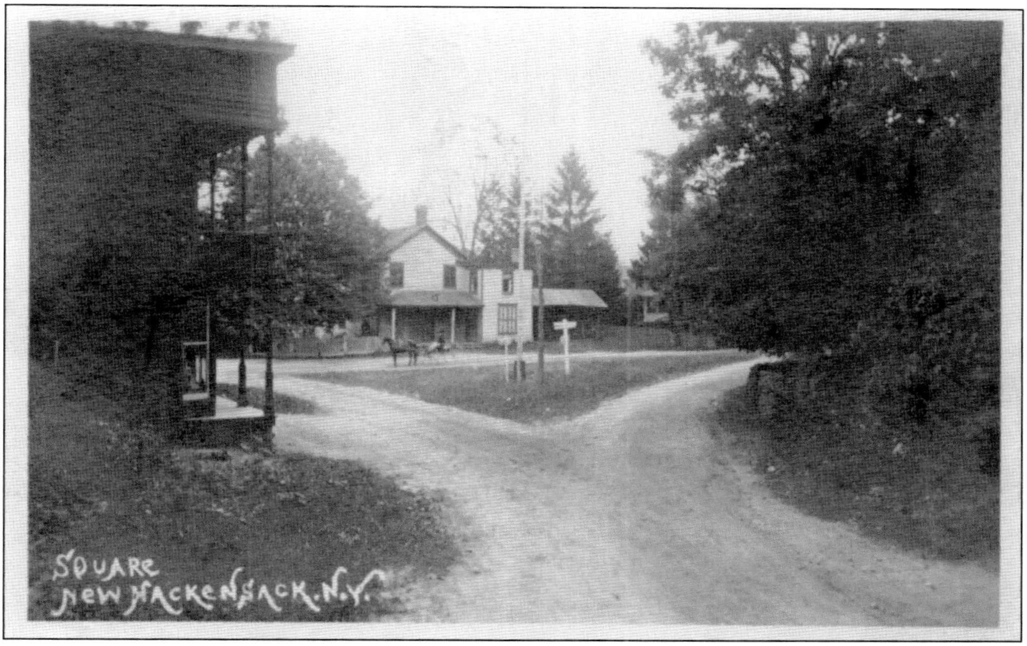

NEW HACKENSACK SQUARE, C. 1910. This view is looking down Route 376 with the old Relyea Store on the left. In the center of the photograph is the hamlet's blacksmith and carriage shop. The road off to the right goes north towards Red Oaks Mill and Poughkeepsie, while the road heading off to the left leads to the village of Wappingers Falls. (Courtesy of Timothy Holls.)

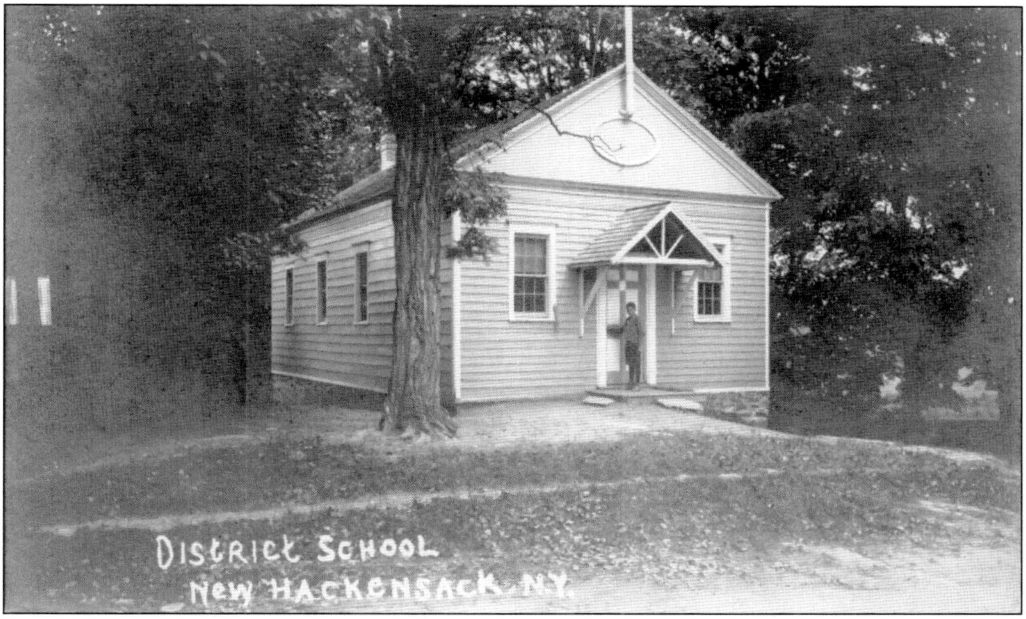

ONE ROOM SCHOOLHOUSE, 1911. A student stands at the door of one of the oldest schools in the town. Located just behind the New Hackensack Store, the building was constructed from stone and timber that was cleared from the nearby fields. Children walked each day to class, even during cold winter mornings, where a small wood-burning stove in the rear of the building was the only comfort. In the late 1930s, the school was closed and children were then bused to more centralized schools in the village of Wappingers Falls.

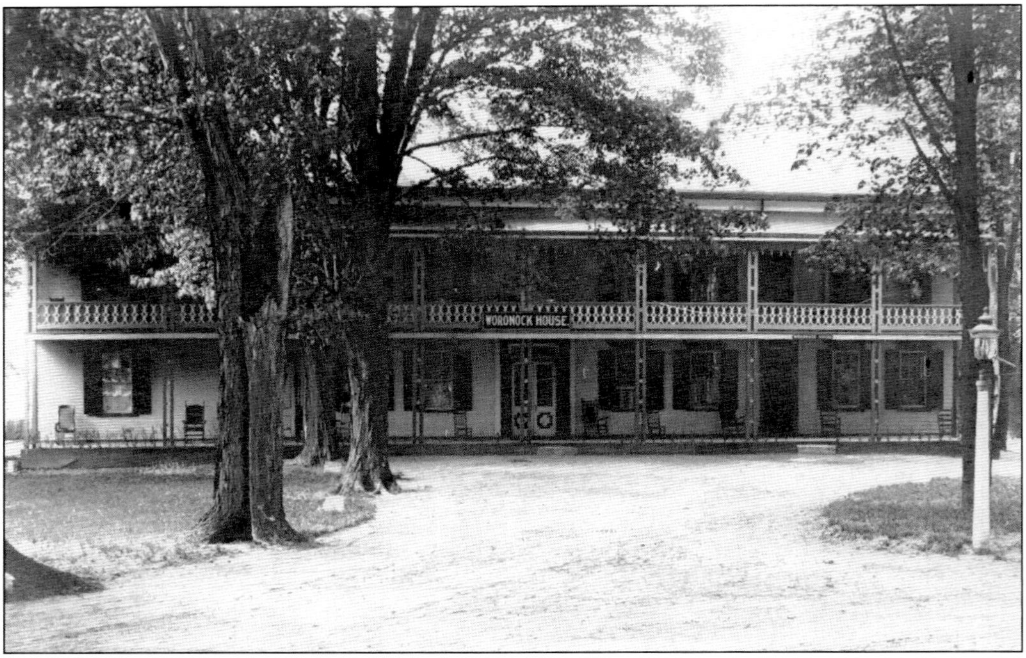

THE WARNOCK HOUSE, 1910. Built in the early 1800s, the Warnock House was a popular stopping point for travelers heading north into Poughkeepsie. The hotel also operated as a boardinghouse for men who worked seasonally in the fields that once surrounded the hotel. To give some relief during the hot summer months, the hotel had both a downstairs porch and upstairs veranda.

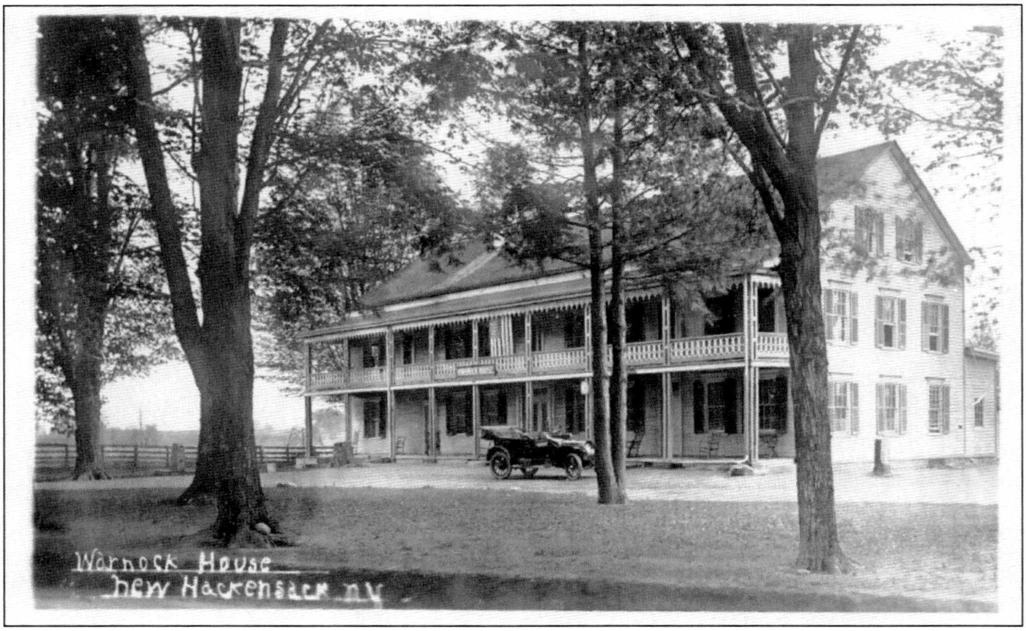

WARNOCK HOUSE'S NORTHERN VIEW, 1921. By the 1920s, the small-town hotel was reaching the end of an era. The main reason for this change is in the center of this photograph. By the 1930s, automobiles moved traffic away from these country roads to Albany Post Road in the village and later Route 9 and the Taconic Parkway. The building, now with its porches enclosed, and a few of the trees in this photograph still stand along Route 376 just east of the airport.

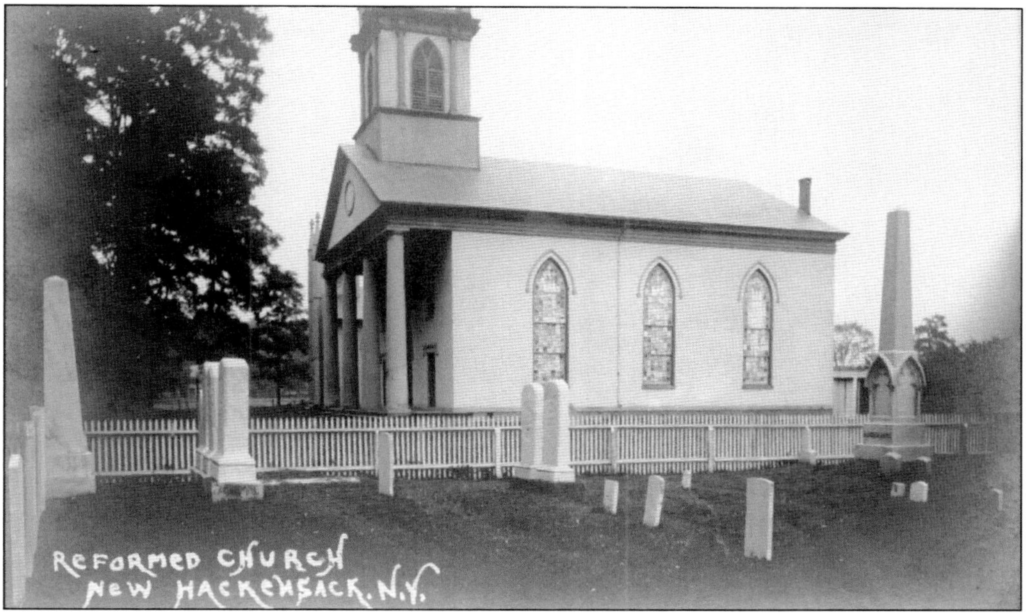

DUTCH CHURCH AND CEMETERY, 1910. The Dutch Church in New Hackensack was organized in 1758. The first church building was constructed in 1766 and was later replaced in 1834 by this structure. The first pastor, Rev. Isaac Rysdyck, also ministered the Dutch churches in Poughkeepsie, Fishkill, and Hopewell. After over 30 years at the church, Isaac's son Dominie Rysdyck took over as pastor. He is now buried in the small cemetery shown in the foreground. In the mid-1900s, the church was destroyed by a fire and never rebuilt.

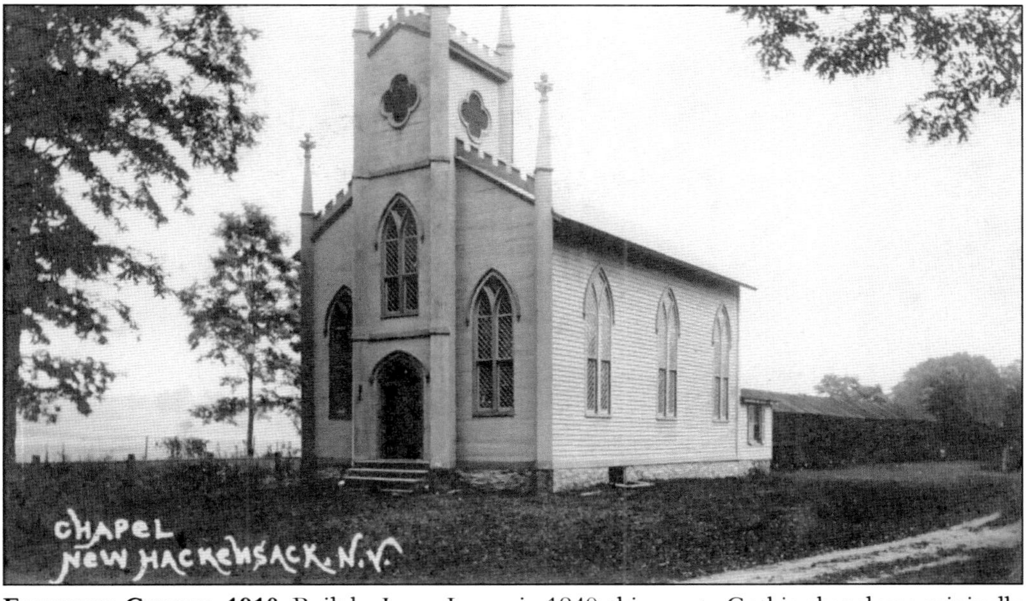

ELLESSDIE CHAPEL, 1910. Built by James Lenox in 1840, this ornate Gothic chapel was originally located on Sheafe Road near New Hamburgh. As the congregation in New Hackensack grew, this chapel was taken apart and moved board by board to be rebuilt just north of the old Dutch Church. A long shed was constructed behind the chapel to shelter members' horses during the service. After spending close to 100 years in New Hackensack, the chapel was again moved in the 1990s, close to its original location on Sheafe Road at the entrance of Bowdoin Park.

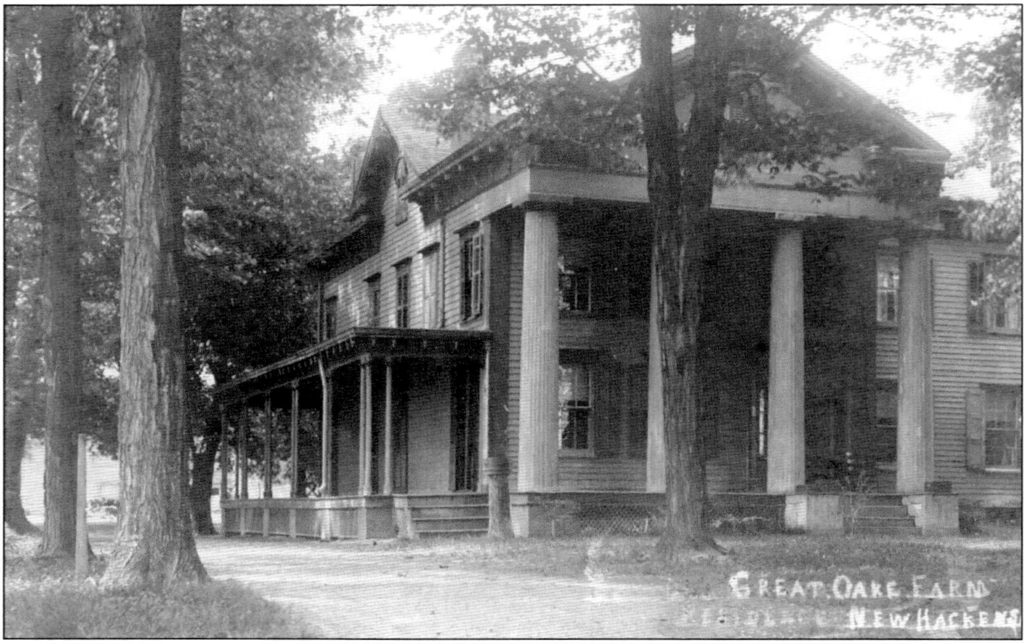

THE GREAT OAK FARM, C. 1907. Once one of the largest farms in the area, the Great Oak Farm stretched far behind the house and comprised much of what is today Airport Road. A large hay barn was constructed in the late 1800s, just north of the main house. During the mid-1900s, the farm fell into disrepair and the large columned porch on the south side of the home was removed.

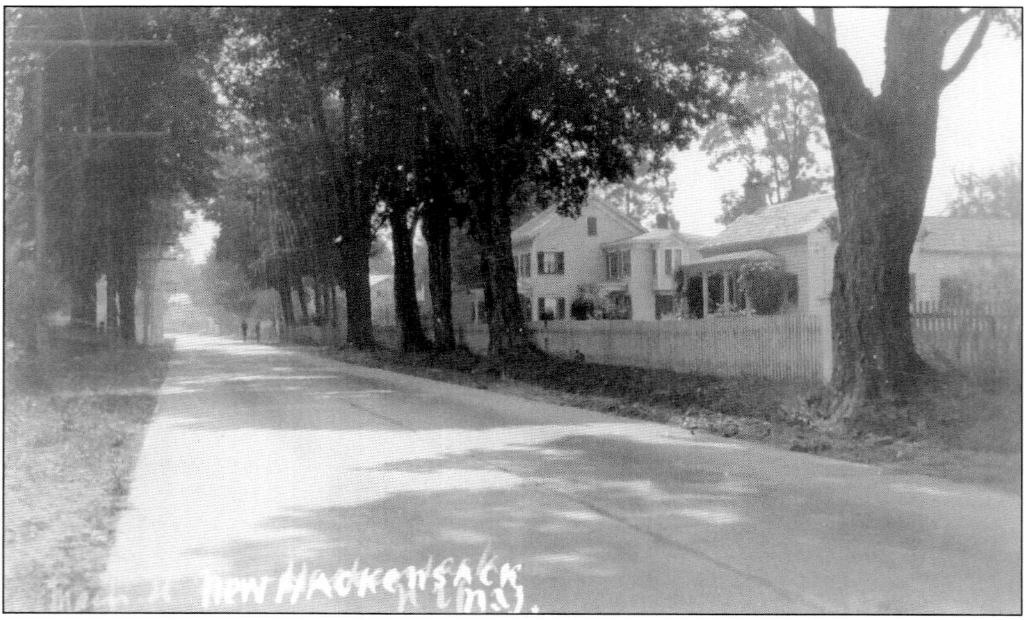

MAIN STREET LOOKING SOUTH, 1929. Even through the 1920s, New Hackensack was a quiet rural community. This view, taken just south of the Warnock House, shows the quaint country setting. Edna Denney writes on the back of the postcard, "This card to show you [*sic*] how the State Road looks in New Hackensack. One can see Freeman and his brother coming home for dinner."

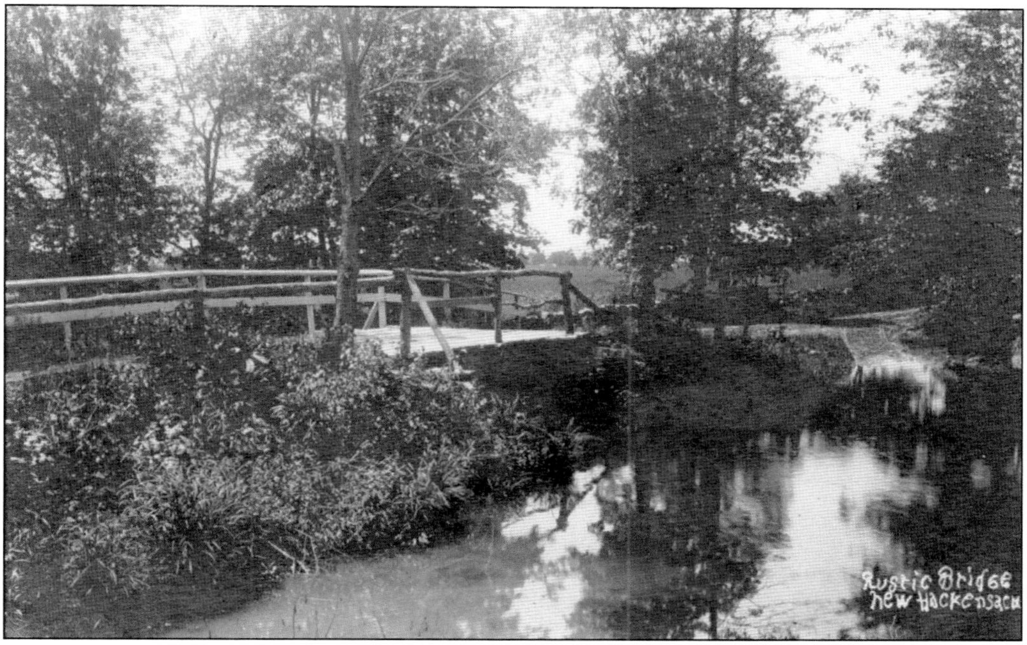

CREEK BRIDGE, 1910. A rustic wooden bridge crosses the small creek just east of the hamlet. The area between New Hackensack and Fishkill Plains was mostly small farms surrounded by large tracts of forest. The small bridge seen here, today near the intersection of Route 376 and Degarmo Hills Road, was washed away during a spring flood and replaced by a concrete structure.

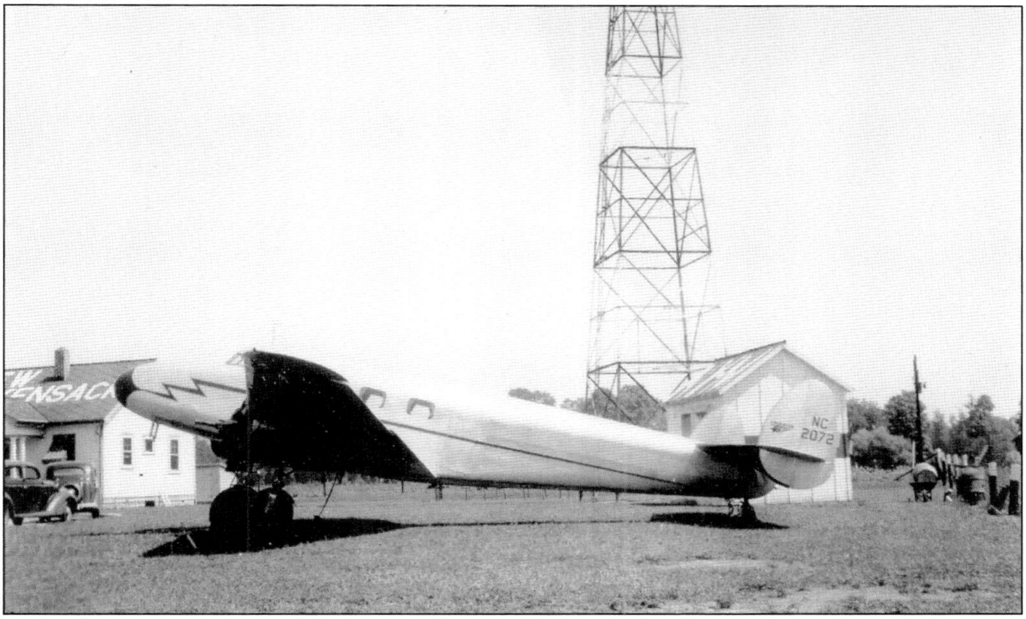

DUTCHESS COUNTY AIRPORT, 1937. During the early 1930s, the land behind the old Warnock House was converted into a small airfield. Mostly used by local amateur enthusiasts, the airstrip was unpaved with only one small building used as the control station. Painted white across the roof was "New Hackensack," which was visible to overhead planes. During the 1940s, the airfield was modernized and renamed the Dutchess County Airport. (Courtesy of the Wappingers Historical Society.)

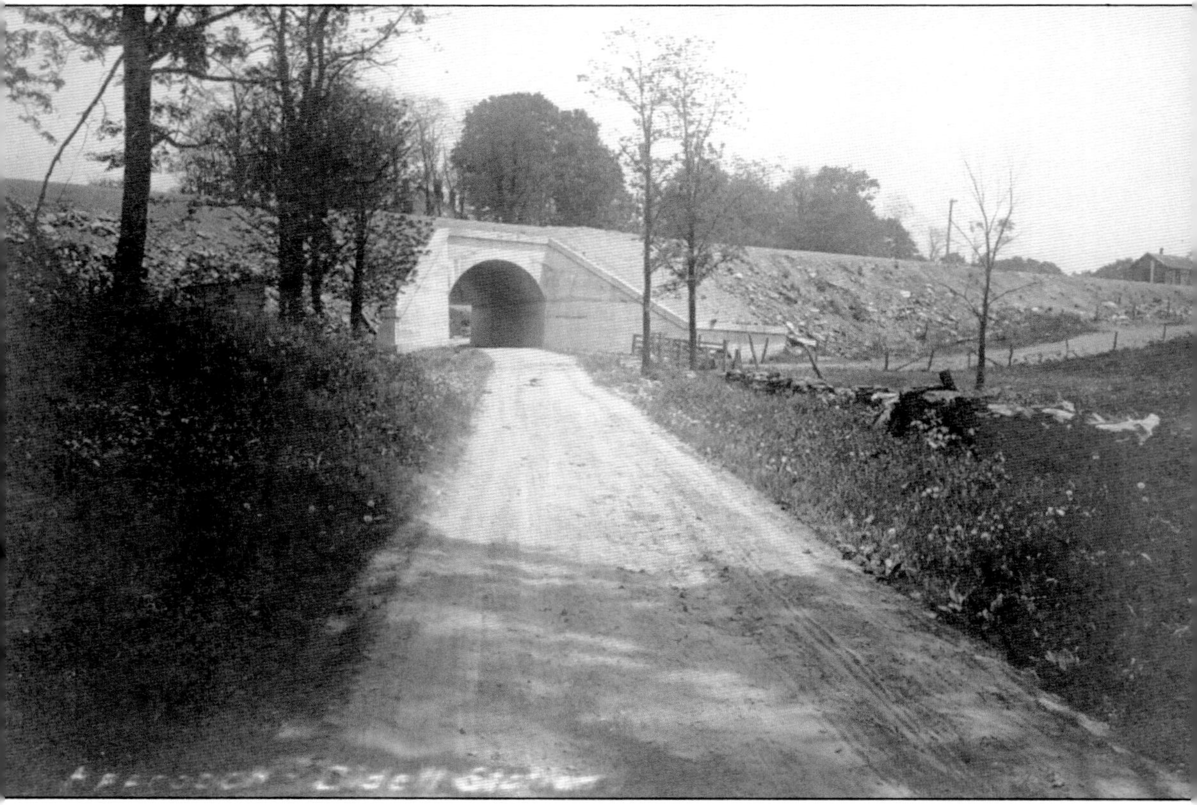

DIDDELL RAILROAD CULVERT, 1911. The small community of Diddell sat just a few miles south of New Hackensack and included a small train station, shown here on the far right. The Maybrook Railroad Line stretched across the county from Pawling to Poughkeepsie and had one stop in the town of Wappinger at Diddell. In 1910, the line was enlarged to two tracks to accommodate larger freight services. As a result, this one lane concrete culvert was erected along Diddell Road.

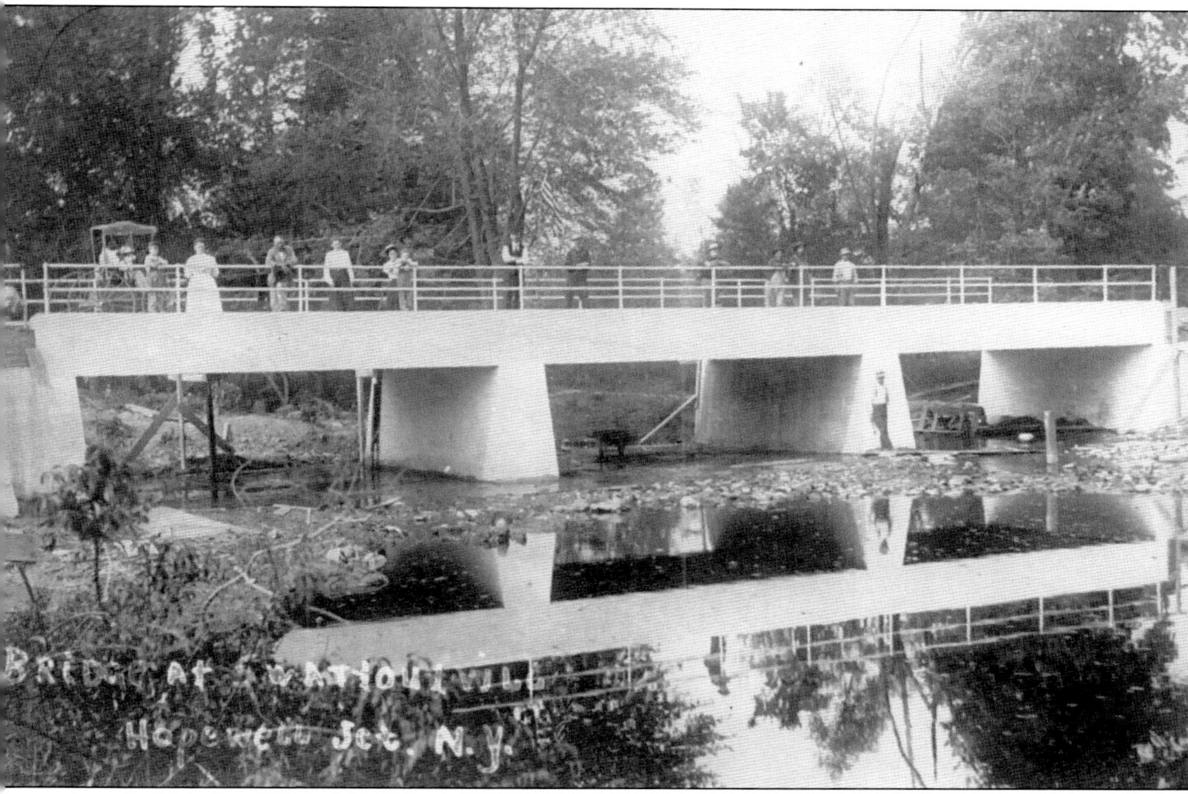

NEW CONCRETE BRIDGE IN SWARTOUTVILLE, C. 1912. At the southernmost tip of the town of Wappinger, at the intersection of Route 82 and All Angel's Hill Road, is the hamlet of Swartoutville. Dating back to the colonial era, the once vibrant hamlet housed George Washington for a few months during the Revolutionary War. This view shows community members standing on the new concrete bridge that was constructed over Fishkill Creek.

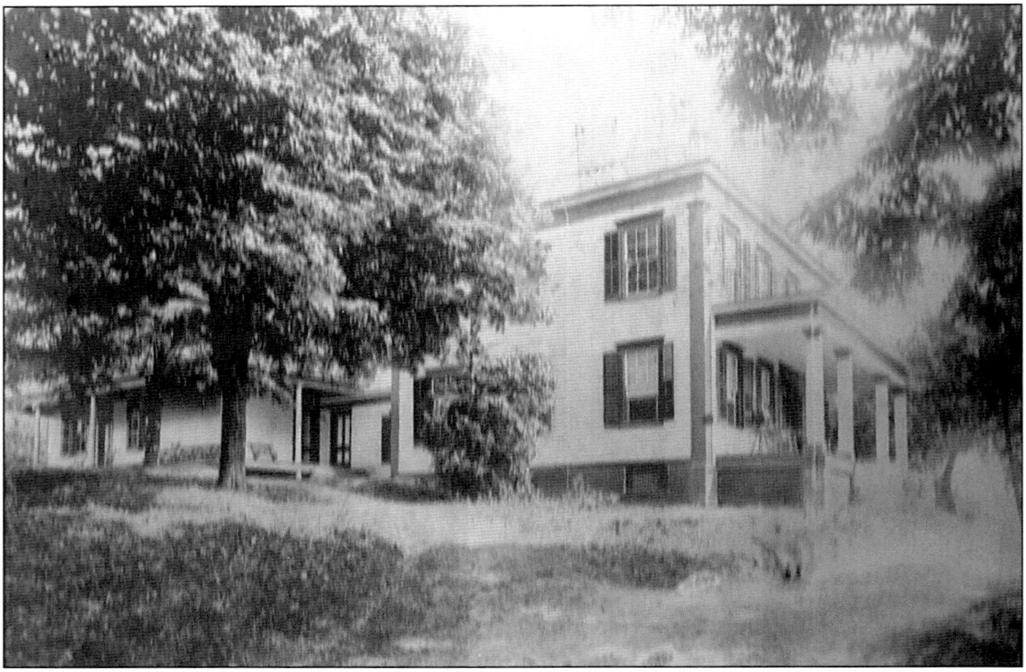

UNDERHILL MANSION, C. 1880. The road now known as All Angels Hill Road was originally called Underhill Road, named after the family that lived in this house. Built in the mid-1800s, the estate comprised much of the land between Pye Lane and Myers Corners Road. (Courtesy of the Wappingers Historical Society.)

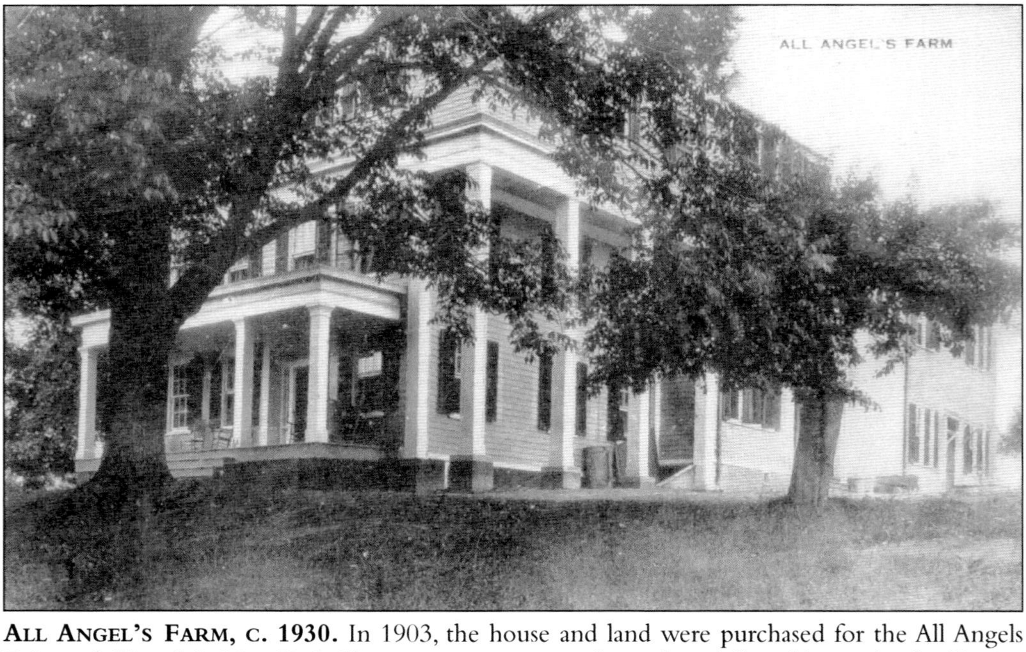

ALL ANGEL'S FARM, C. 1930. In 1903, the house and land were purchased for the All Angels Episcopal Church in New York City as a summer retreat for underprivileged inner city families. To accommodate over 100 mothers and children, a third story and a large addition behind the house was built. After being sold and used as a chicken coop, the house fell into disrepair and was torn down to make way for new housing.

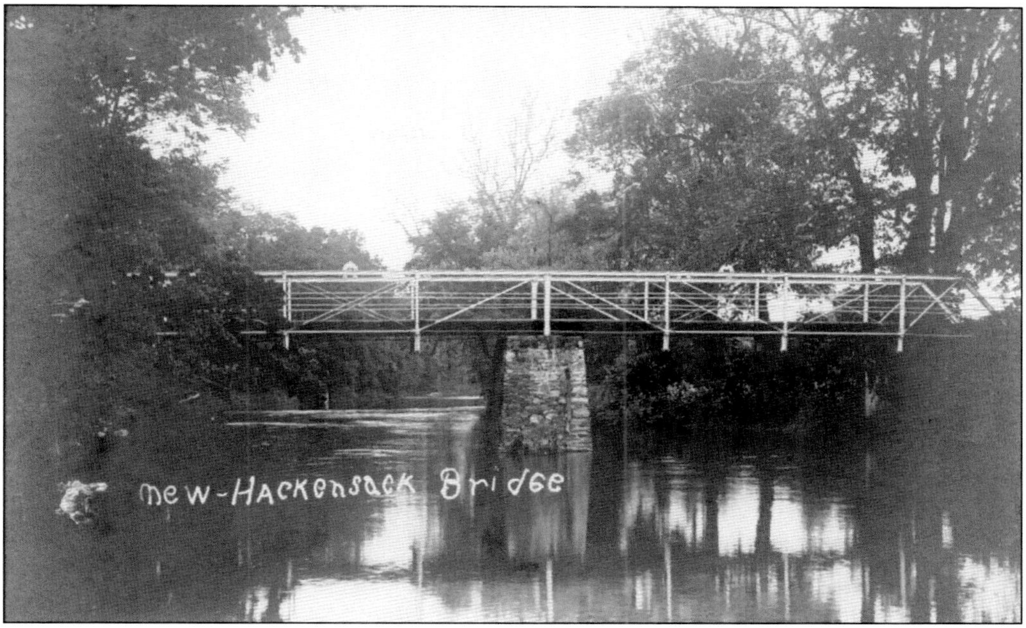

NEW HACKENSACK BRIDGE, C. 1909. The first bridges across the Wappingers Creek in New Hackensack were constructed of wood. After numerous floods destroyed these early structures, a new stone and steel bridge was erected in the early 1900s. This stronger bridge lasted for a few decades until the Dutchess County Airport expanded in the 1960s. As Jackson Road was moved, a new bridge was built slightly upstream. The middle stone support shown here can still be seen in the middle of the creek below the new bridge.

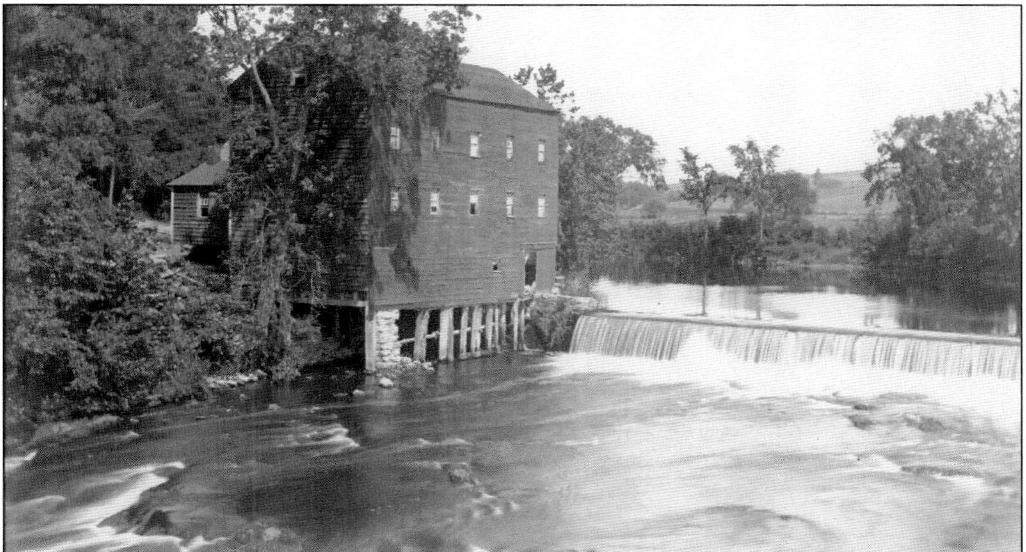

OLD RED OAKS MILL, C. 1890. Just north of the hamlet of New Hackensack was Red Oaks Mill. At the time of this photograph, the mill was the longest continuously operating gristmill in the town and was already 100 years old. Rapids along the relatively flat banks made this part of Wappingers Creek an optimal place to process the wheat from the surrounding farms. Although the mill no longer stands, the dam can still be seen from the Route 376 Bridge. (Courtesy of the Wappingers Historical Society.)

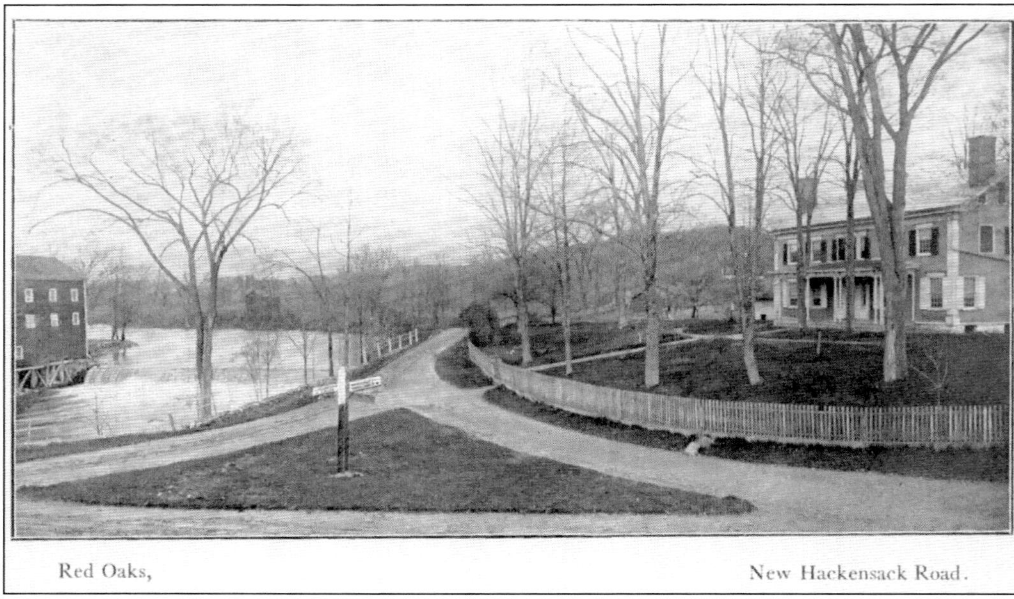

MILL HOUSE, RED OAKS, 1906. Looking up Red Oaks Mill Road, the small dirt lane wound north along Wappingers Creek to the hamlet of Manchester Bridge. The large Federal-style home on the right was constructed by Benjamin La Verge to be his house. It is located across the creek from the old Red Mill.

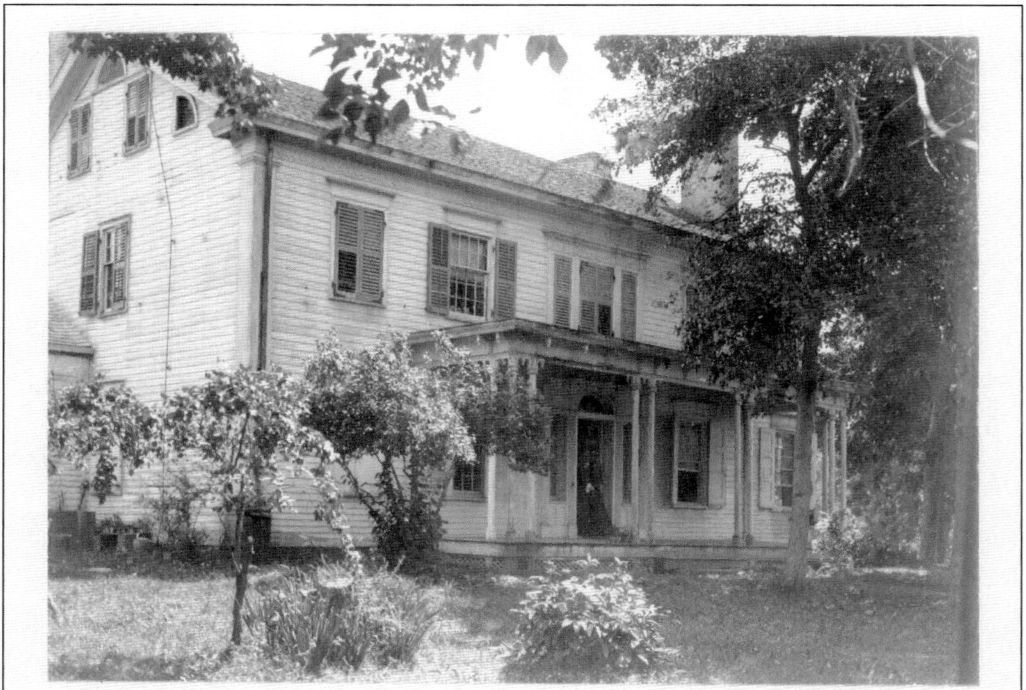

MILL HOUSE, C. 1920. A woman stands at the doorway to the old LaVerge House. Once the Red Mill closed, the Wodell family split up the large property and sold the mill house. As seen here, the house quickly fell into disrepair. Today, the house has been renovated and converted into a business. (Courtesy of the Wappingers Historical Society.)

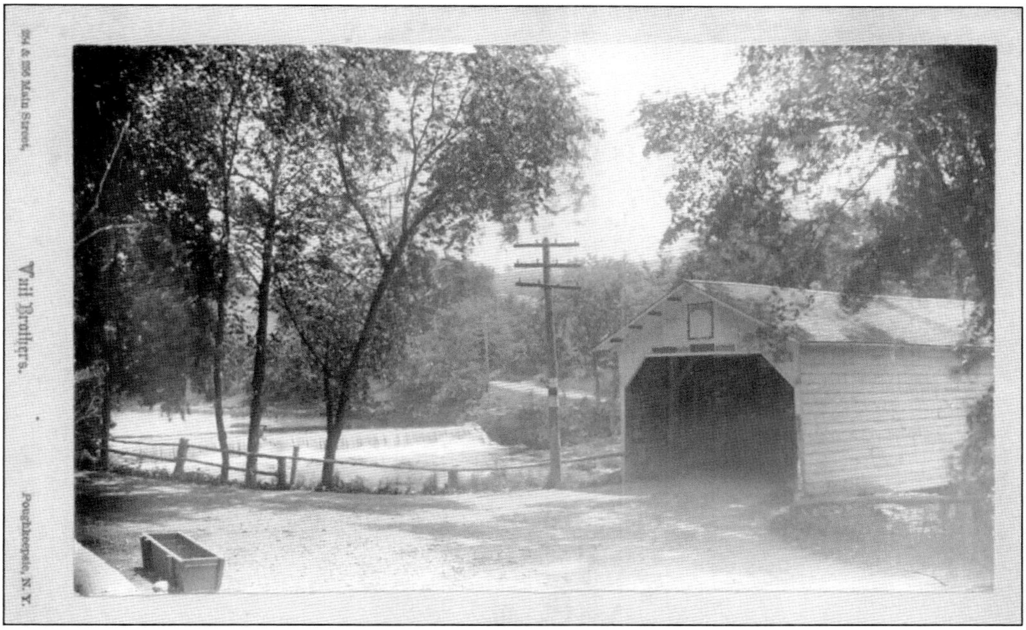

COVERED BRIDGE OVER WAPPINGERS CREEK, C. 1890. Just below the mill and falls was a small wooden covered bridge. As with many other bridges along the Wappingers Creek from Pleasant Valley to New Hamburgh, a strong spring flood washed the bridge away in 1897. (Courtesy of the Wappingers Historical Society.)

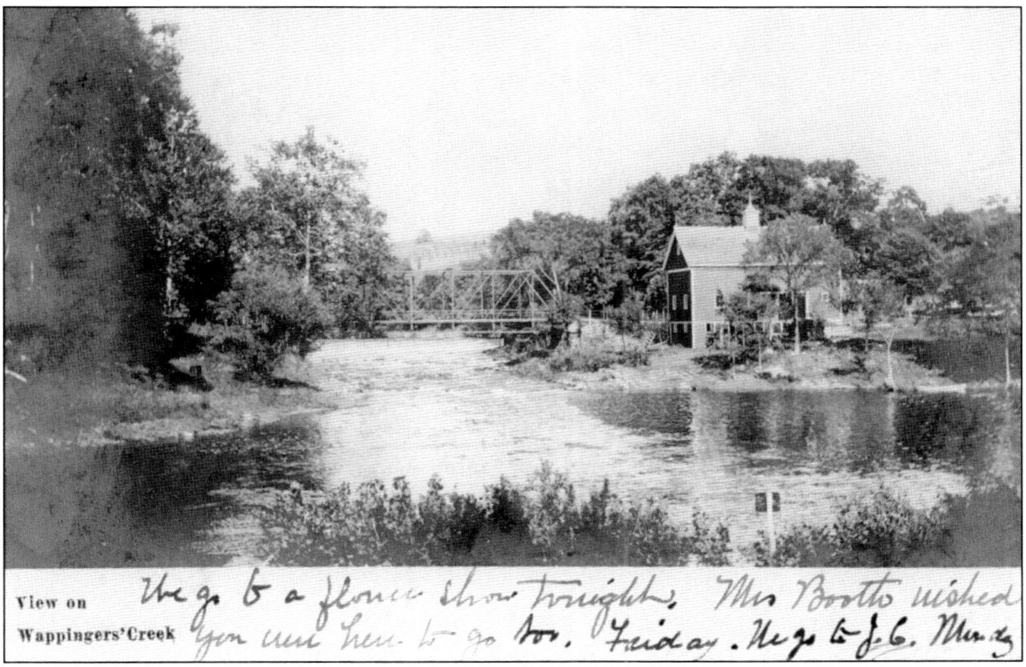

WAPPINGERS CREEK BY RED OAKS MILL, 1905. Shortly after the covered bridge was destroyed, a new steel bridge was constructed at the same point along the creek. Taken from the west side of the creek, the photograph shows a popular swimming hole in the hamlet. The building next to the bridge was originally a lumber mill and was later converted into the barn for the mill house across the street.

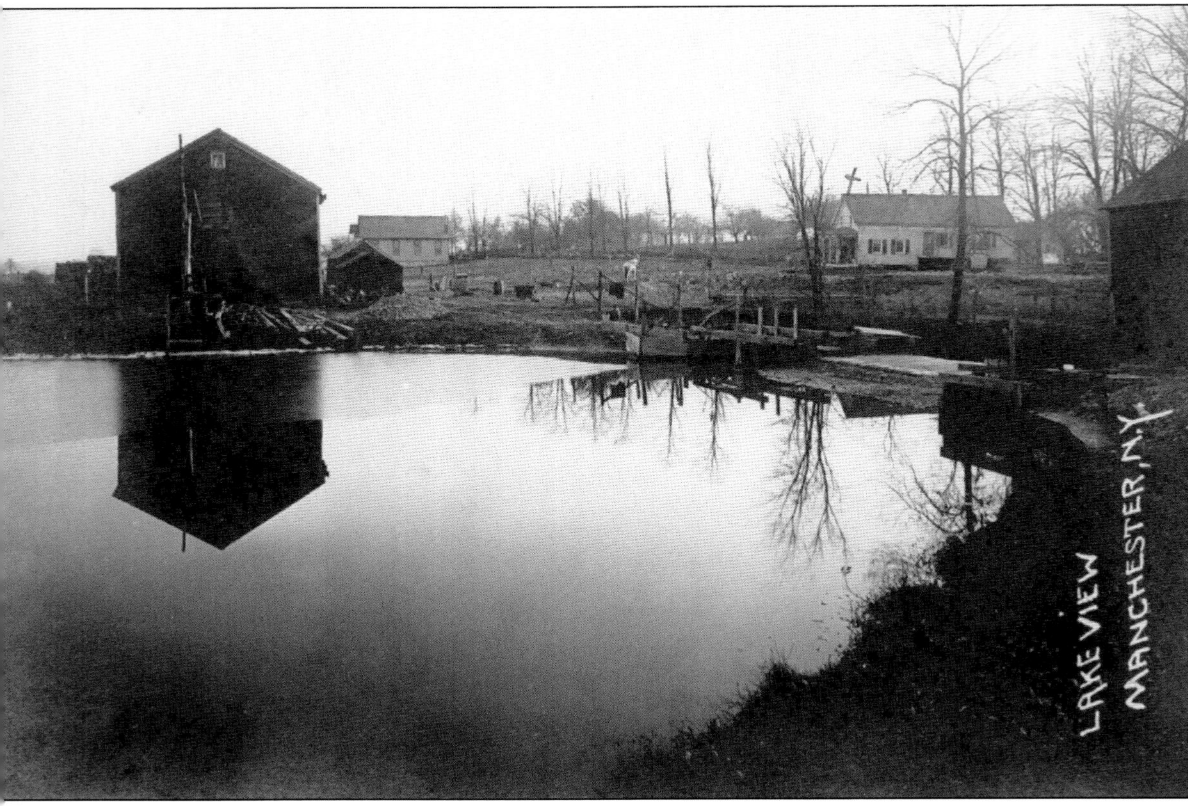

TITUSVILLE MILL, c. 1908. Just north of Red Oaks Mill was the small hamlet of Titusville. Also situated on Wappingers Creek, the hamlet had its own small flour mill, shown here on the far right by the small dam. The house on the right with the small cross above it is being moved so that the small dirt road can be widened.

Three

Chelsea-on-Hudson
A Hudson River Hamlet

Originally called Low Point, the hamlet of Chelsea had many names, including Carthage and Carthage Landing. Settled in the early 1800s, the community had a small dock to export goods farmed in the interior of the county. In the mid-1800s, a large flour mill was erected on the dock and soon the hamlet had grown into a thriving shipping community.

The railroad came to town in 1848, and a small station was built. Trying to avoid confusion with another Carthage in upstate New York, the railroad renamed the hamlet Chelsea-on-Hudson. Throughout the late 19th and early 20th century, the hamlet prospered and established the first public school in the town. A yacht club was organized in the late 1800s for the purpose of ice yachting. Although mostly concentrating on sailing today, the yacht club still operates and is one of the last gathering places in the now residential community.

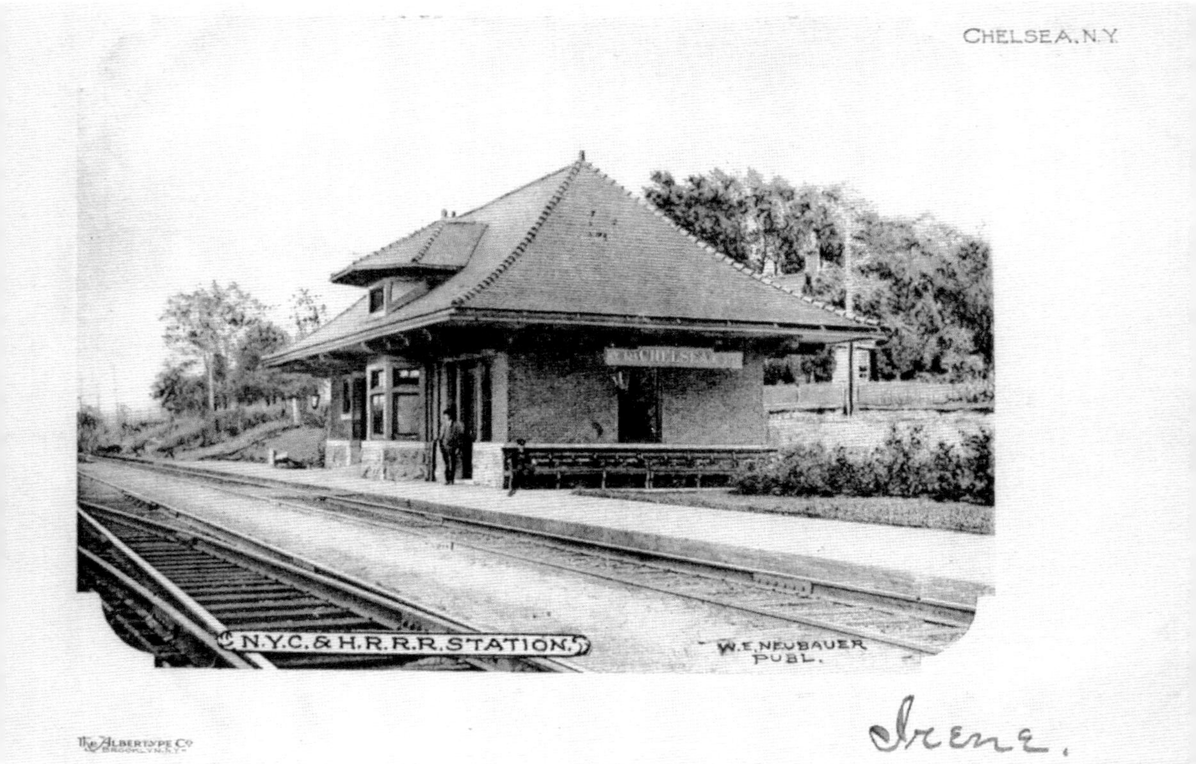

RAILROAD STATION AT CHELSEA-ON-HUDSON, 1908. Sitting on the New York City and Hudson River Railroad, the hamlet of Chelsea was the only station between Beacon and New Hamburgh. The railroad was so influential to the hamlet that it allowed the railroad company to change the name from Carthage Landing to Chelsea. The impressive stone and brick station replaced a smaller wooden building in 1901 to accommodate both passengers and freight services.

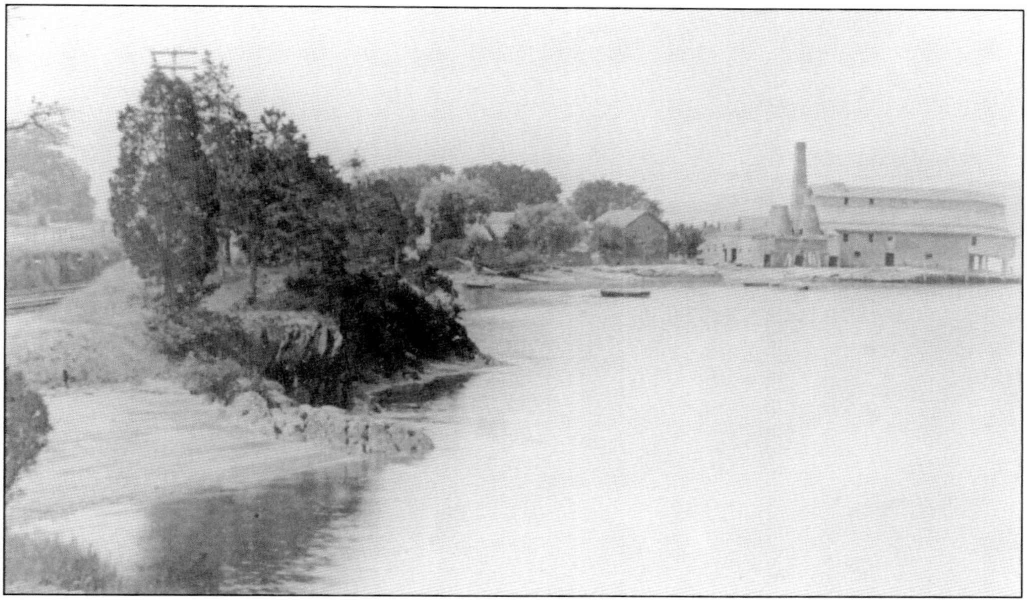

CHELSEA DOCK AND FACTORY, 1875. Stretching into the Hudson River on a long wooden dock, the old Carthage Landing Mill was constructed for the production of flour in the 1860s. In the early 1870s, the mill was purchased and was converted into a cement factory. Owners hoped that a new train bridge proposed over the Hudson River in Poughkeepsie would increase the demand for locally made cement. Sadly, the train bridge would be delayed for another decade and the factory closed. (Courtesy of the Beacon Historical Society.)

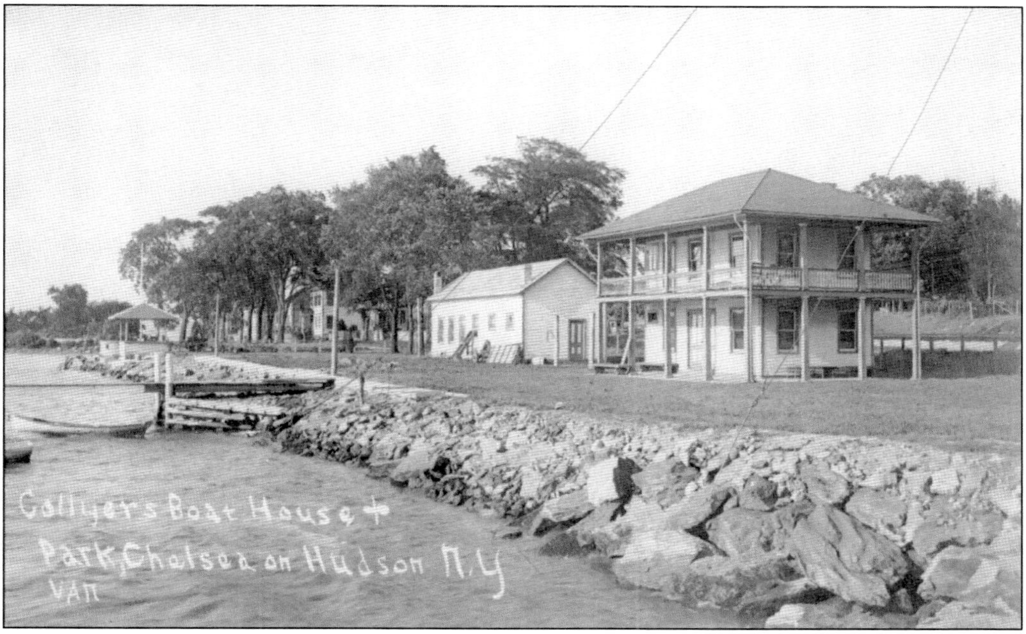

CHELSEA YACHT CLUB, 1910. Organized in 1881, the Chelsea Yacht Club was built on a small strip of land along the river just beyond the railroad tracks. First called the Carthage Yacht Club, member's main interest was ice yachting. This winter sport, usually reserved for the wealthy, was a community-wide event when races with other local yacht clubs in Hyde Park, Poughkeepsie, and New Hamburgh came to town. (Courtesy of Timothy Holls.)

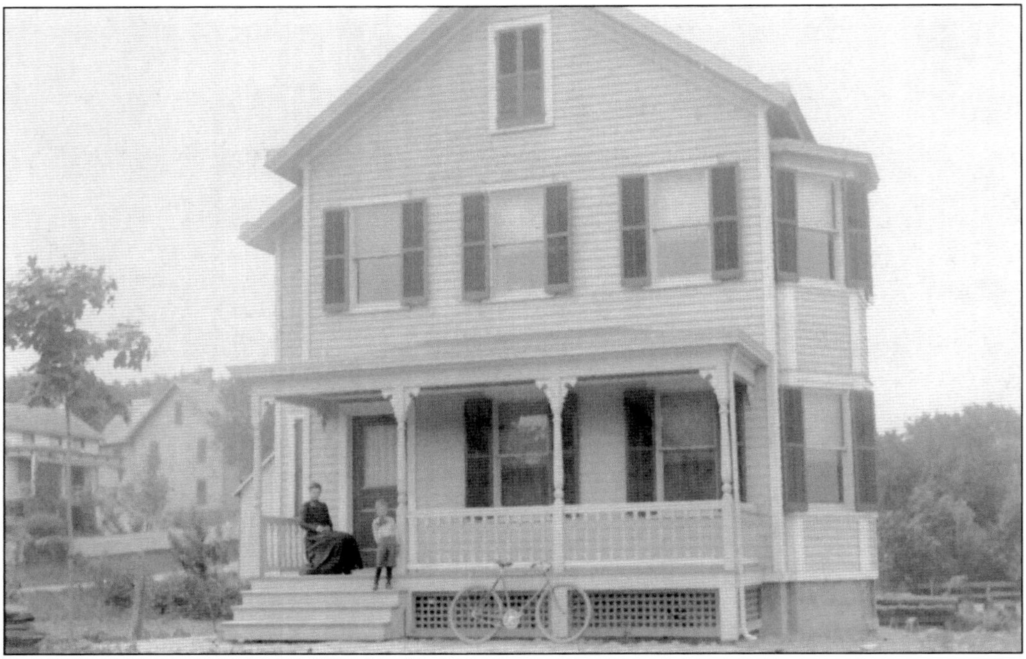

HAGER FAMILY HOME, 1909. One of the prominent homes in the village was the Hager family residence. Sitting on the corner of Liberty and Bank Streets, it was constructed for Ulysses and Sarah Hager in 1900. One of the wealthier families in Chelsea, they were the first residents to own an automobile. (Courtesy of the Beacon Historical Society.)

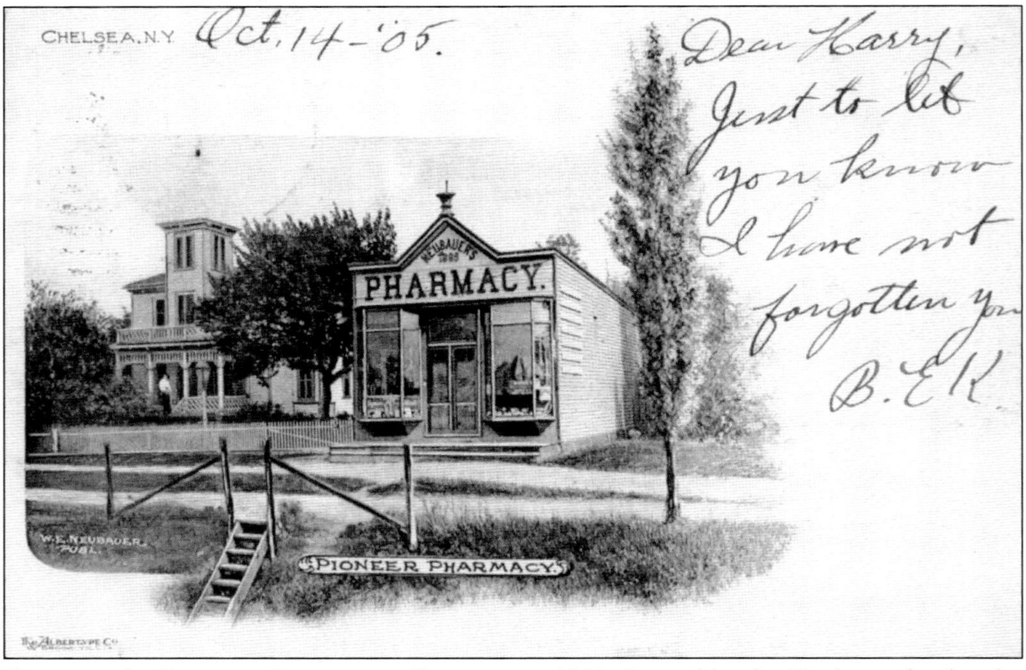

NEUBAUER'S GENERAL STORE AND PHARMACY, 1905. Owned by the Neubauer family who occupied the house next door, the pharmacy opened its doors in 1889. Standing on River Road North just above of the railroad station, Neubauer's Store carried a variety of local food and other goods brought up from New York City.

METHODIST CHURCH, C. 1912. Across Liberty Street from the old schoolhouse is the Methodist Church. First organized in 1823, the church was constructed a decade later in 1833. In 1870, alterations to the interior and the facade cost the church $1,600; almost twice as much as it cost to originally construct the building.

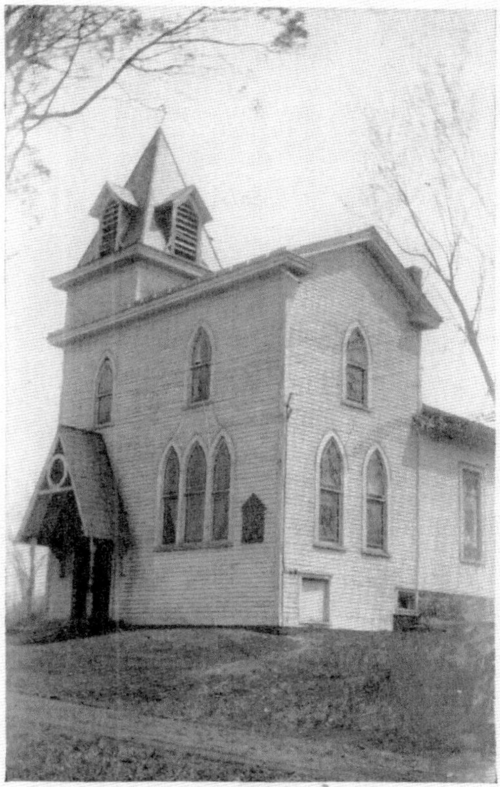

M. E. Church, Chelsea, N. Y.

BRICK SCHOOLHOUSE, 1898. The class of 1898 stands in front the schoolhouse on South Liberty Street. The first public schoolhouse in the town of Wappinger, the Chelsea School housed children up until high school. It was common for children to walk for miles from nearby farms to attend class each day. Today, the building is used as the hamlet's post office. (Courtesy of the Beacon Historical Society.)

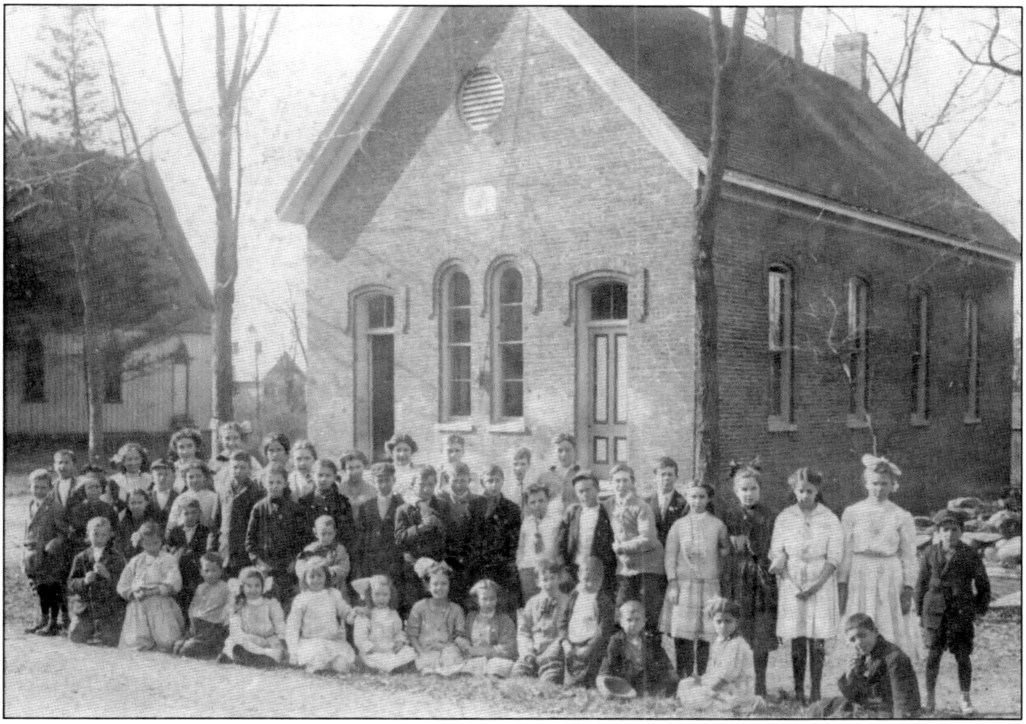

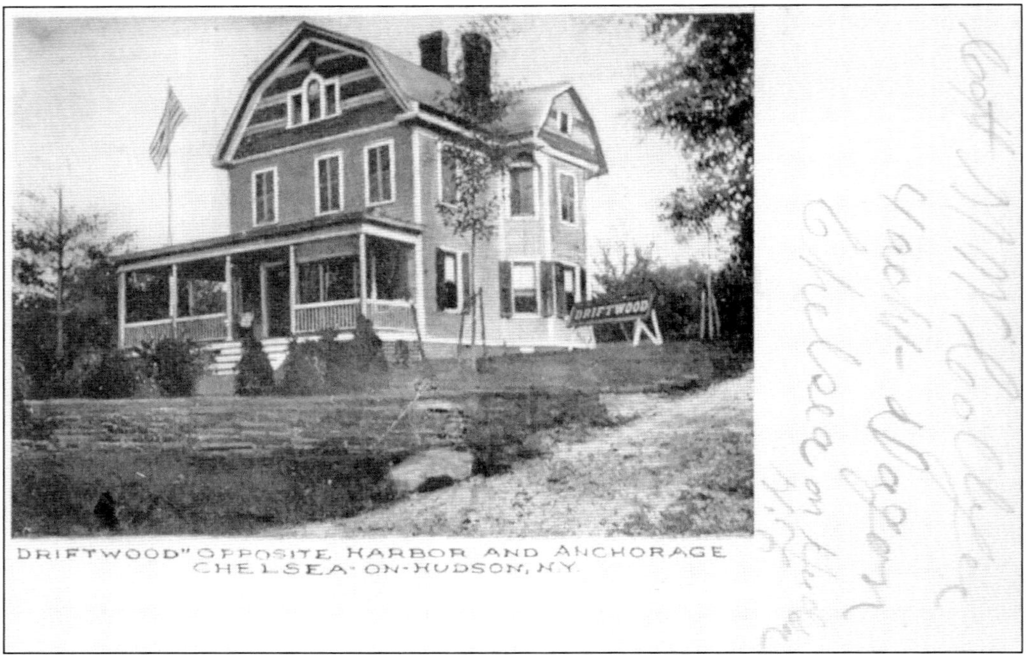

DRIFTWOOD INN, 1906. Fronting the railroad on River Road South, the Driftwood Inn was a popular boardinghouse for people traveling up and down the river. Chelsea's deepwater dock allowed travelers sailing up the Hudson River to dock their boat and spend a weekend in a quaint, country setting.

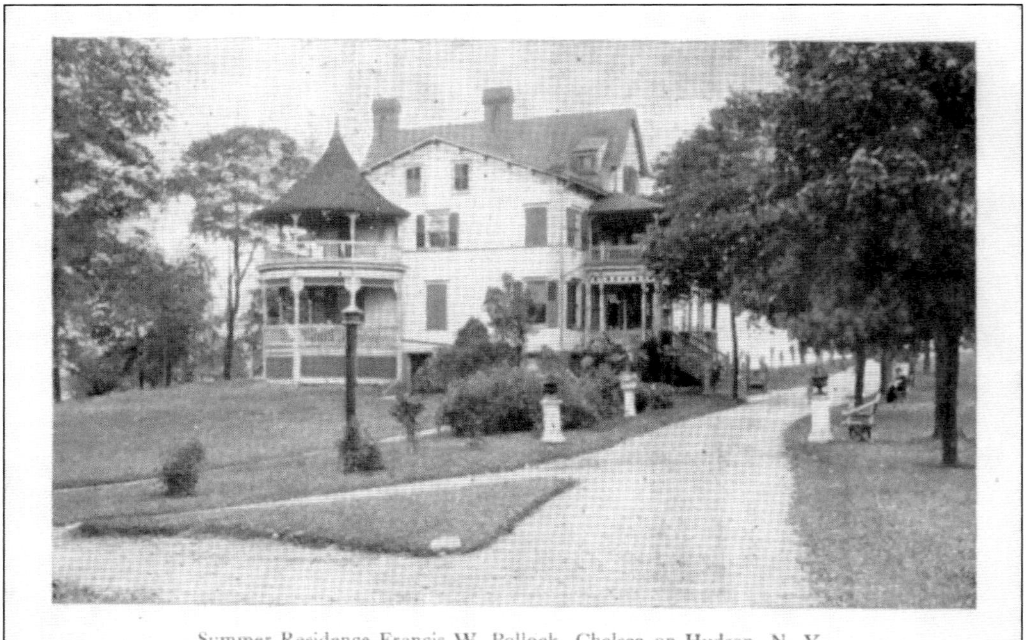

FRANCIS POLLOCK MANSION, 1911. Sitting on a bluff on the north side of the hamlet with a commanding view of the river was the home of Francis Pollock. Pollock made his money in New York City as a prominent lawyer. During the summer months, he would travel here with his sister Mary, until 1913 when the house burned to the ground.

Four

Hughsonville
The Crossroads

The small crossroads at Albany Post Road, New Hamburgh Road, and Old Hopewell is the community of Hughsonville. Named after the Houghson family in the early 1700s, many of the original families, loyal to England, left during the American Revolution to settle in Canada.

The small hamlet grew slowly over the decades with the only industry being the Faulkner Mill near Middlebush Road. A small Presbyterian Church was constructed near the major intersection and became the main gathering place for the community. Once housing two stores, a number of small bars, a hotel, and a few workshops, the hamlet never grew to more than 200 people. Today, the community is mostly known for its firehouse, a bright pink shop on the corner, and long lines of cars during rush hour.

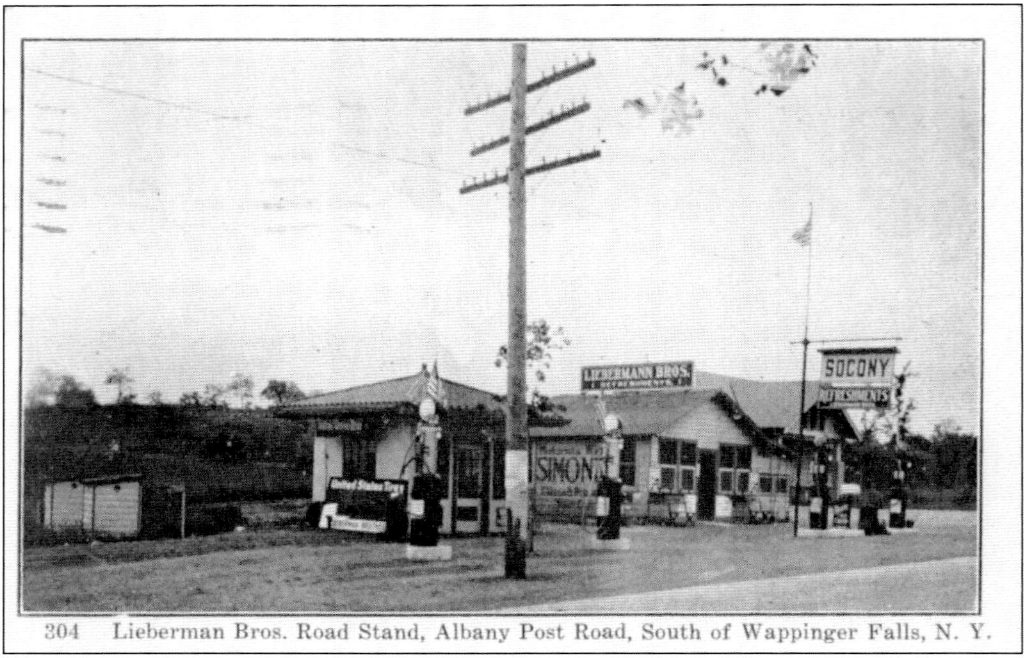

LIEBERMAN BROTHERS ROAD STAND, 1935. By the 1930s, car culture already started to shape the town of Wappinger. Before the Route 9 bypass was constructed, Albany Post Road, or Route 9D, was the major route north from Beacon. As one approached the hamlet of Hughsonville from the south, the Lieberman brother's road stand was the only point one could fill up with gas. The full service station sold tires and car parts and even had a small restaurant.

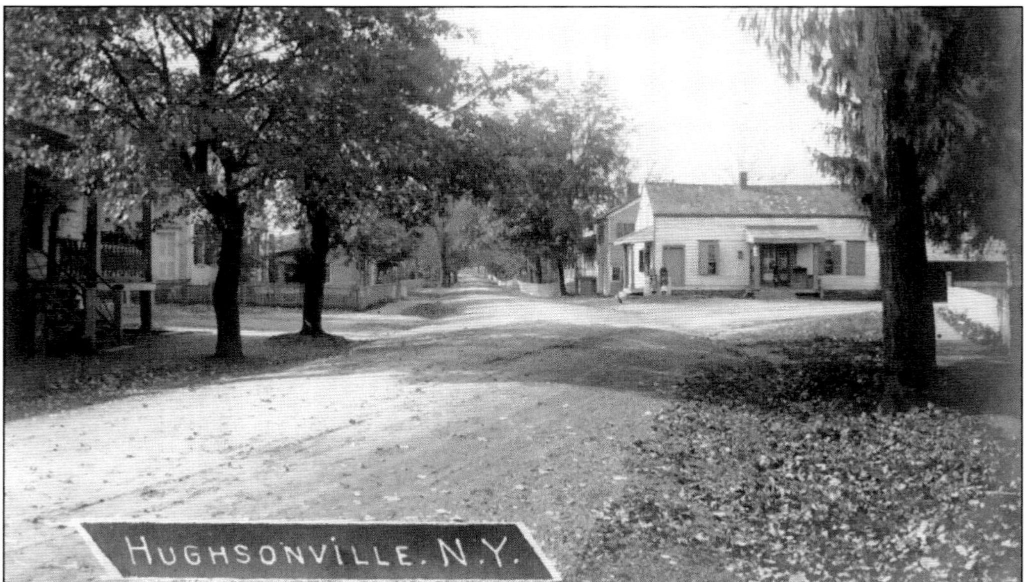

HUGHSONVILLE INTERSECTION, 1908. The small hamlet of Hughsonville sat at an important intersection in the town of Wappinger. Here, looking south on Albany Post Road, the road off to the right in front of the Hughsonville Store leads west to New Hamburgh. The road leading east on the left is Hopewell Road, a vital artery for inland farms to bring their goods to the railroad station and riverfront docks.

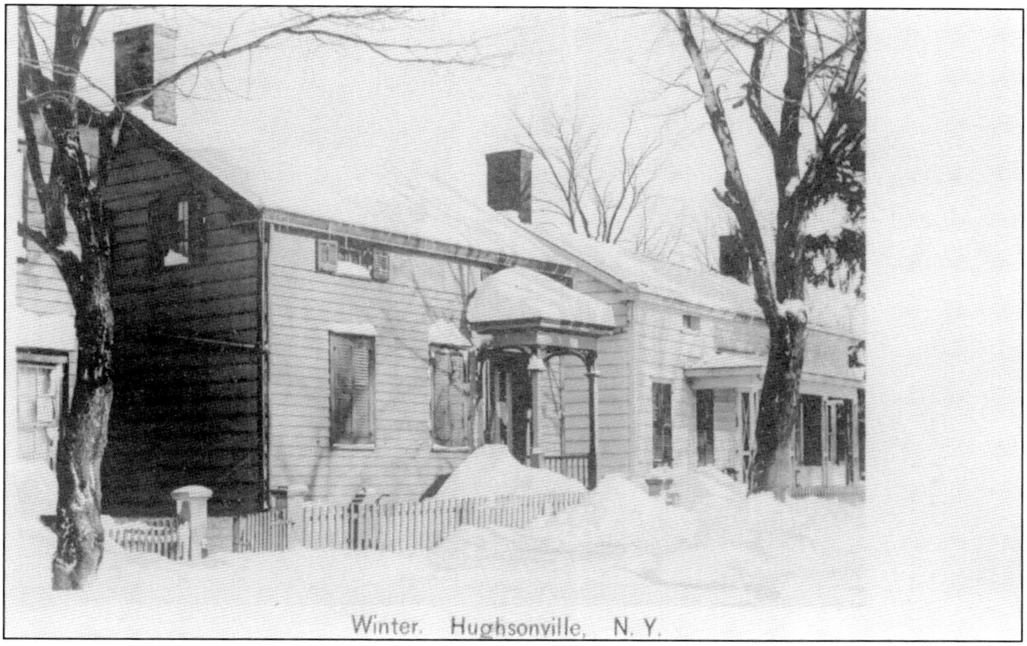

MAIN STREET HOMES, C. 1907. Piles of snow blanket a row of colonial homes just north of New Hamburgh Road. Ever since the hamlet was founded, it had always been a quiet crossroad. The first census for the hamlet was in 1800, showing only 25 people living in the area. By 1880, the community numbered 150 people with many people working in the village of Wappingers Falls nearby. (Courtesy of the Wappingers Historical Society.)

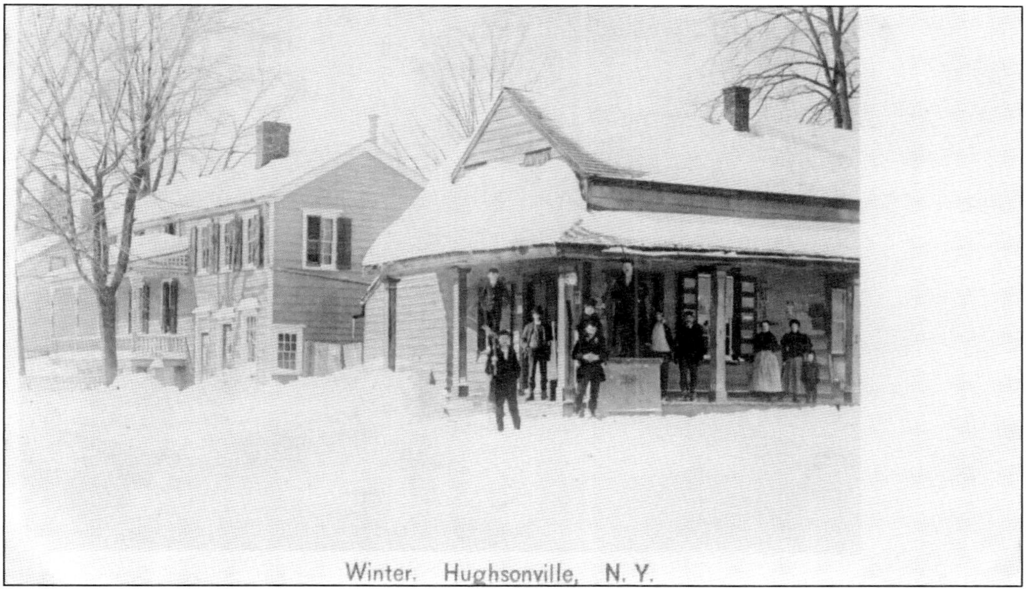

HUGHSONVILLE STORE, 1908. Residents stand on the porch of the general store after a large snowstorm. Standing on Albany Post Road and New Hamburgh Road, this small store serviced the entire hamlet. With goods ranging from local farm produce, tools, housewares, and animal feed, the store provided all the necessities for local residents. Today, the store still stands and serves as a local landmark, painted bright pink on one of the town's busiest intersections. (Courtesy of the Wappingers Historical Society.)

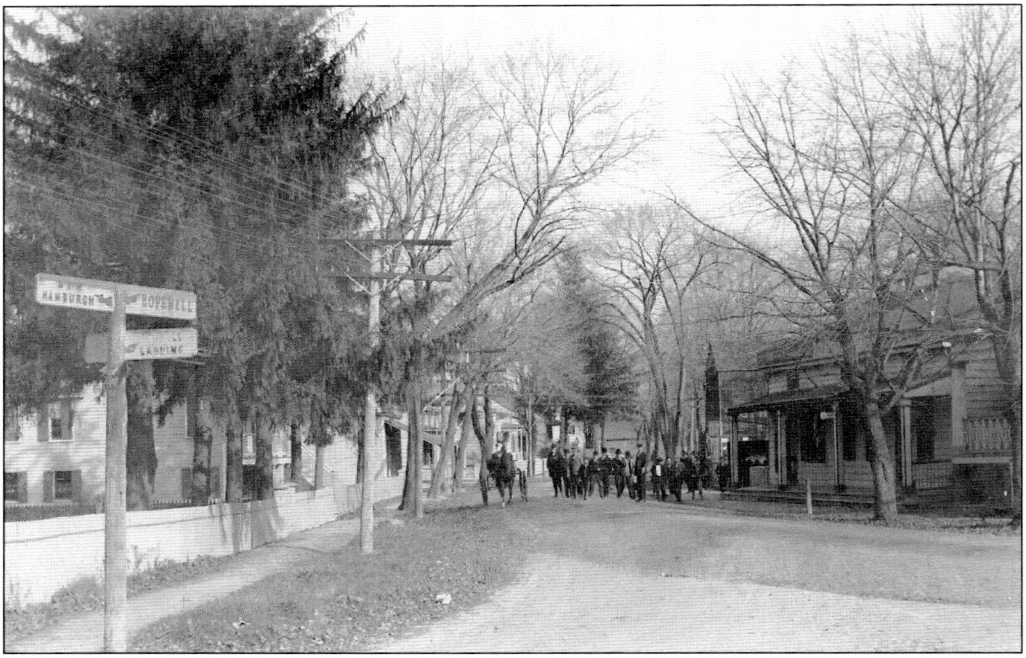

Election Day, 1908. The 1908 presidential election saw William Howard Taft win by a comfortable margin. Using his post under Theodore Roosevelt to gain popular support, he carried the vote in New York with ease. This view, looking north on Albany Post Road, shows prominent men of Hughsonville walking home after casting their ballot.

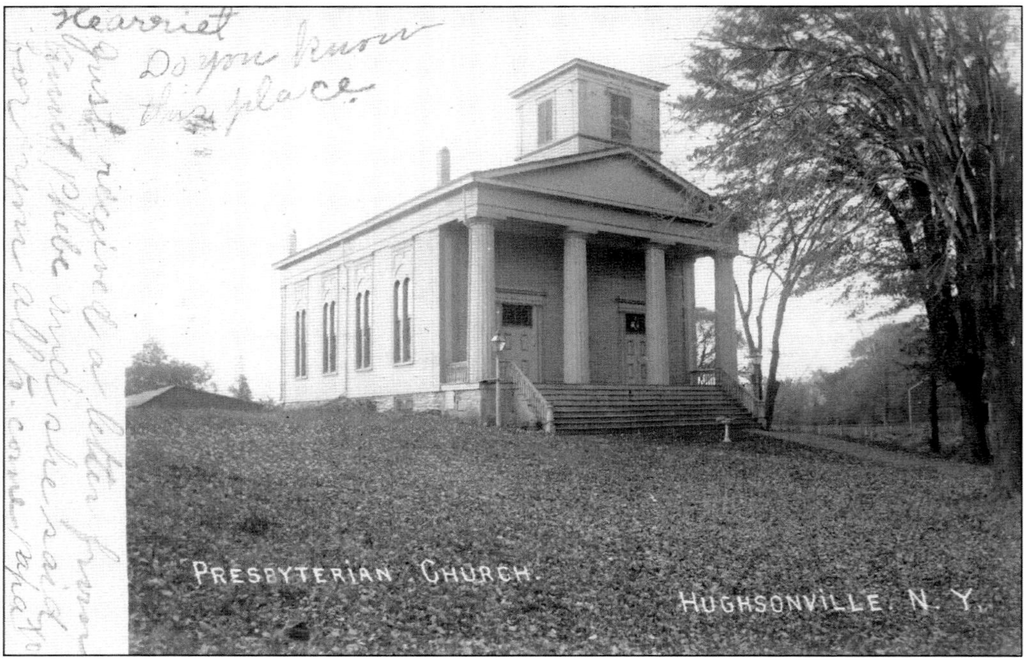

Presbyterian Church, 1915. Constructed in 1840, the Federal-style building was originally a local meetinghouse for the community. In 1892, Rev. Calvin Wright established the church, moving some of the congregation from the New Hamburgh Presbyterian Church. The pastor brought new life into the building, making it the center for community and social activities.

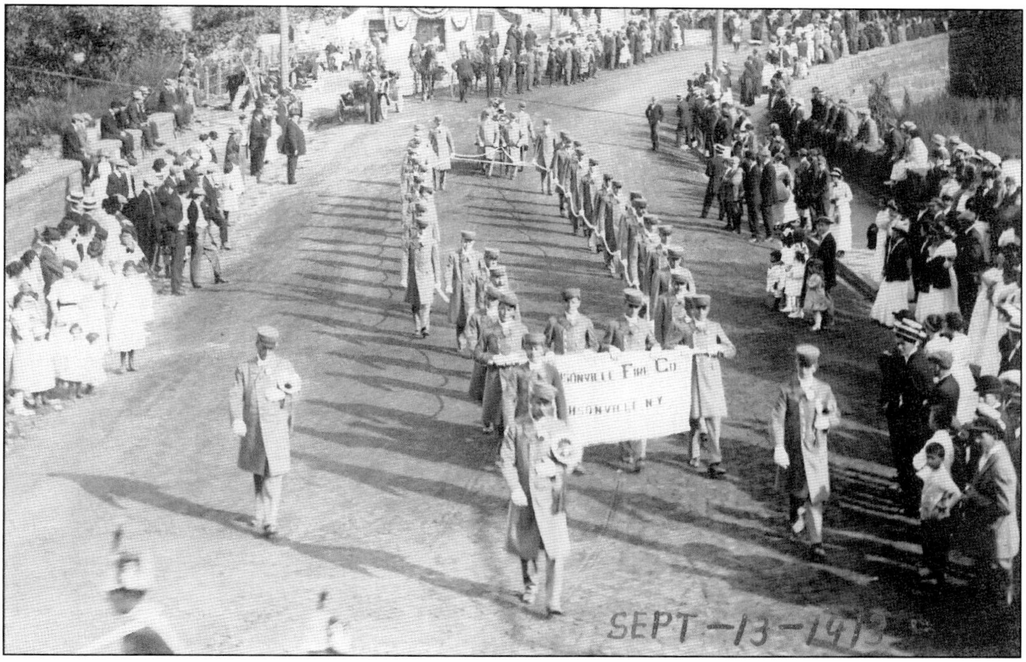

HUGHSONVILLE FIRE COMPANY, 1913. Hughsonville had its own small fire company, shown here just months after being organized. Fires were a common occurrence during this period with many fire companies only equipped with a hand-powered water pumper. This company, comprised of local volunteers, was also present during many of Wappingers Fall's large fires. Today, the Hudsonville Fire Company has its own station on Old Hopewell Road.

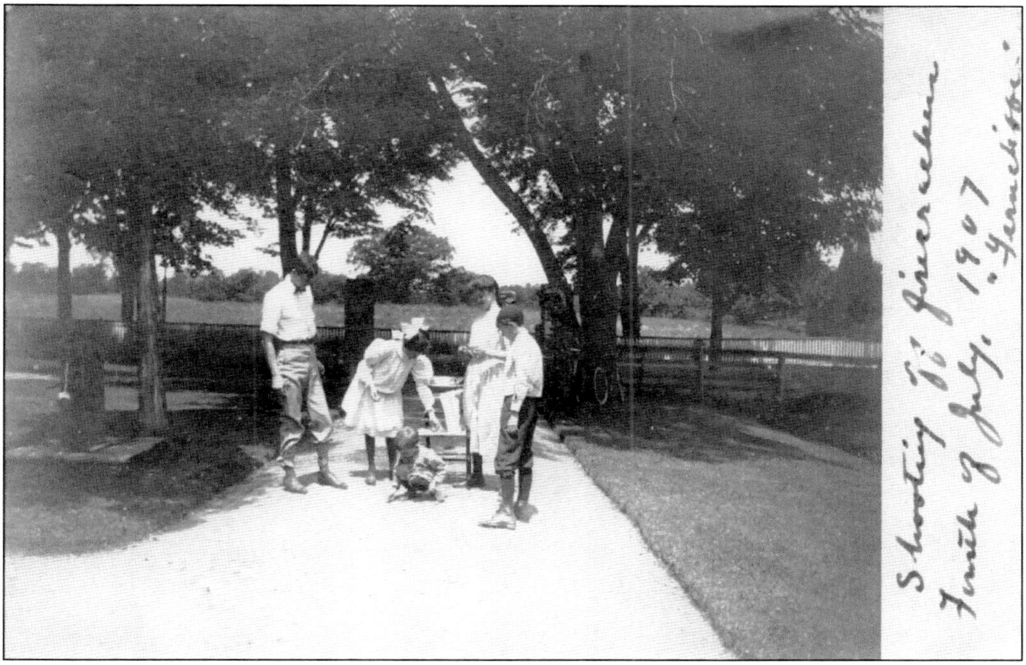

FERNCLIFF ESTATE ON FOURTH OF JULY, 1907. Dressed in their Sunday best, a family plays with firecrackers on the Fourth of July just outside the hamlet. Each estate in the town had its own nickname, including this house on New Hamburgh Road called Ferncliff.

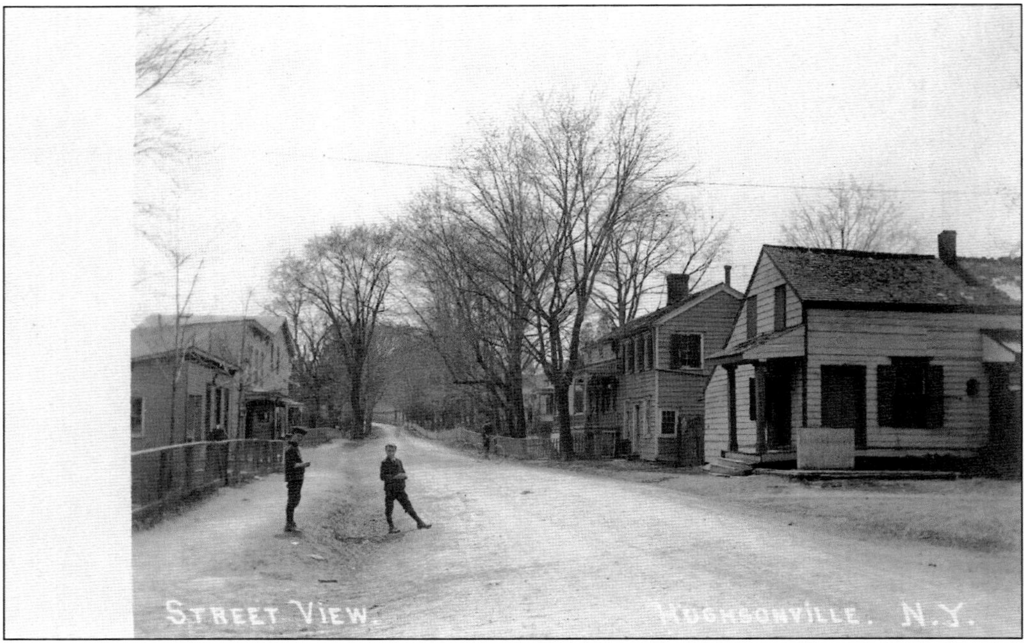

MAIN STREET SOUTH, 1908. Children play on the side of Albany Post Road across the street from the Hughsonville Store. The small buildings on the left are some of the old workshops, including one of the hamlets blacksmith shops. The west side of the street behind the general store was a row of large colonial homes. Only two of these houses now stand, both converted into businesses and apartments.

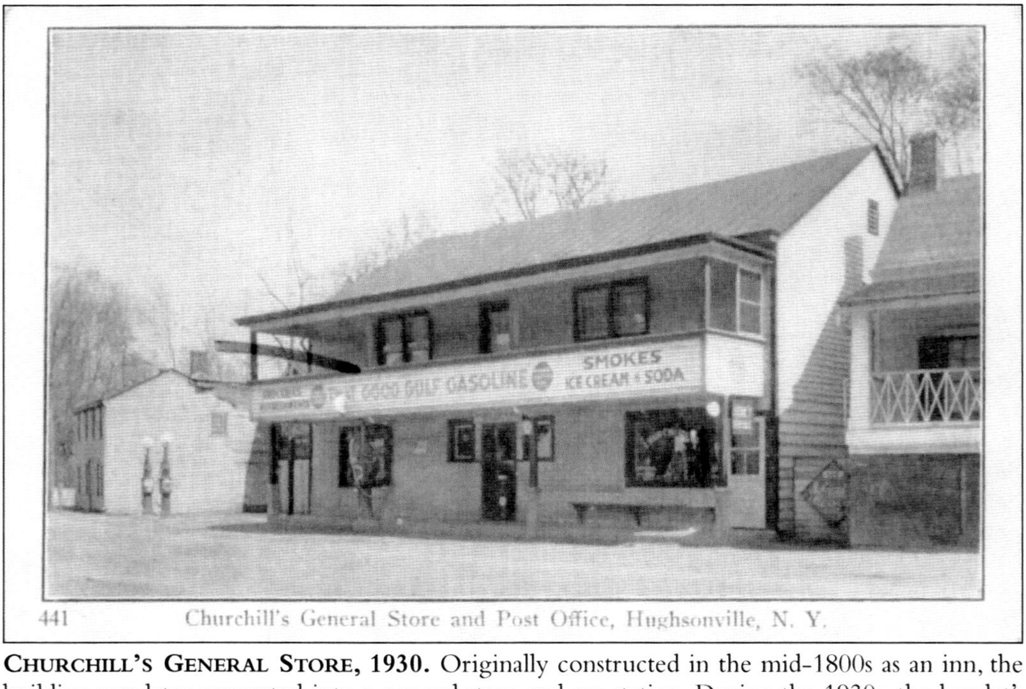

CHURCHILL'S GENERAL STORE, 1930. Originally constructed in the mid-1800s as an inn, the building was later converted into a general store and gas station. During the 1930s, the hamlet's post office was housed in a corner of the store. As car traffic increased on Albany Post Road, Churchill's Store became a thriving pit stop of passing travelers.

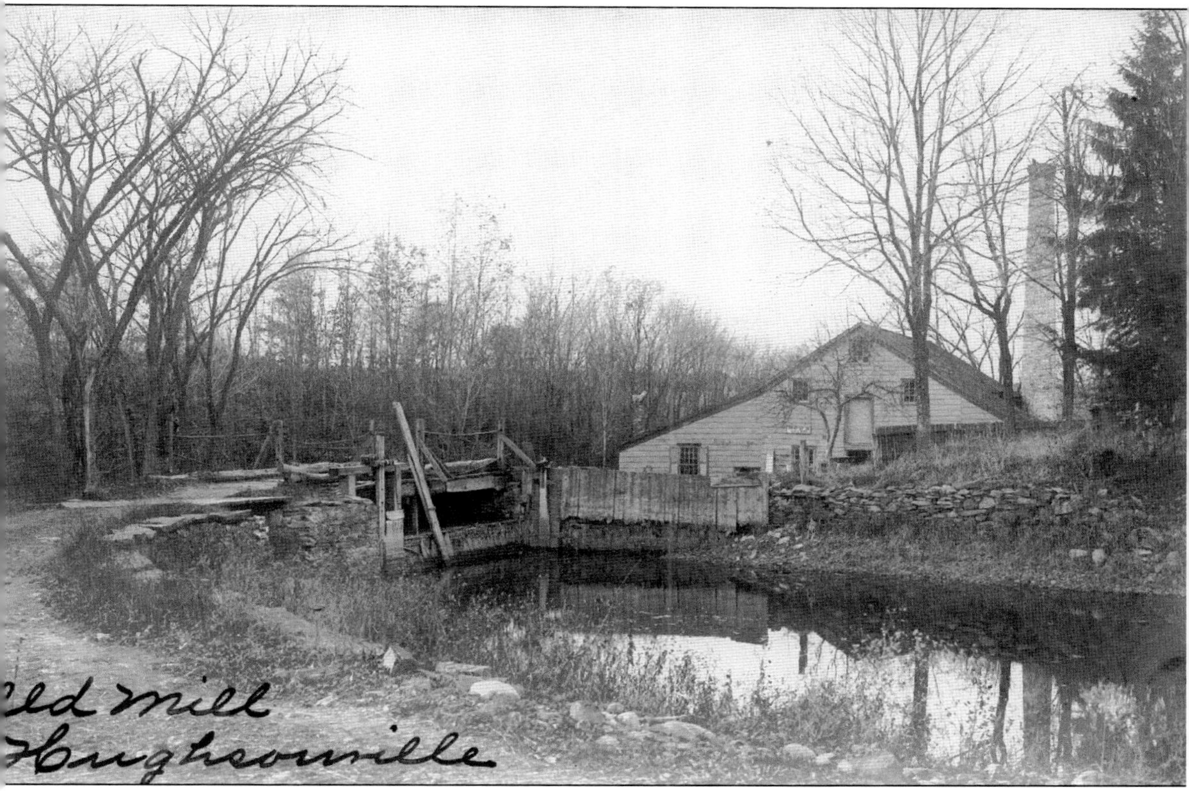

FAULKNER MILL, 1910. Constructed prior to the 1870s, the mill was owned and operated by the Faulkner family, one of the hamlet's original residents. Decedents of the Faulkners would later be instrumental in the creation and operation of the Wappingers Savings Bank and the Garner Print Works. Their humble beginnings originated here on the outskirts of Hughsonville, milling flour and harvesting ice in the winter.

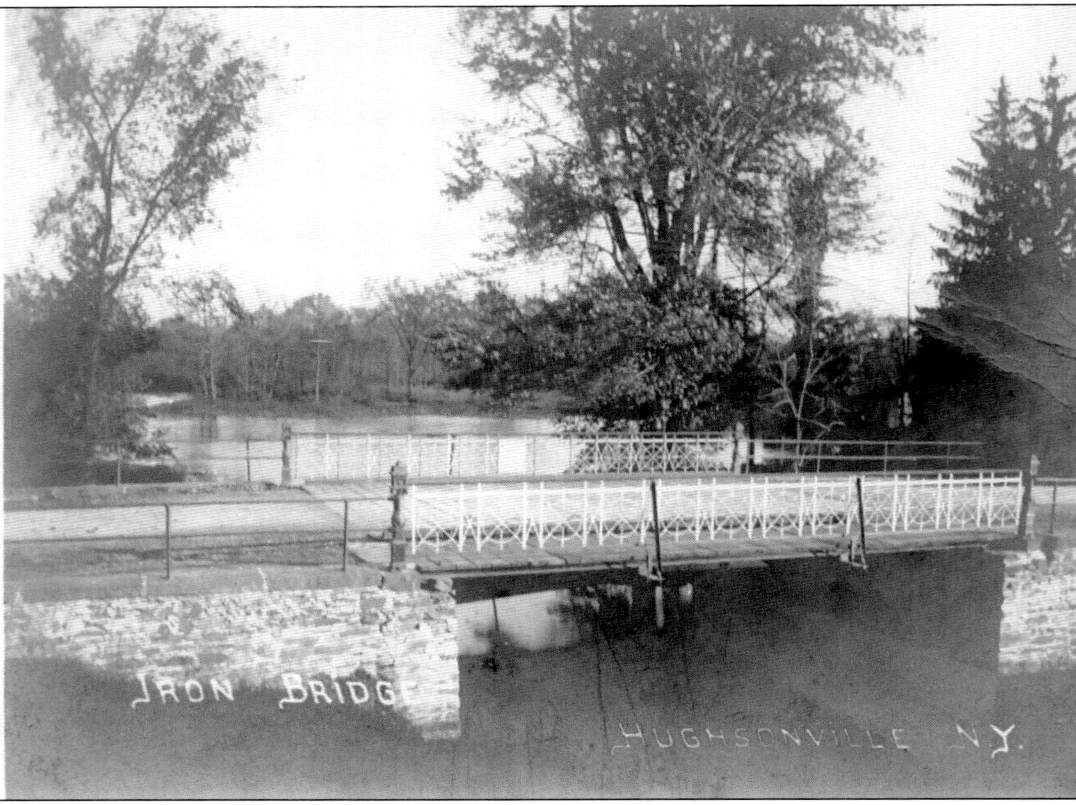

IRON BRIDGE OVER CREEK, 1910. Replacing an old wooden bridge on Albany Post Road near Middlebush, the new iron bridge was a modern improvement allowing for cars and trucks to pass through the community. Composed of field stone and timber from the surrounding woods, the bridge was reinforced by iron beams under the road deck, allowing heavier loads.

Five

New Hamburgh
Where the Wappinger Meets the Hudson

Technically in the town of Poughkeepsie, New Hamburgh was integral to the development of the town of Wappinger. Sitting at the mouth of Wappingers Creek, the hamlet's first industry was fishing along the Hudson River. A lime quarry was built on the north edge of the hamlet while docks were constructed on the deep water channel along the river.

Having many names, including High Point, Wappinger Creek, and Wappingers Landing, the hamlet continued to grow throughout the 19th century as a major shipping point. In 1849, the railroad reached the hamlet from New York City. Many thought the railroad would eliminate the need for the docks, but the railroad only added to commerce. At the mouth of the Wappingers Creek, the railroad company built a drawbridge so that barges could migrate up the creek to the Dutchess Print Works. Today, the riverfront still has a large marina and a popular yacht club. Although Metro North Railroad has a station stop in New Hamburgh, the hamlet remains quiet and mostly unknown to outsiders.

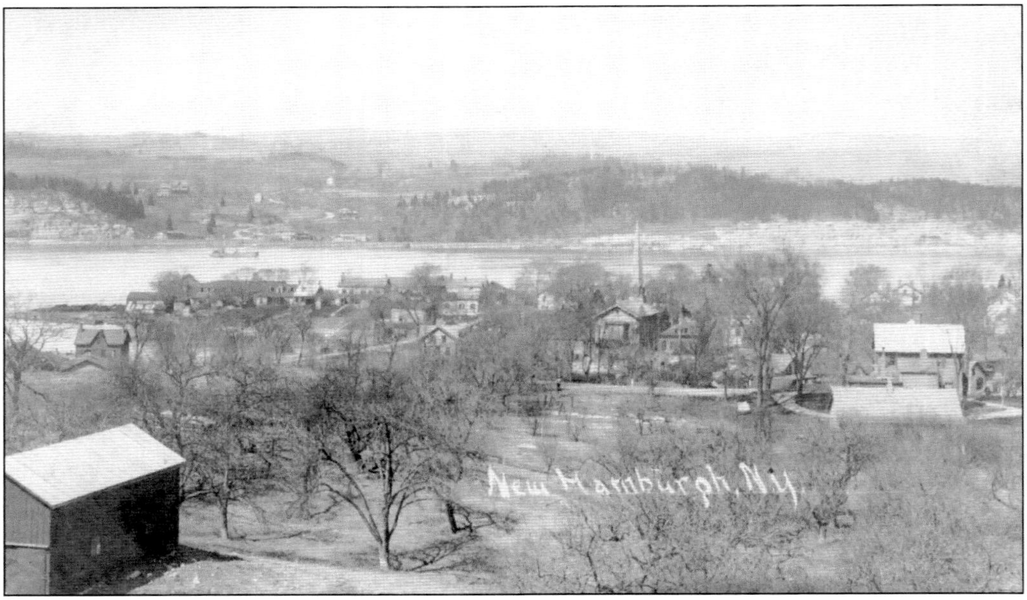

GENERAL VIEW OF NEW HAMBURGH, C. 1906. This bird's-eye view shows a cross section of downtown New Hamburgh. The peninsula on the far left is the Millard Dock, which had a long store house along the Hudson River for the Garner Print Works. Across the river was the hamlet of Cedar Point, which was demolished when the Trap Rock Mining Company purchased it. (Courtesy of Timothy Holls.)

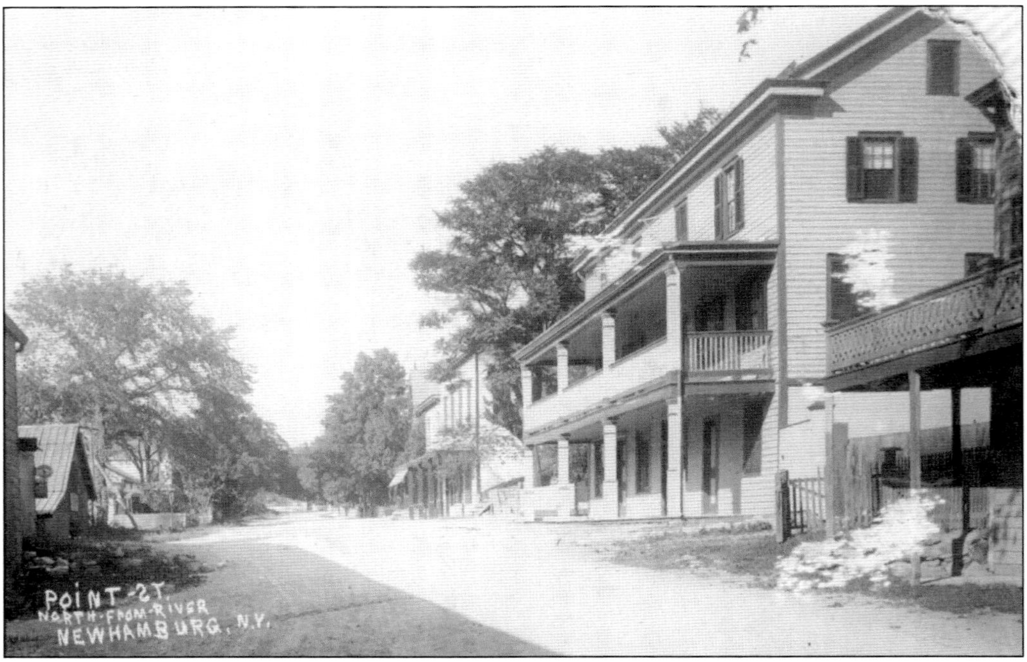

POINT STREET, C. 1910. Looking up Point Street from what is today White's Marina, the large white building on the right was the old New Hamburgh Hotel, which no longer stands. The largest hotel in the hamlet, many of the guests were passing visitors or businessmen who stopped before either catching the *Mary Powell* dayliner to New York or heading inland to nearby Wappingers Falls. (Courtesy of Lawson Edgar.)

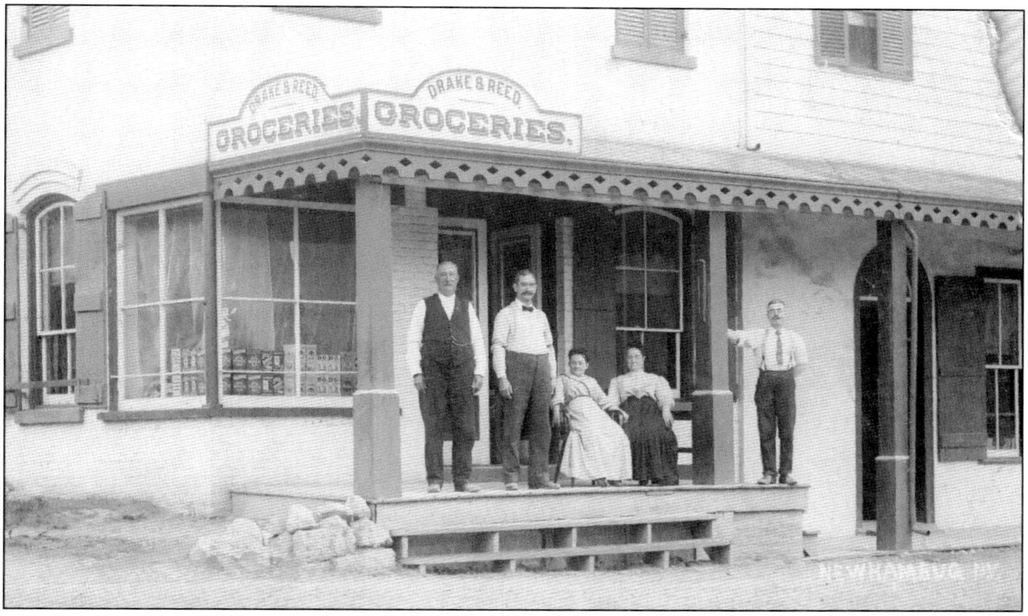

GROCERY STORE, C. 1908. Just north of the New Hamburgh Hotel was Drake and Reed Groceries. Standing on the porch are the owners, whose store sat on the corner of Point and River Roads. The very successful business lasted until the 1940s, when it closed after the death of Mr. Reed. (Courtesy of Lawson Edgar.)

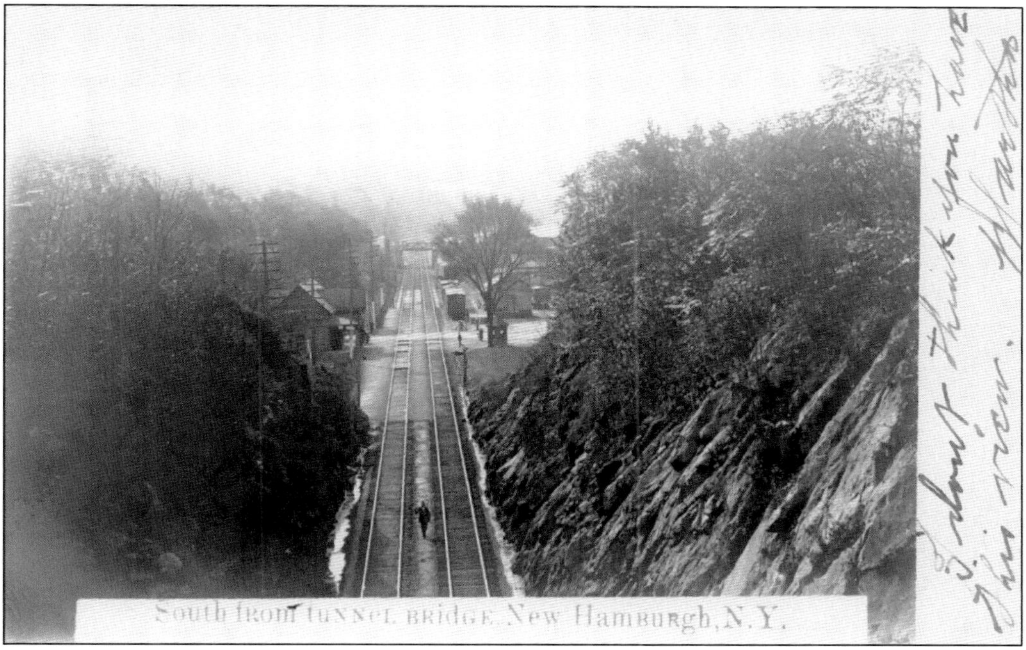

SOUTH FROM RAILROAD TUNNEL, 1908. This old photograph shows a lone railroad worker walking north towards the tunnel. Although New Hamburgh had a thriving lime quarry, the economy boomed when the railroad finally reach the village from New York City. Just north of the Main Street crossing, a line of train cars stand along a small spur line in front of the freight depot. Farmers from as far away as Beekman traveled to New Hamburgh for a fast and easy way to get their goods down to New York City.

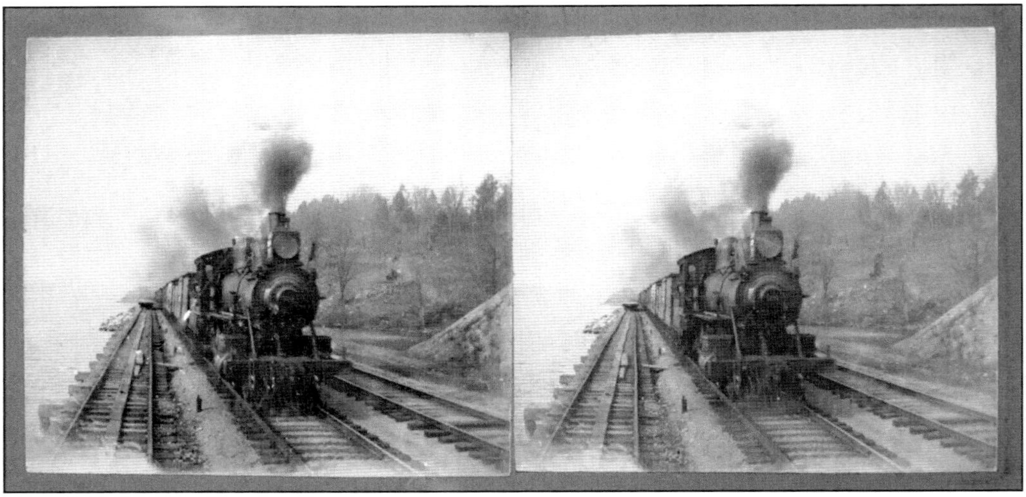

HUDSON RIVER RAILROAD, C. 1890. Constructed in 1847 and later owned by Cornelius Vanderbilt, the Hudson River Railroad was a vital link between New York City and communities along the eastern shore of the Hudson River. Most of the line had two tracks to allow both freight and passenger trains to pass. The track on the far left was an auxiliary track used only when one of the other tracks was under repair.

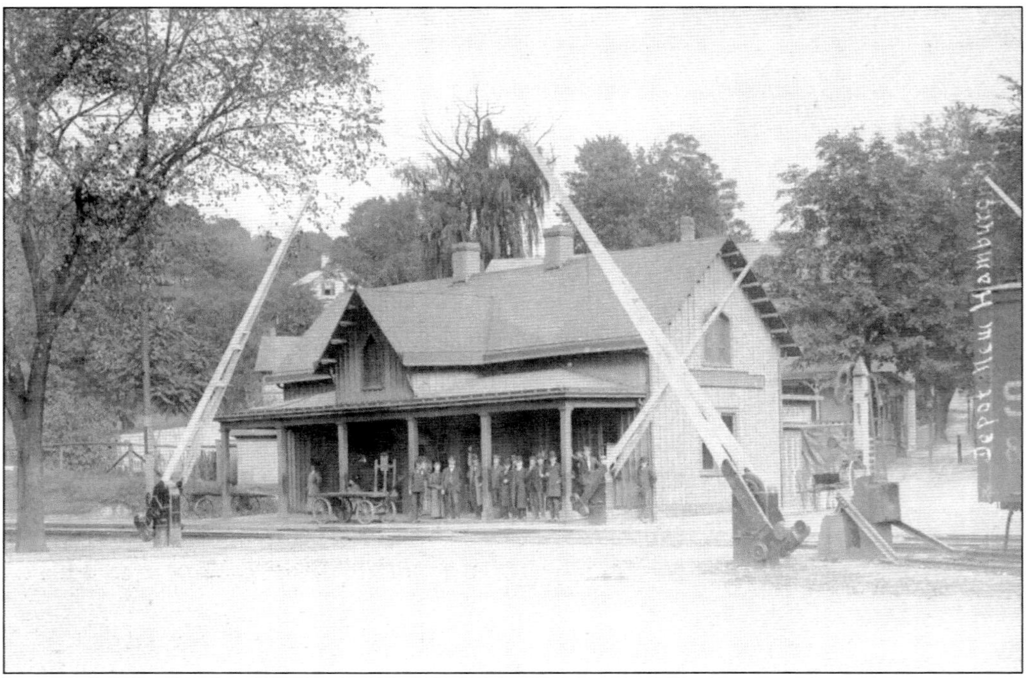

NEW HAMBURGH PASSENGER RAILROAD STATION, 1908. Passengers stand on the porch of railroad station on Main Street waiting for the train down to New York City. Constructed in 1850, the large wooden station dramatically changed both the small hamlet of New Hamburgh and the town of Wappinger. Passenger service, which ran twice daily from the station, allowed residents to travel to New York City and also enabled wealthy city residents easy access to their summer cottages that lined the river.

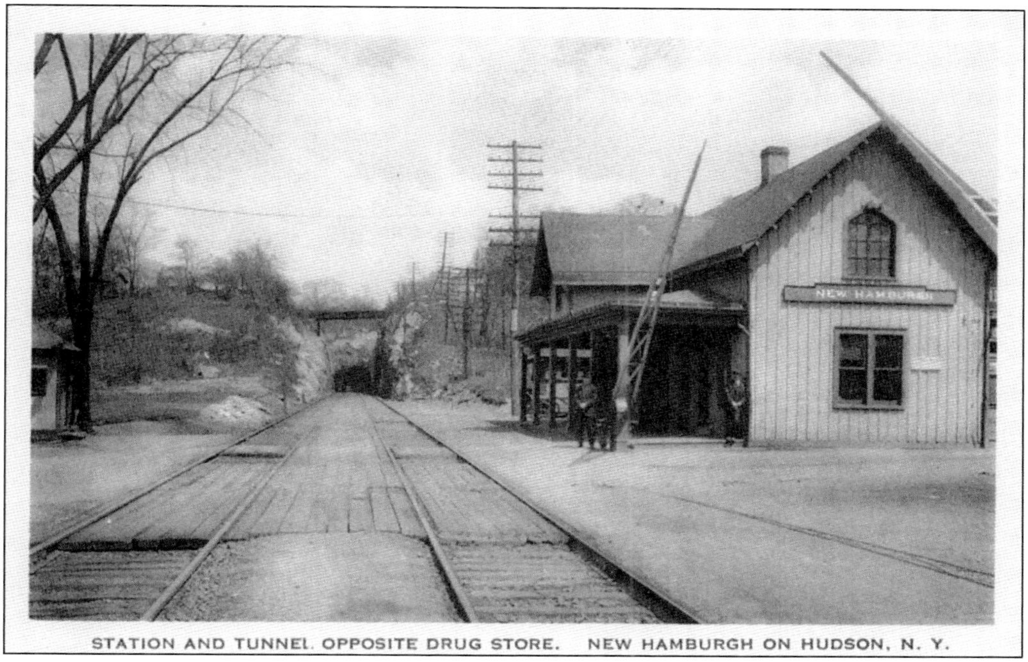

NYC&HR Railroad Tunnel, c. 1910. Just north of the railroad station, a large wall of rock proved to be a roadblock for the Hudson River Railroad Line. Even though the railroad reached the village in 1849, the tunnel through the hillside was not completed until 1851. During that two-year interval, passengers continuing north would have to disembark the train and board a boat at the mouth of the Wappingers Creek. The boat would then take them north around the point to an awaiting train on the other side of the rock hillside.

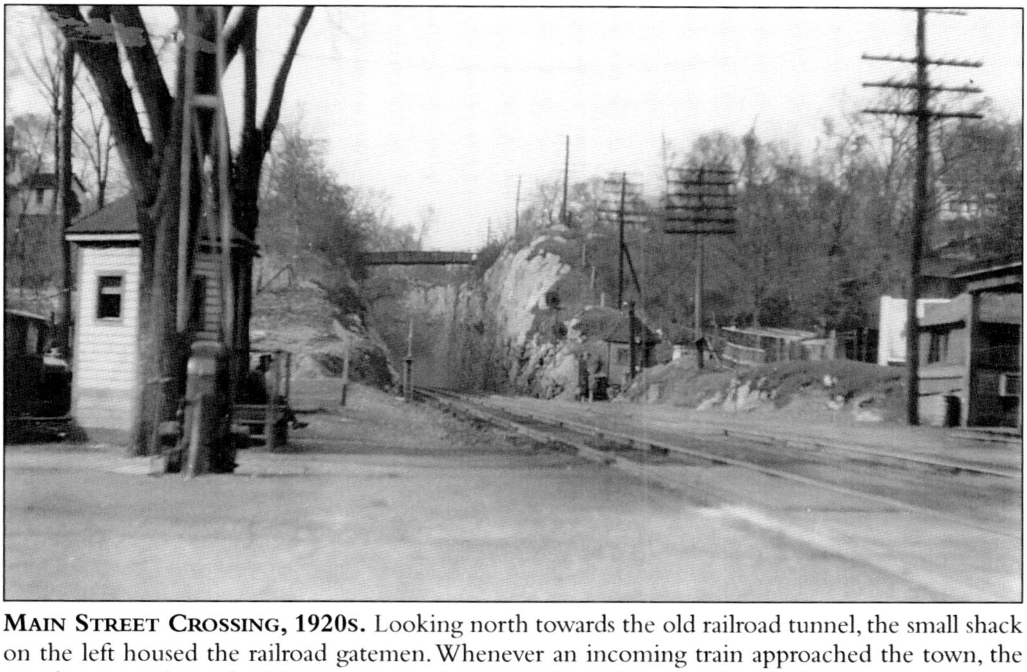

Main Street Crossing, 1920s. Looking north towards the old railroad tunnel, the small shack on the left housed the railroad gatemen. Whenever an incoming train approached the town, the signal towers telegraphed the gatemen to lower the Main Street barriers by hand to stop crossing traffic. (Courtesy of Lawson Edgar.)

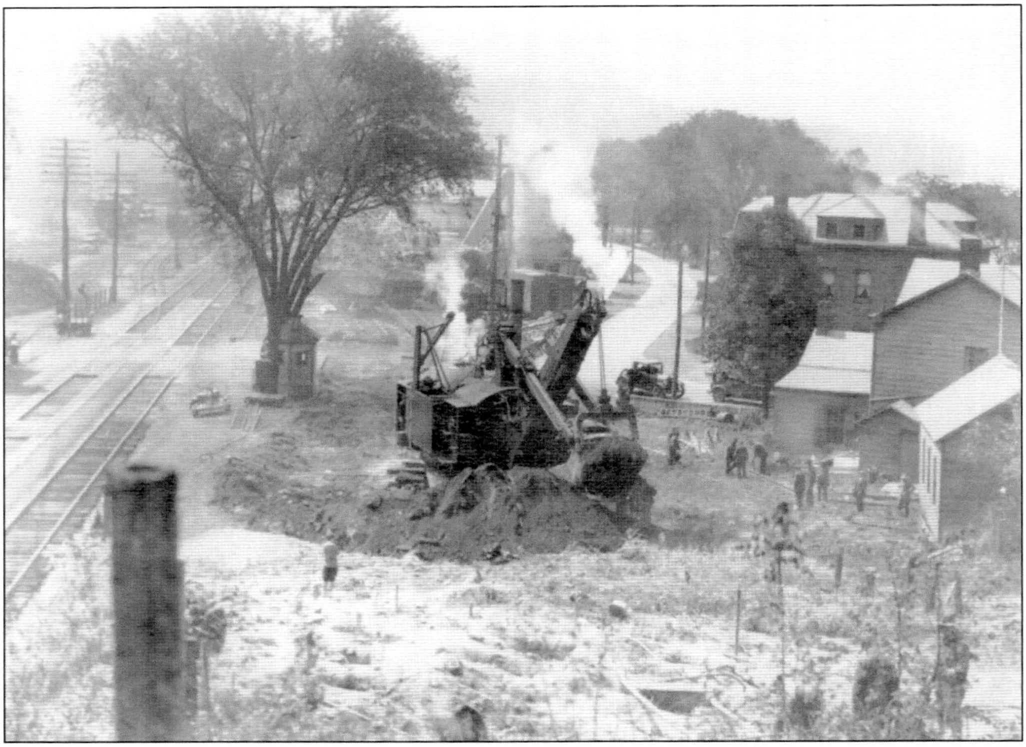

Hudson River Railroad Expansion, 1930s. The Hudson River Railroad was expanded during the 1930s to four tracks. Shown here, a steam operated shovel begins the work digging into the hillside for a new railroad cut. The tunnel continued to be used throughout the construction work so that train service would not be interrupted. (Courtesy of Lawson Edgar.)

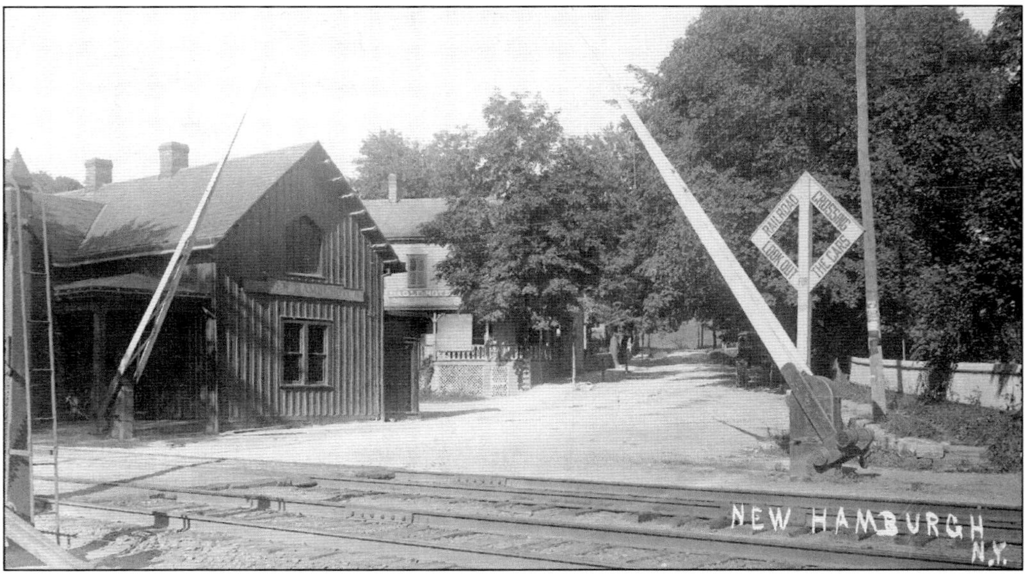

Main Street East, 1912. A quiet scene is shown here, looking east from the Main Street railroad crossing. The wooden building to the left is the passenger station, which was removed during the expansion of the Metro-North Commuter line in the mid-1900s. The building directly behind the station is the Eagle Hotel, a popular resting spot for railroad travelers passing through.

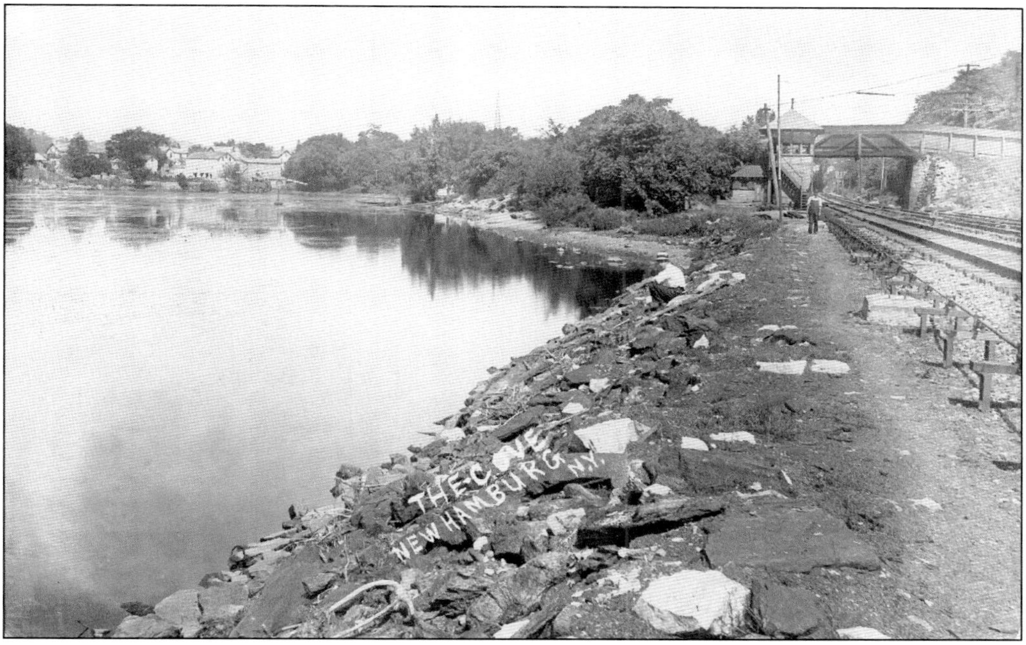

THE COVE, C. 1905. A railroad signalman stands along the railroad tracks just north of the mouth of Wappingers Creek. The tower behind him was used to warn northbound trains of the upcoming station stop. The bridge behind the tower once connected New Hamburgh Road to Railroad Avenue. The buildings to the far left were along North River Road and were used by the Drake Dock at the end of Point Street.

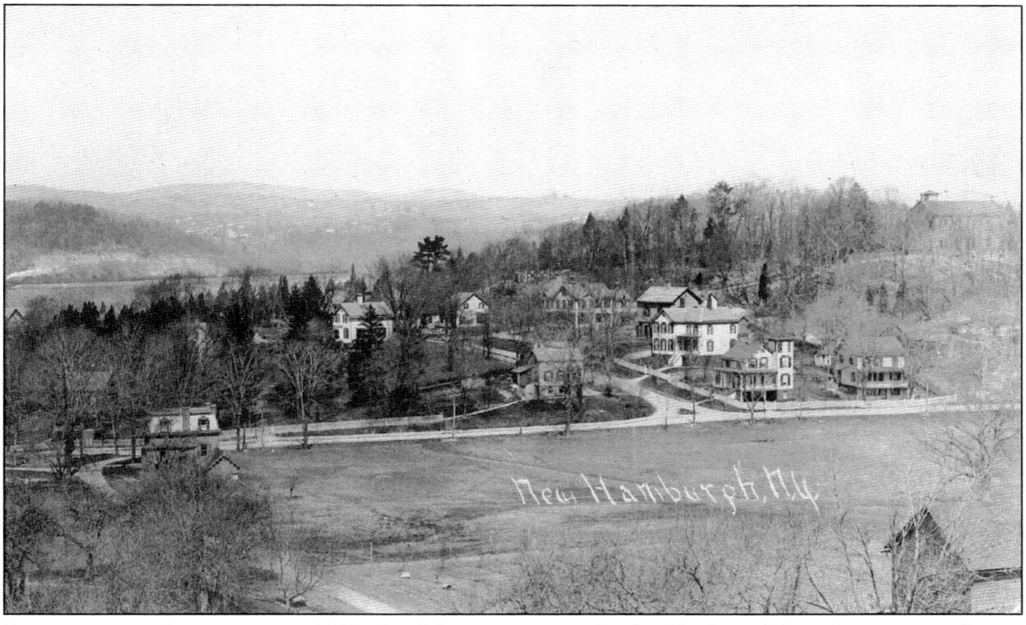

RESIDENTIAL SECTION, C. 1910. Looking west towards the Hudson River, houses are shown along North Main Street and Division Street, present-day Conklin Street. Many of the homes in this photograph were constructed from 1800 to 1870, as the village moved east away from the Hudson River. Main Street, the road going horizontally across the photograph, turned into Channingville Road as it led north to West Main Street in Wappingers Falls.

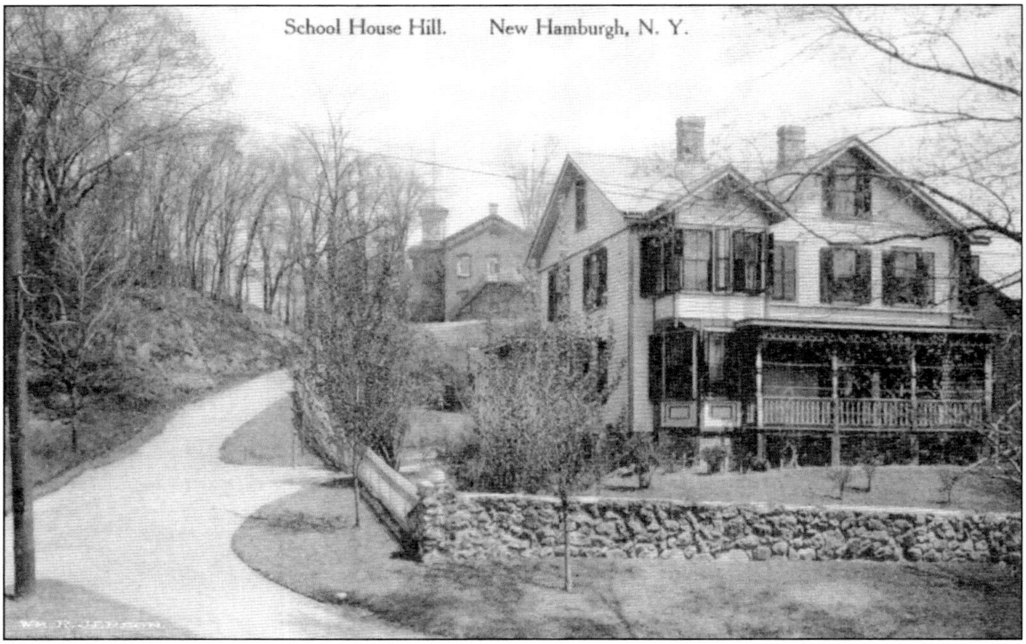

SCHOOL STREET, C. 1915. For many residents in the village, the school at the top of the hill was known as Crow Hill Seminary for the large amount of crows that would congregate in the trees along School Street. A Mr. Graham, the head landscaper for the nearby Reese estate called Obercreek, owned the house on the corner.

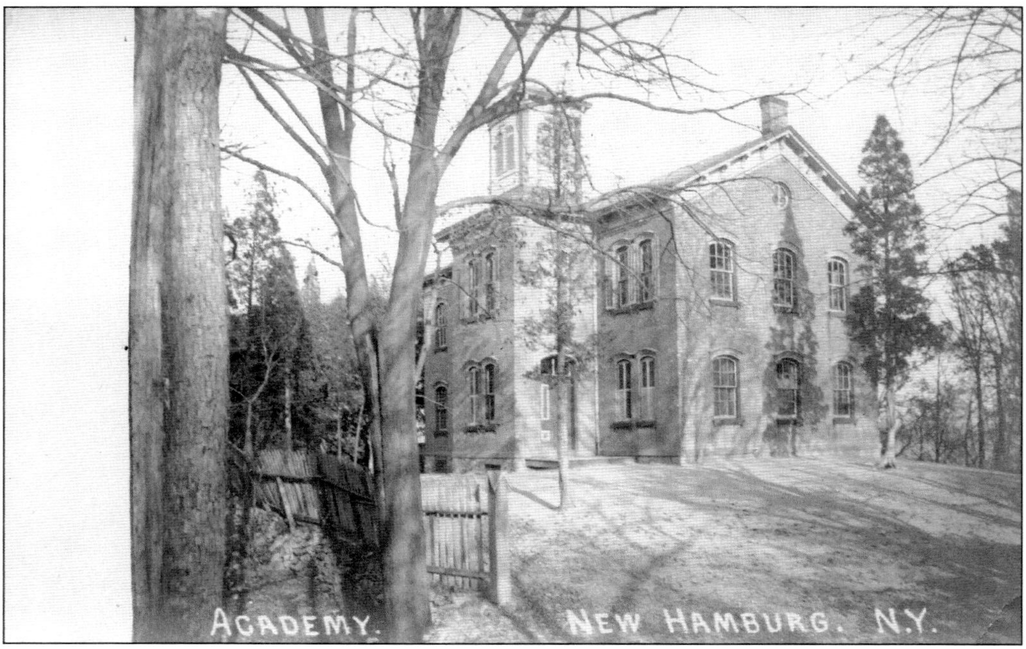

THE ACADEMY SCHOOL, C. 1910. At the top of "School House Hill" was the Academy School building. The large brick building, similar in design to the schools in Hughsonville and Wappingers Falls, housed all grades up to high school. The school closed in the early 1940s, when students were bused to the central school in Wappingers Falls. Today, the old school classrooms have been converted into apartments.

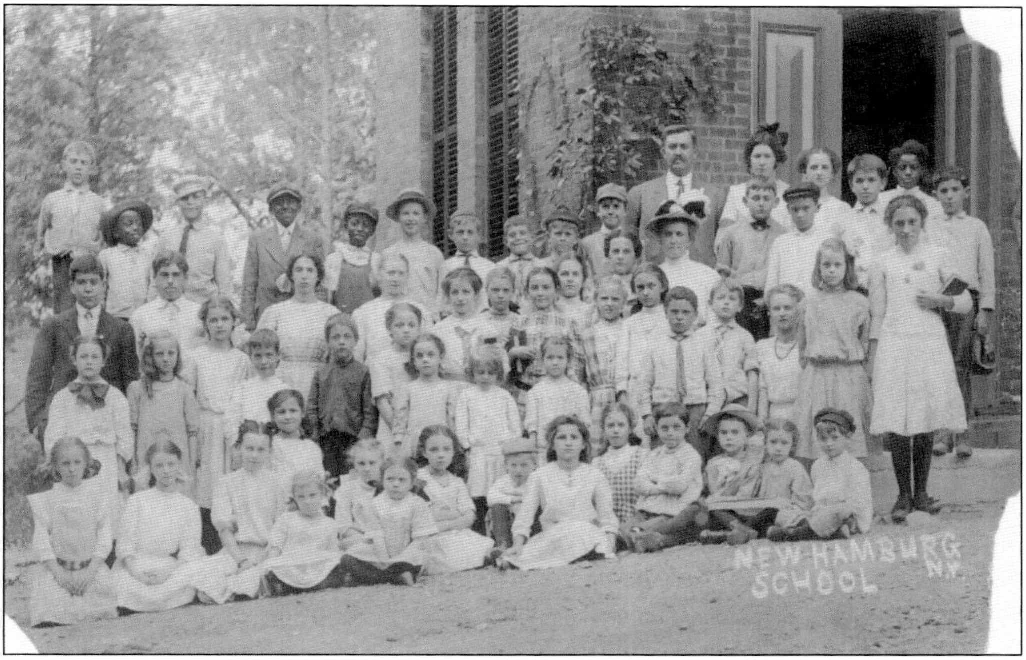

School Photograph, c. 1910. The village's children are sitting for a class photograph. Although mostly from the village, some of the children traveled miles from homes along Sheafe Road to attend class each day. (Courtesy of Lawson Edgar.)

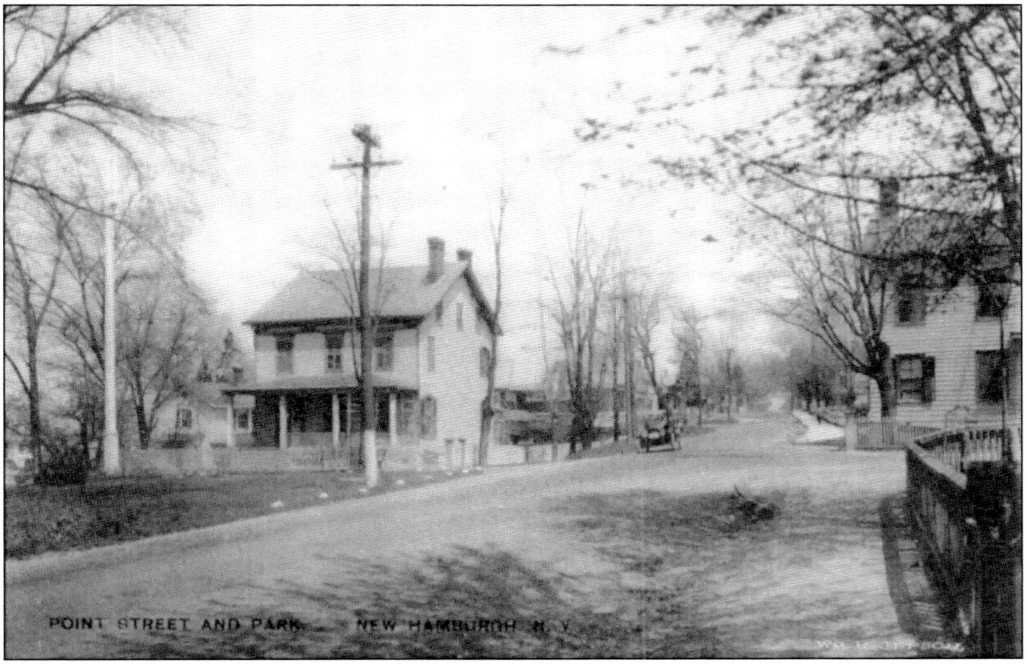

Point Street, c. 1915. At the intersection of Point Street and Main Street, the village established a park overlooking the Hudson River. A large ship mast was placed at the center of the park surrounded by benches and gardens. The house on the left was owned by Captain Drake, an accomplished ice yacht sailor and owner of a few Hudson River excursion boats.

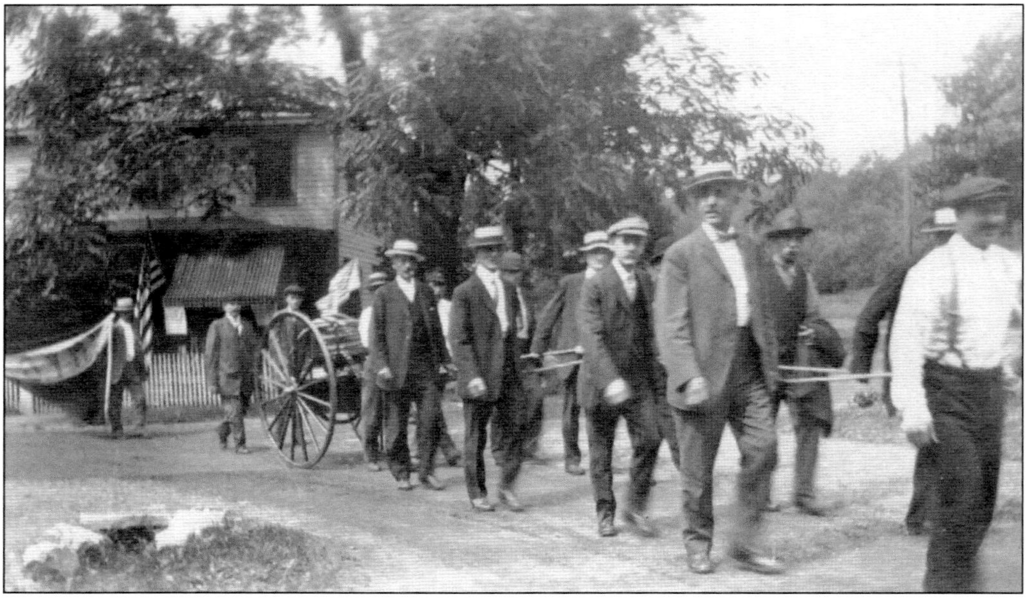

New Hamburgh Fire Company, 1919. The New Hamburgh Fire Company was established in a house in 1917. Shown here, the early fire company carries their hand pumper during a World War I parade. The all-volunteer company included some of the town's most prominent men, whose families have carried on the tradition over the generations. (Courtesy of Lawson Edgar.)

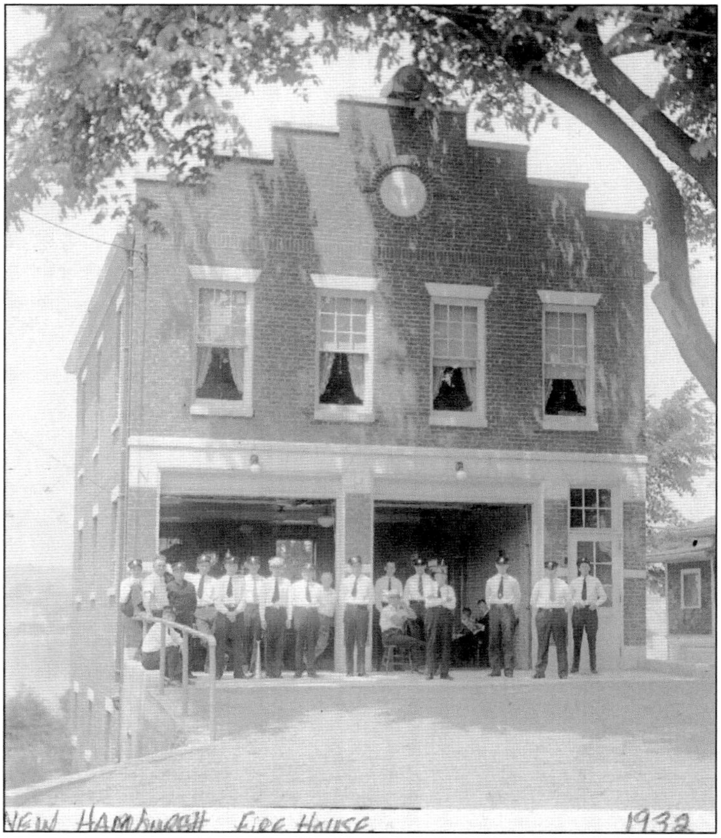

New Firehouse, 1932. The New Hamburgh Fire Company built this firehouse on Point Street near the intersection of Main Street in the early 1930s. The first fire commissioners for the hamlet were Warren C. Edgar, John Pawl, and William Workman. The company used the first floor to house their fire truck while the upstairs was used as a meeting room and social hall. (Courtesy of Lawson Edgar.)

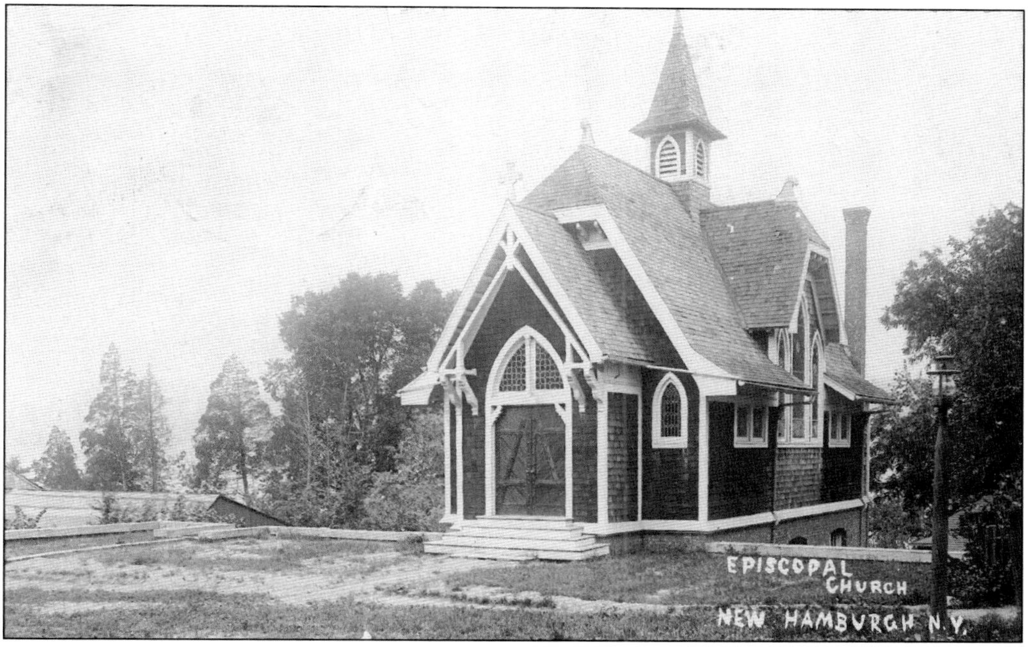

EPISCOPAL CHURCH, 1909. Overlooking the river on Point Street, the Episcopal Church was constructed in 1903 in a mix of Gothic and carpentry architectural styling. First called the Zion Chapel after the church in Wappingers Falls, the church soon became a landmark for the community. Today, renamed St. Nicholas-on-the-Hudson, the building has continuously housed an Episcopal parish for over 100 years.

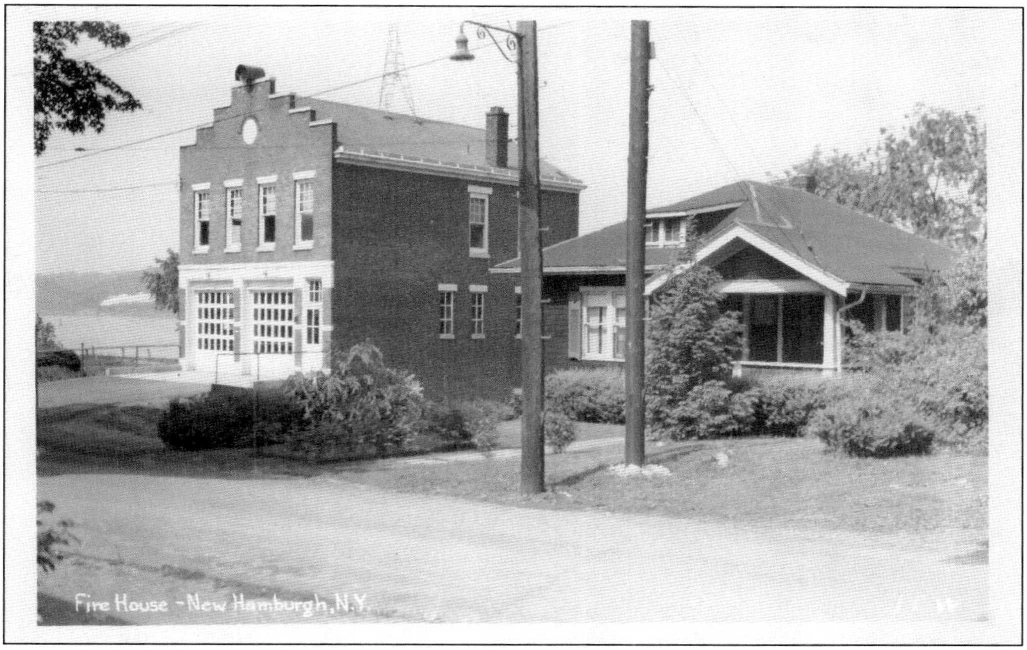

NEW HAMBURGH FIRE COMPANY, C. 1935. The local firehouse moved in 1967 to its present site on Channingville Road, just north of the hamlet. The house next door, today owned by the Edgar family, was a Sears and Roebuck catalog home that was brought into town by train and assembled in 1926. (Courtesy of Lawson Edgar.)

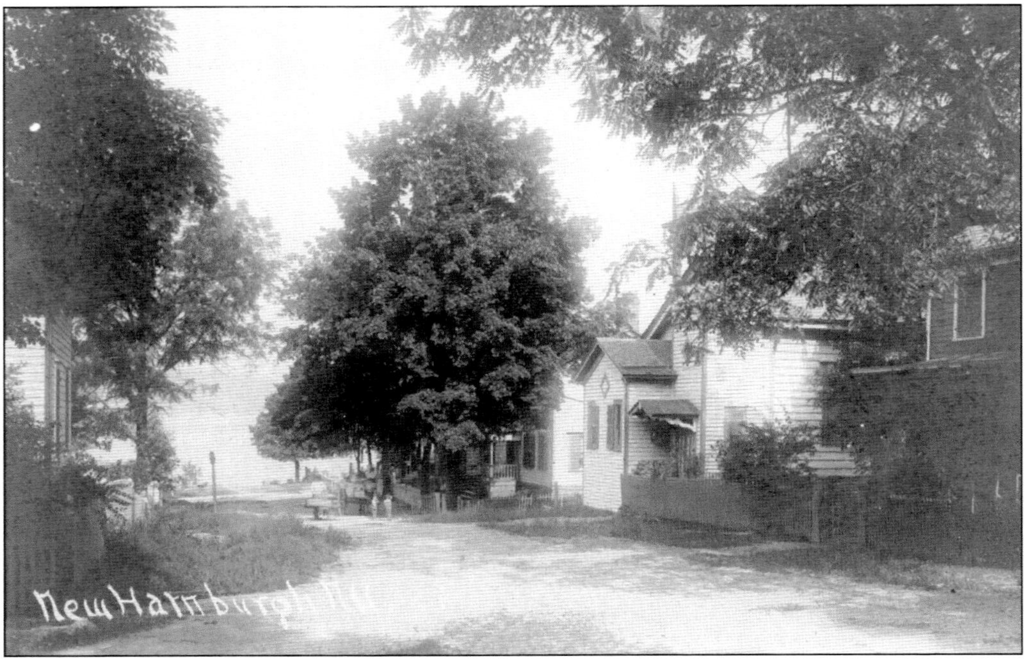

DIVISION STREET, C. 1905. Looking west from Point Street, the small stretch of Division Street is one of the oldest settled areas of New Hamburgh. The light-colored building on the right is the Methodist Church and parsonage. At the end of the street was the Brower home and a small riverside park.

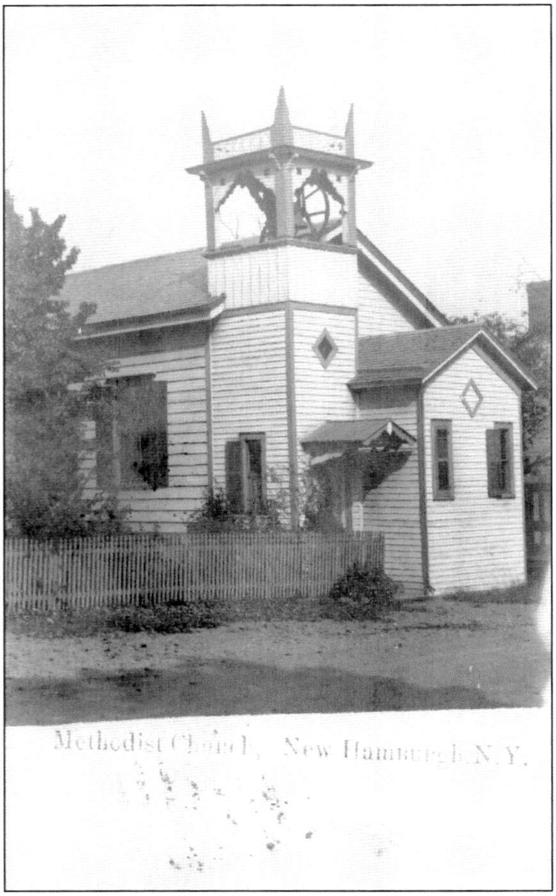

METHODIST CHURCH, 1908. The small Methodist Chapel was constructed for $800 in 1856. The first pastor, Rev. F. Sellick, presided over a small congregation numbering less than 35 people. The chapel was the only church building in the village that had a bell, which was usually used on Sunday to call parishioners to service and children to Sunday school.

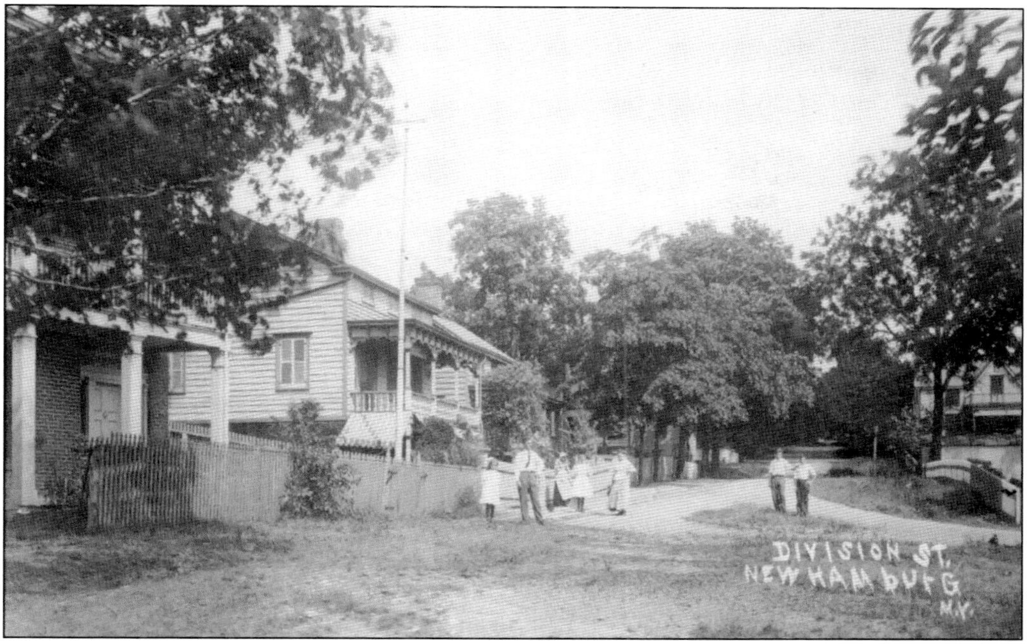

DIVISION STREET EAST, C. 1910. Residents stand on Division Street during a quiet afternoon. The house on the left was owned by Mildred Sinsabaugh, a longtime resident of the hamlet. Division Street once connected to Main Street until the rock cut was built. Since no bridge was constructed to connect both halves, the eastern section of the street was renamed Conklin Street. (Courtesy of Lawson Edgar.)

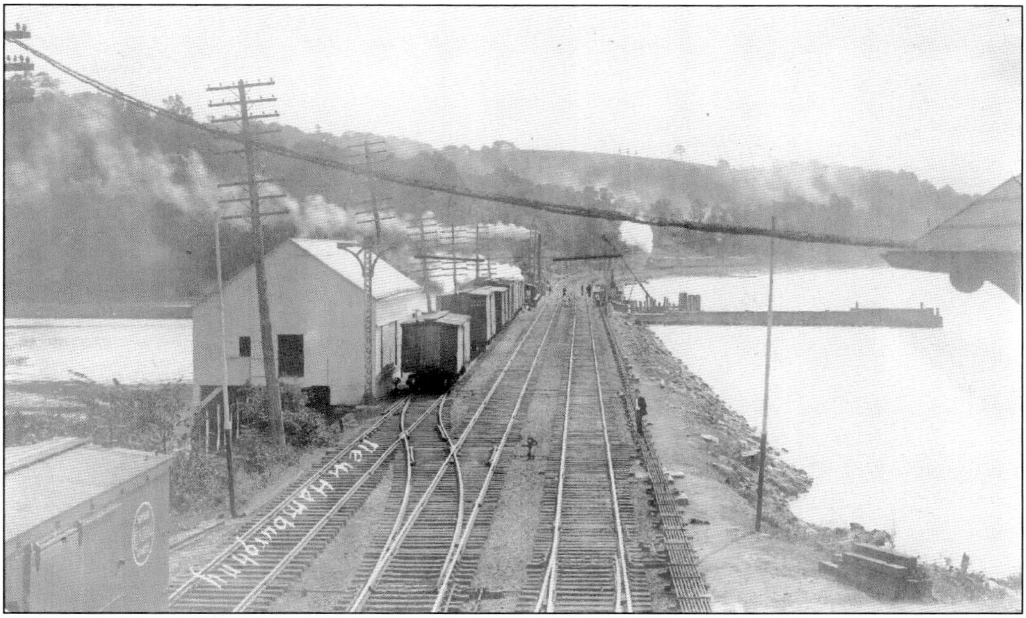

NYC&HR RAILROAD TRACKS LOOKING SOUTH. Looking south from the old freight yard, one can see how important New Hamburgh was as a railroad town. The freight trains along the left were most likely bringing goods in for the Dutchess Bleachery just upstream. The large slip on the right was the entrance to the Wappingers Creek, where boats could enter through a small drawbridge. (Courtesy of Lawson Edgar.)

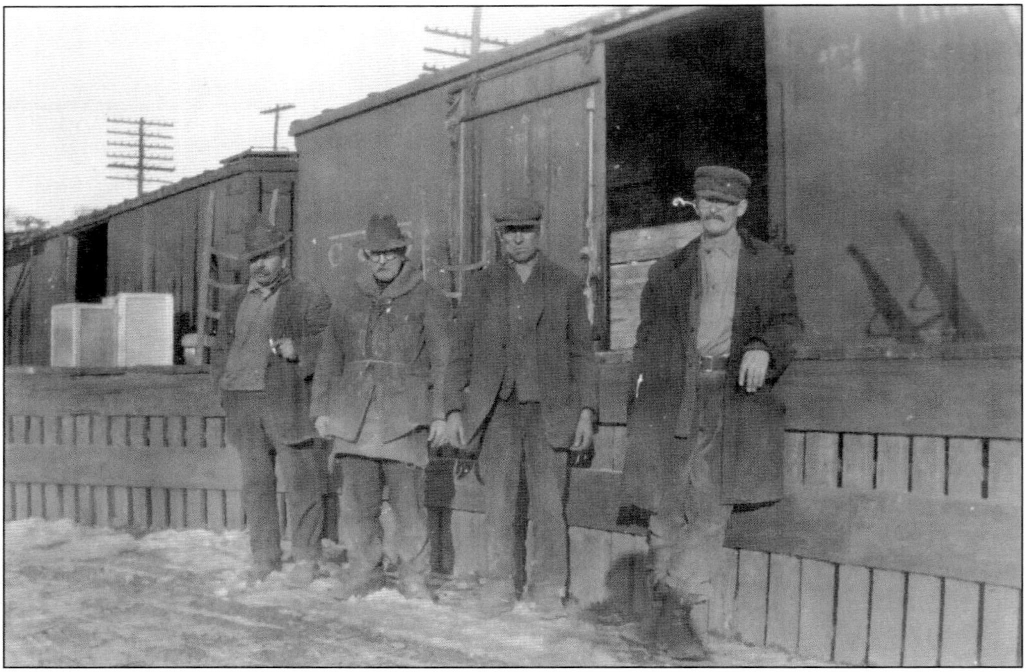

RAILROAD YARD, C. 1920S. The Hudson River Railroad was the main source of income for many of the town's residents. Standing in a line is a group of rail workers while on break. Trains arrived daily with boxcars full of merchandise for local stores and factories. (Courtesy of Lawson Edgar.)

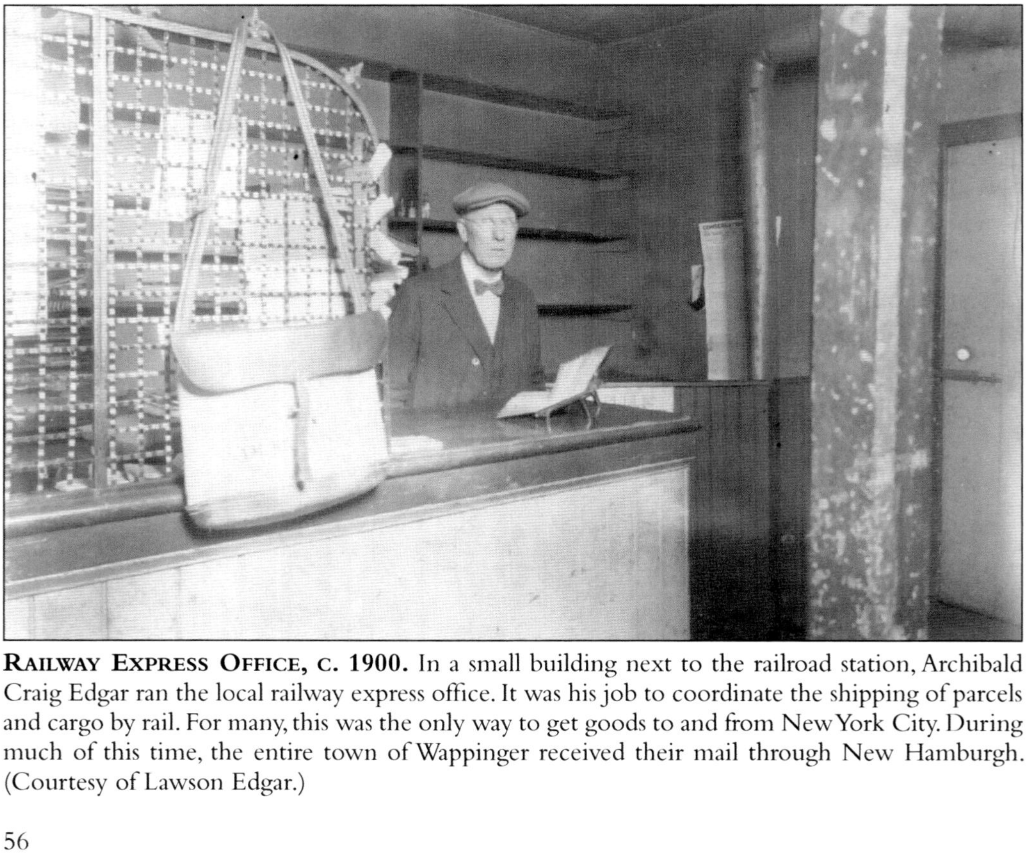

RAILWAY EXPRESS OFFICE, C. 1900. In a small building next to the railroad station, Archibald Craig Edgar ran the local railway express office. It was his job to coordinate the shipping of parcels and cargo by rail. For many, this was the only way to get goods to and from New York City. During much of this time, the entire town of Wappinger received their mail through New Hamburgh. (Courtesy of Lawson Edgar.)

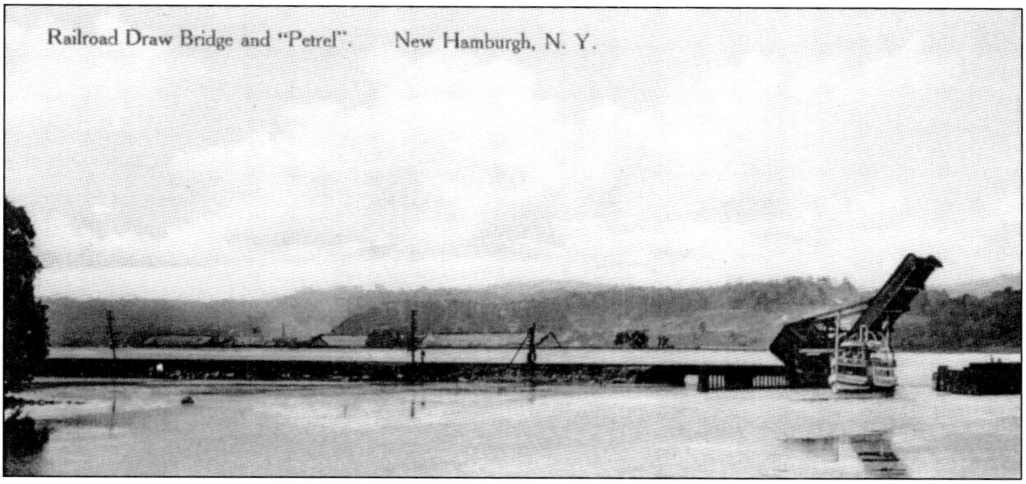

RAILROAD DRAWBRIDGE OVER WAPPINGERS CREEK, C. 1915. Since no railroad line went east from New Hamburgh, the village of Wappingers Falls had no rail service. The best way to get goods from the river to the factories along the creek was by barge. To ensure easy passage for boats up and down Wappingers Creek, the New York City and Hudson River Railroad (NYC&HRRR) built a drawbridge at the creek's mouth. Shown here, the drawbridge opens for the excursion *Petrel* to enter the creek from the Hudson River.

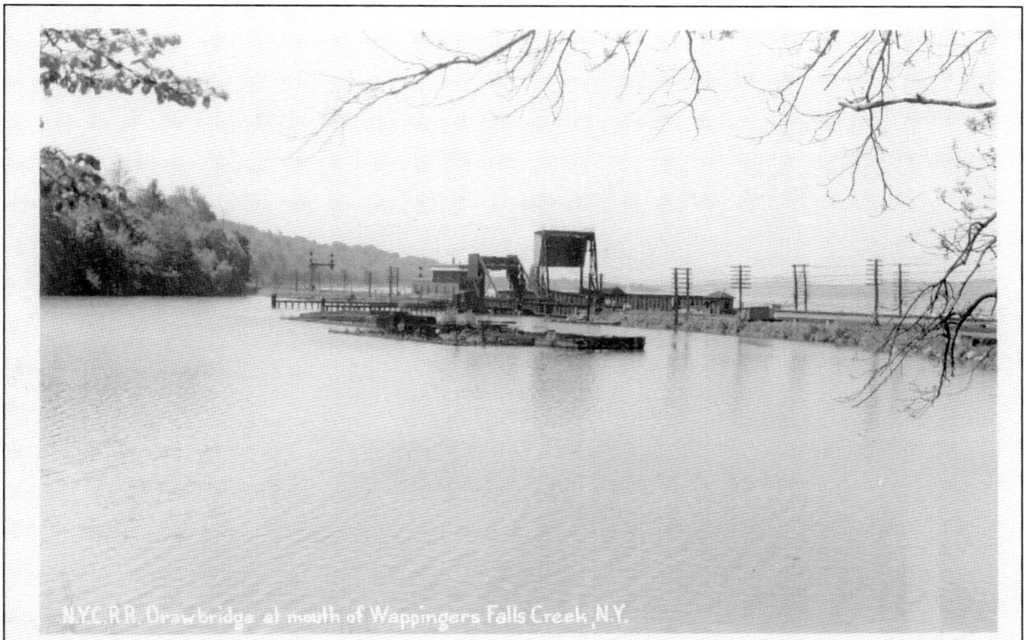

NEW YORK CITY & HUDSON RIVER RAILROAD DISASTER. The original drawbridge over Wappingers Creek at New Hamburgh was constructed in the 1850s but was destroyed in the winter of 1871 during the worst railroad accident of the Hudson River Railroad Company. It occurred when a passenger train heading north collided with a derailed oil train. A fire ensued, consuming both trains and the drawbridge mainly constructed of wood. When the bridge finally collapsed into the Hudson River, it pulled a number of passenger cars with it under the ice. The collision and subsequent sinking killed 40 passengers and the conductor, David Simmons, who sacrificed his life to save those still trapped.

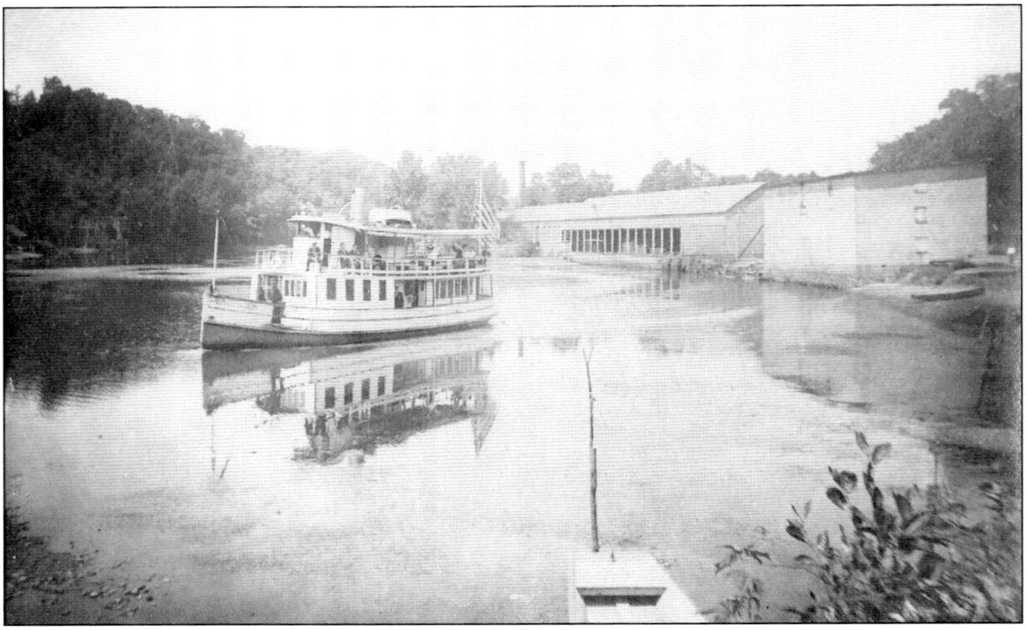

PASSENGER FERRY *MESSENGER*, C. 1905. Operated by Frank Drake, the *Messenger* ferryboat brought factory workers from across the river to the Garner Print Works. The boat made two trips daily from New Hamburgh to Newburgh, stopping at Roseton and Marlboro along the way. Shown here on Wappingers Creek below the print works, the boat passes the old power plant and lumber mill that stood on Creek Road. (Courtesy of Timothy Holls.)

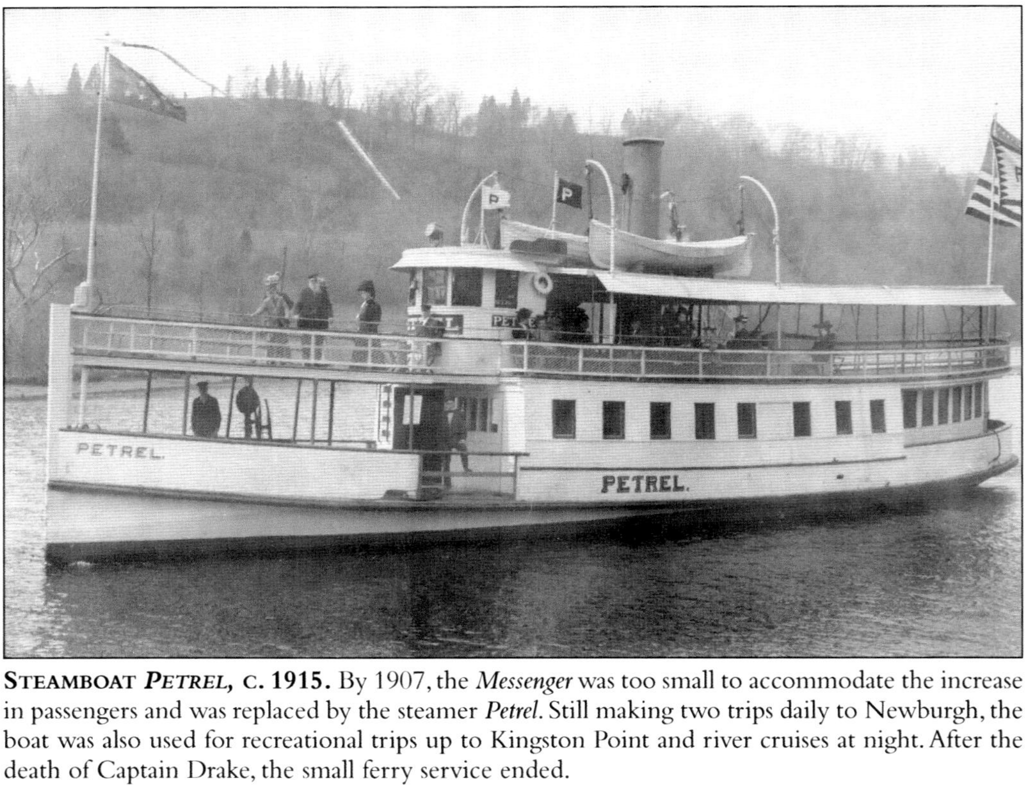

STEAMBOAT *PETREL*, C. 1915. By 1907, the *Messenger* was too small to accommodate the increase in passengers and was replaced by the steamer *Petrel*. Still making two trips daily to Newburgh, the boat was also used for recreational trips up to Kingston Point and river cruises at night. After the death of Captain Drake, the small ferry service ended.

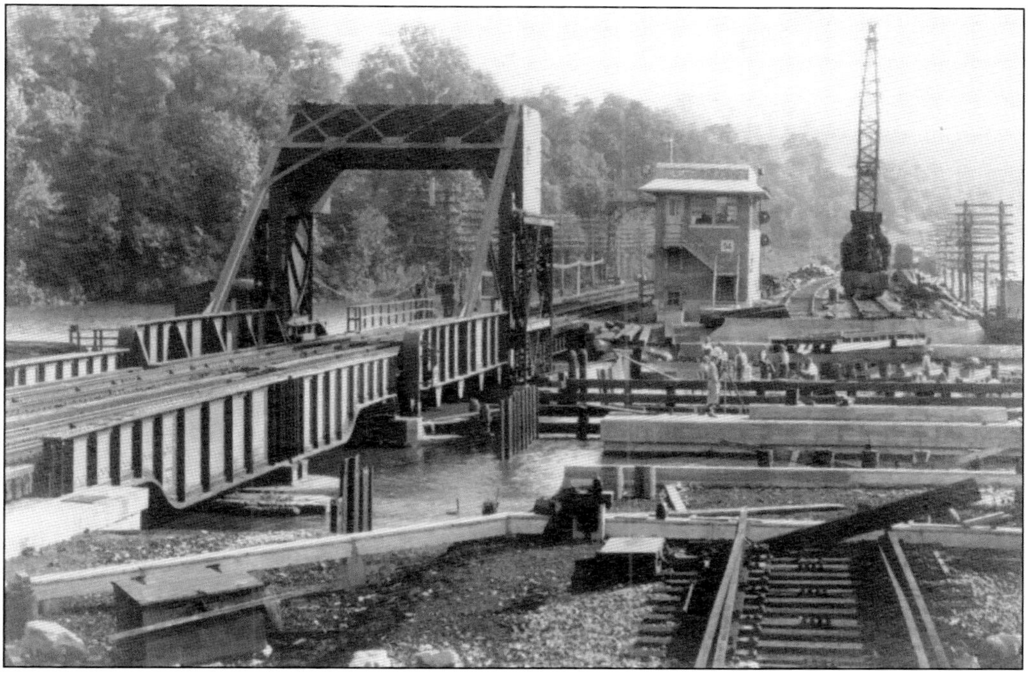

CONSTRUCTION OF NEW RAILROAD BRIDGE, C. 1930. With the addition of two more tracks, a new bridge was constructed next to the old drawbridge. On the right, men stand in the outlet of Wappingers Creek, securing pilings for the larger drawbridge. Today, the bridge no longer opens, and it blocks access to the creek from the Hudson River. (Courtesy of Lawson Edgar.)

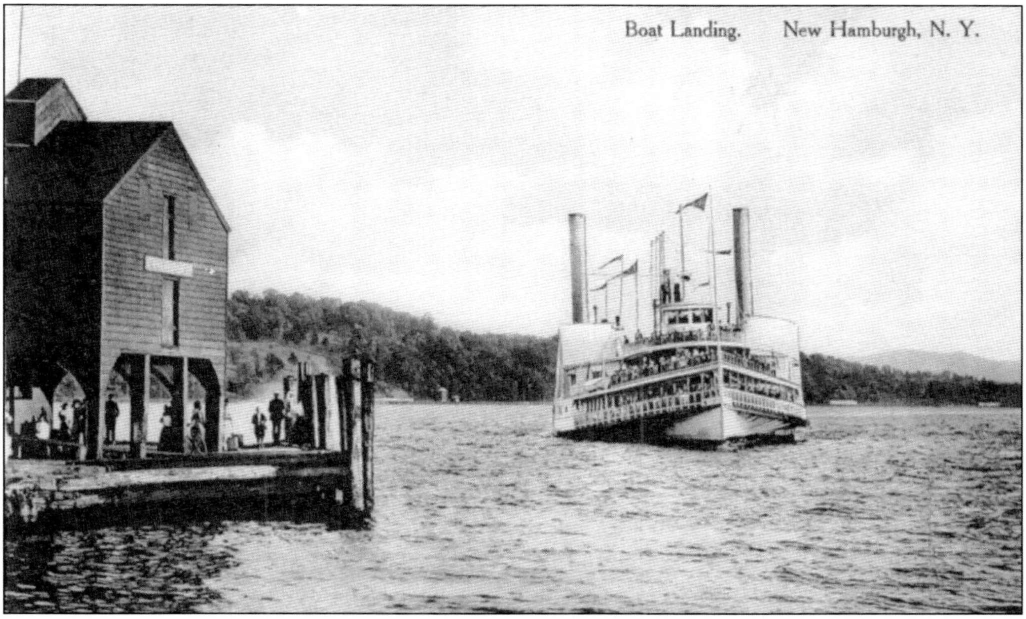

DAYLINER ARRIVING AT NEW HAMBURGH DOCK, C. 1915. This old postcard shows the Hudson River Dayliner, the *Mary Powell*, arriving from New York City. The dock and building were operated by Vermilyea and Jackson and was referred to as "Lower Dock." The *Mary Powell* stopped at New Hamburgh twice daily, once in the morning to take residents south towards the city and once in the afternoon as it headed north towards Albany.

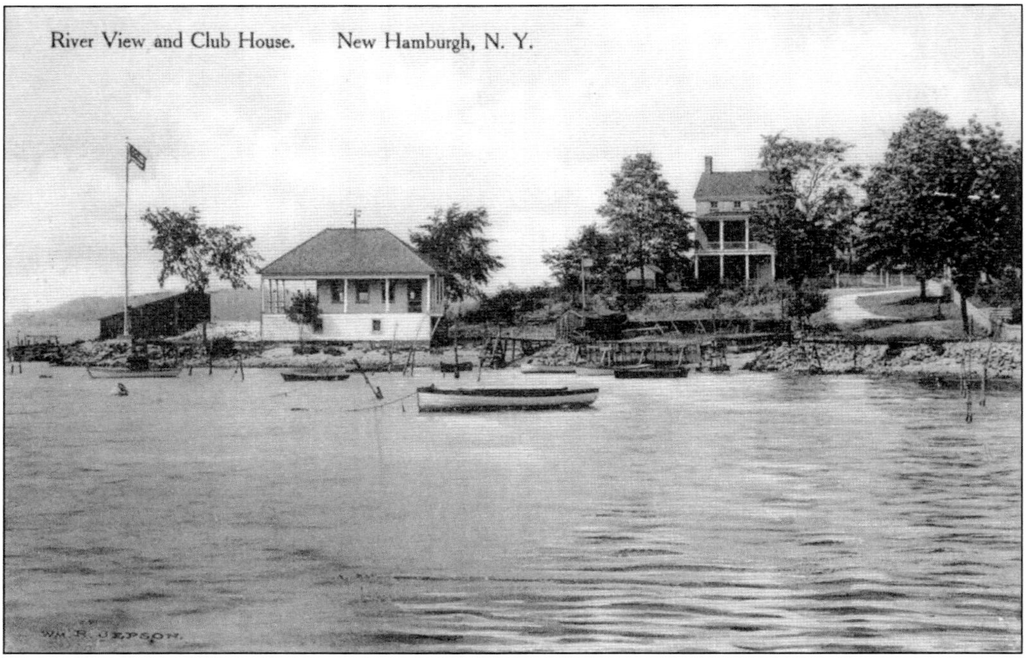

NEW HAMBURGH YACHT CLUB, C. 1915. One of the oldest yacht clubs in the country, the New Hamburgh Yacht Club's incorporation was spirited by local millionaire Irving Grinnell in 1869. Until the mid-1900s, the club was mainly focused on the winter sport of ice yachting. The one-story building on the left was the organization's clubhouse, which was later enlarged to two floors. Adolph Brower, who owned the nearby limekilns, constructed the house in the background in 1845.

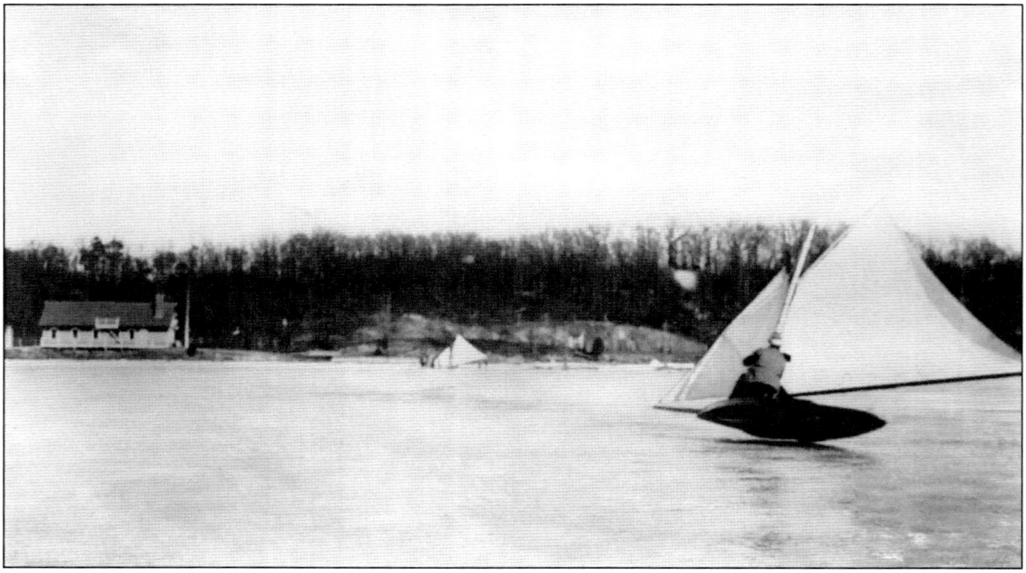

ICE YACHTING ON THE HUDSON RIVER, C. 1890. Ice yachting is a high speed, daring sport only possible with a smooth, flat sheet of ice. Shown here is Archibald Rogers, relative of Franklin D. Roosevelt and friend of Irving Grinnell, taking a sharp turn near the Hyde Park Yacht Club. Although the Hudson River still freezes every winter, ice-breaking ships run by the Coast Guard carve a channel through the ice, creating a jagged and unstable surface for ice yachting.

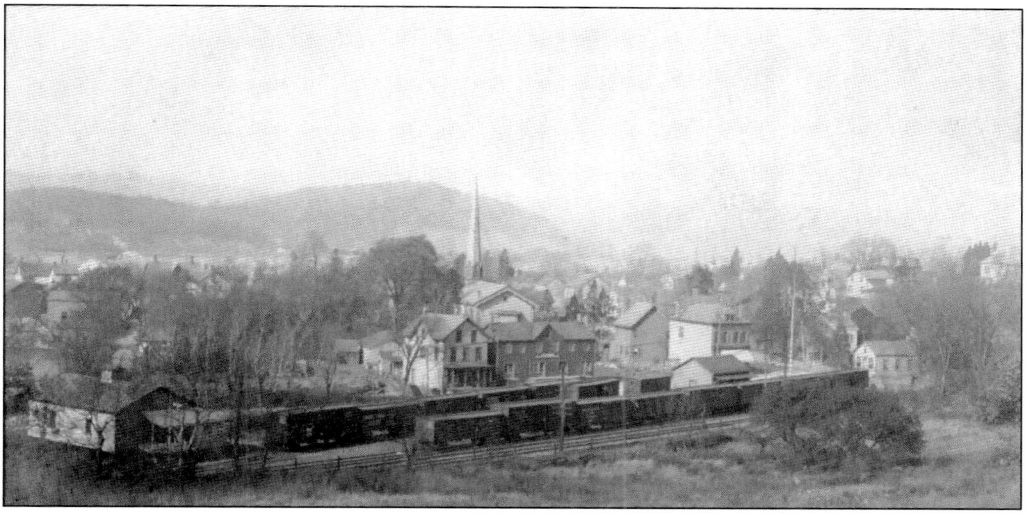

OVERLOOKING RAILROAD AVENUE, C. 1908. Freight cars line the track in front of Railroad Avenue. One of the major businesses on the street was J.A. Flemming's Lumber Supply. His store on Railroad Avenue was just a small part of his operation, which also included a large dock, where White's Marina stands today. His lumber company helped fuel the building boom in New York City during the turn of the 20th century. (Courtesy of Lawson Edgar.)

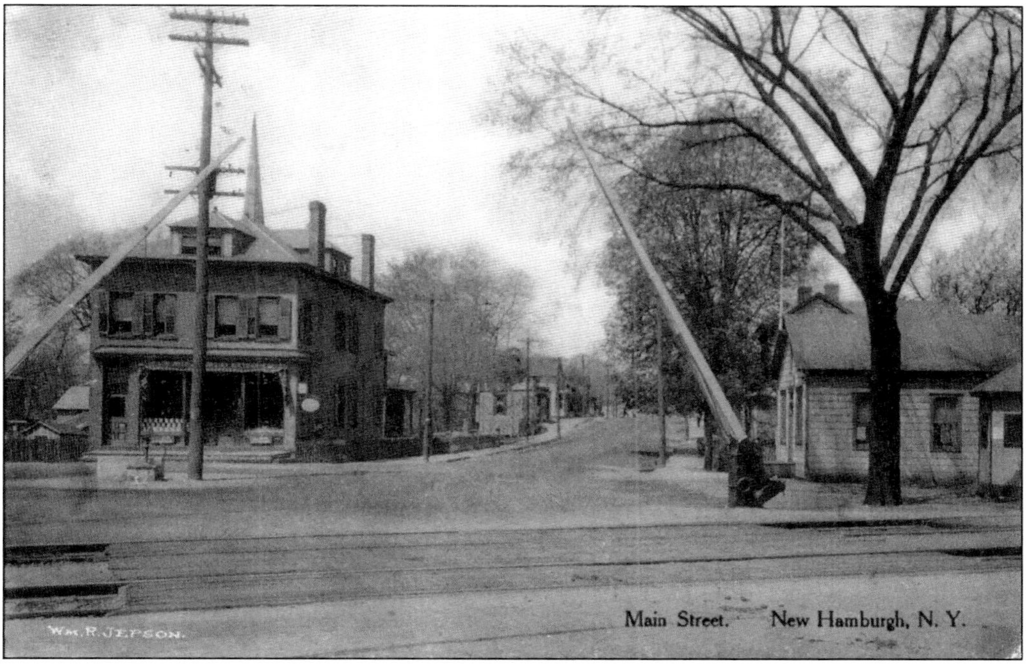

MAIN STREET WEST, C. 1915. Fronting the railroad at the intersection of Railroad Avenue and Main Street was the family-run Jepson Drug Store. The owner, William Jepson, received his goods each morning from the station across the street. Just above the drugstore, the steeple of the Presbyterian Church is visible.

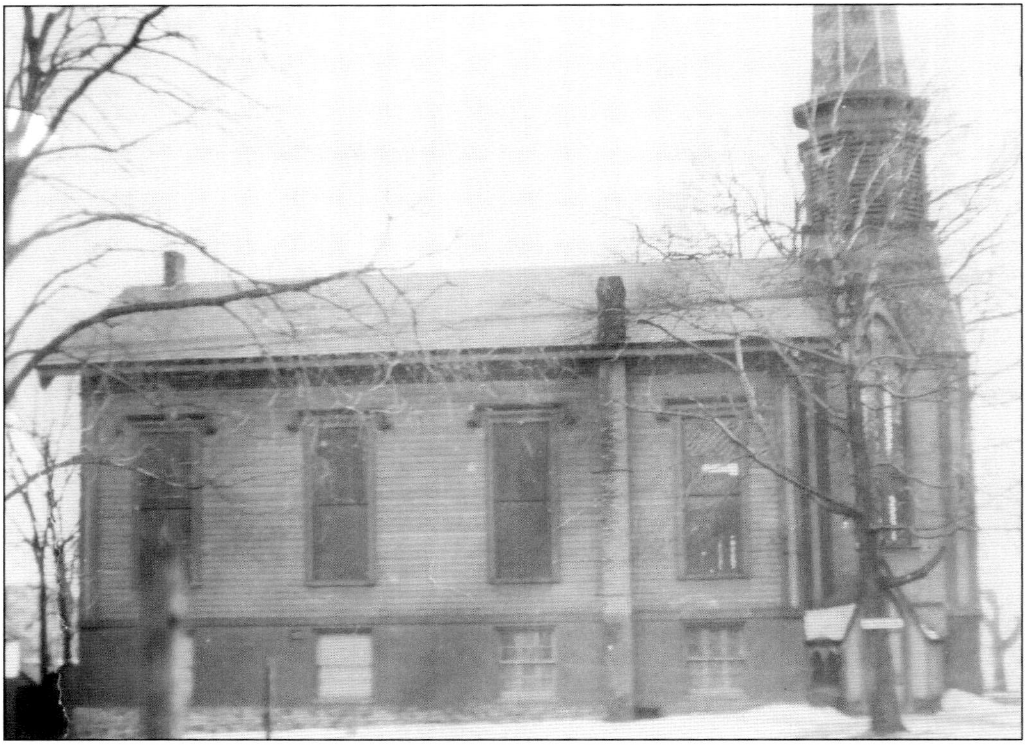

PRESBYTERIAN CHURCH, C. 1915. Situated on Main Street, the Presbyterian Church was by far the largest church in the village. Constructed in 1845, the church first sat on a bluff overlooking the village. As the congregation grew, the building was moved behind Railroad Avenue. After World War II, the congregation declined and the church closed its doors. Today, the building still stands with its steeple now removed and its interior converted into apartments. (Courtesy of Lawson Edgar.)

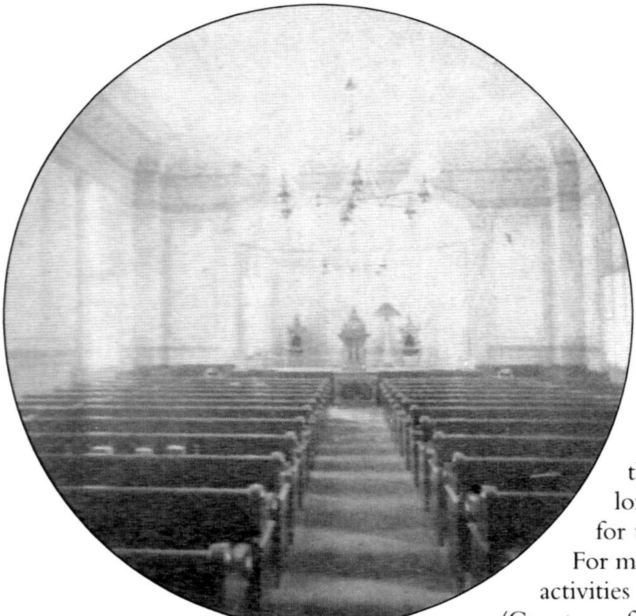

INTERIOR OF THE PRESBYTERIAN CHURCH, C. 1900. The inside of the church was lined by pews with a long center aisle. The front pews were for the town's most prominent families. For many years, most of the village's social activities were centered around the church. (Courtesy of Lawson Edgar.)

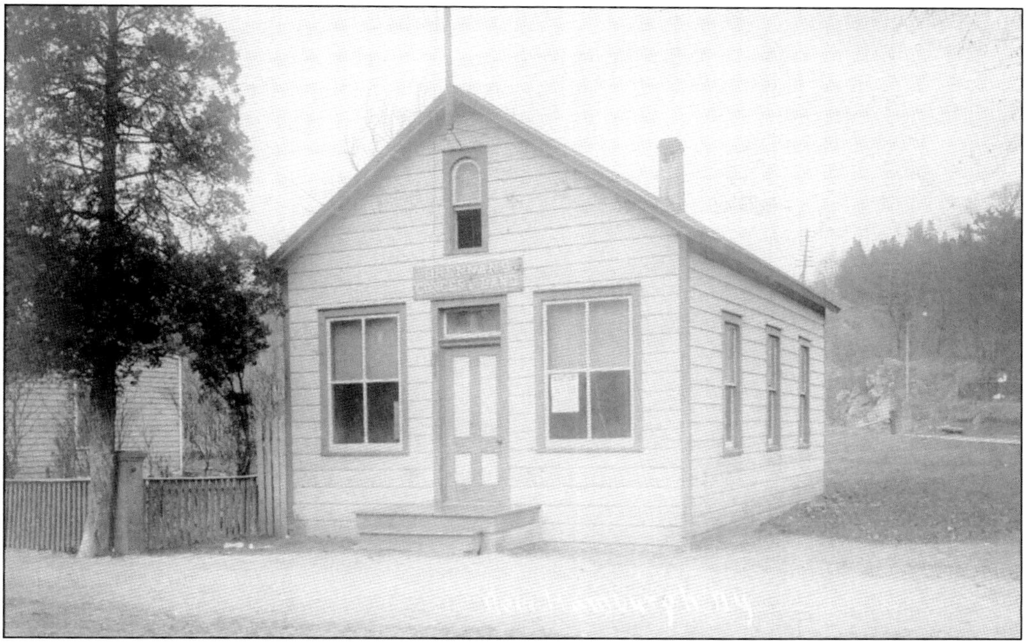

BRENNAN'S BAND HEADQUARTERS, c. 1910. Across Main Street from Jepson's Drug Store was the meetinghouse for Brennan's Band. The wood-frame building was mostly used as a practice hall and storage when the band was not performing. The small building was removed when the railroad was enlarged to four tracks.

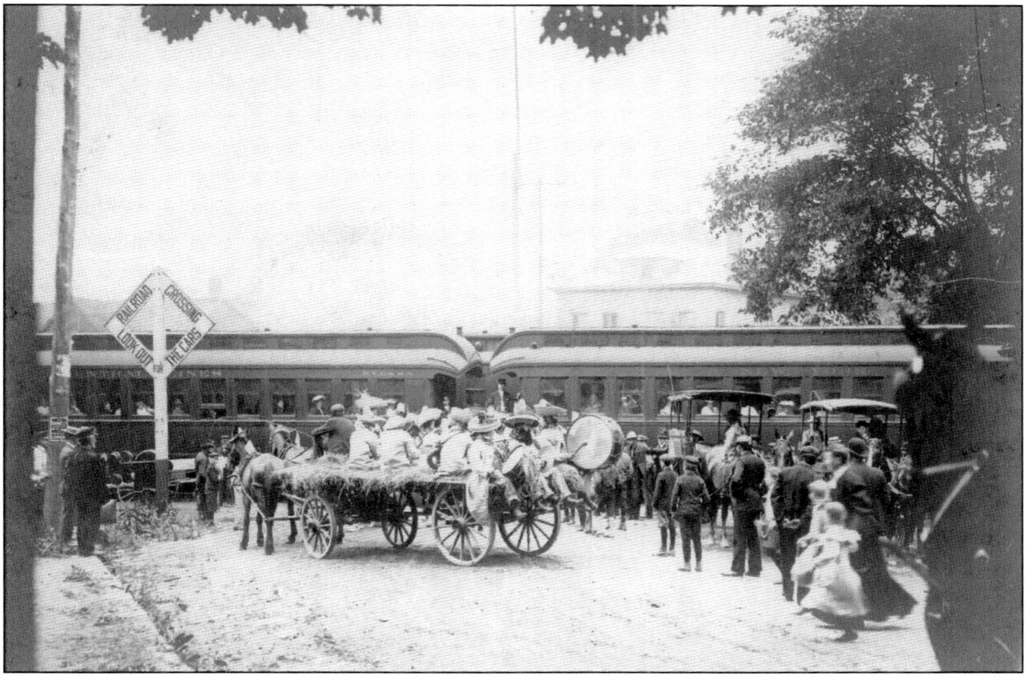

NEW YORK LYRICAL STRING ORCHESTRA ARRIVAL, 1909. The entire village stopped and converged on the railroad station to welcome one of the most popular musical acts from New York City. Brennan's Band arrived on a hay cart in matching costumes to greet the orchestra as the train rolled into the town. (Courtesy of the Wappingers Historical Society.)

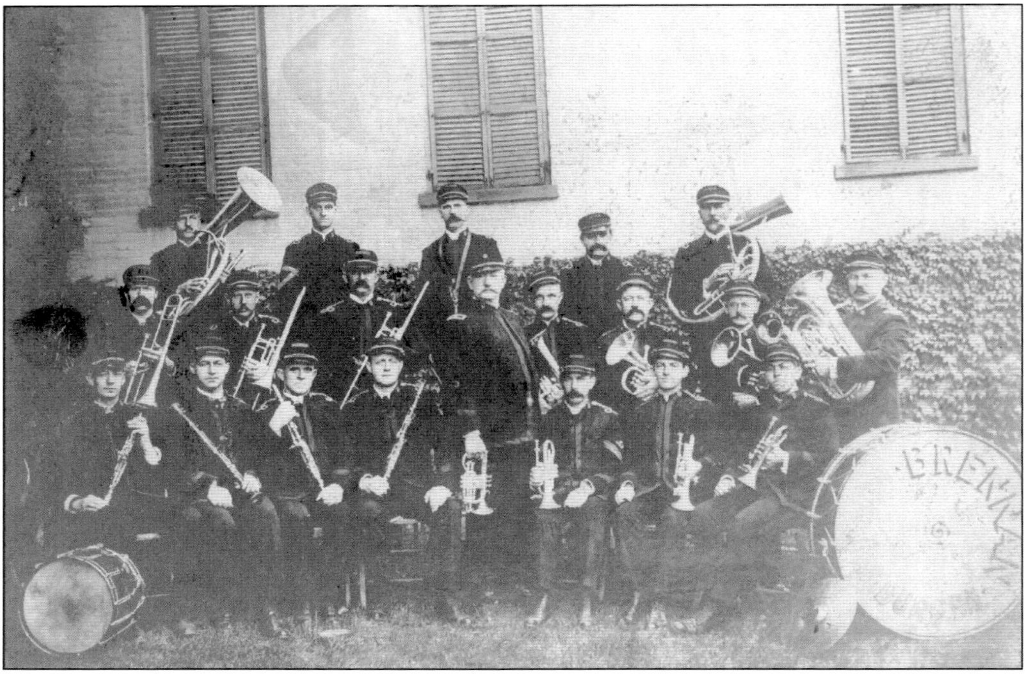

Brennan's Band, c. 1909. All of the men in Brennan's Band were local residents. Mr. Brennan, standing in the center of the photograph, was the band's leader and was the driving force in its creation. After his death, the remaining members disbanded and joined other local musical groups in the area. (Courtesy of the Wappingers Historical Society.)

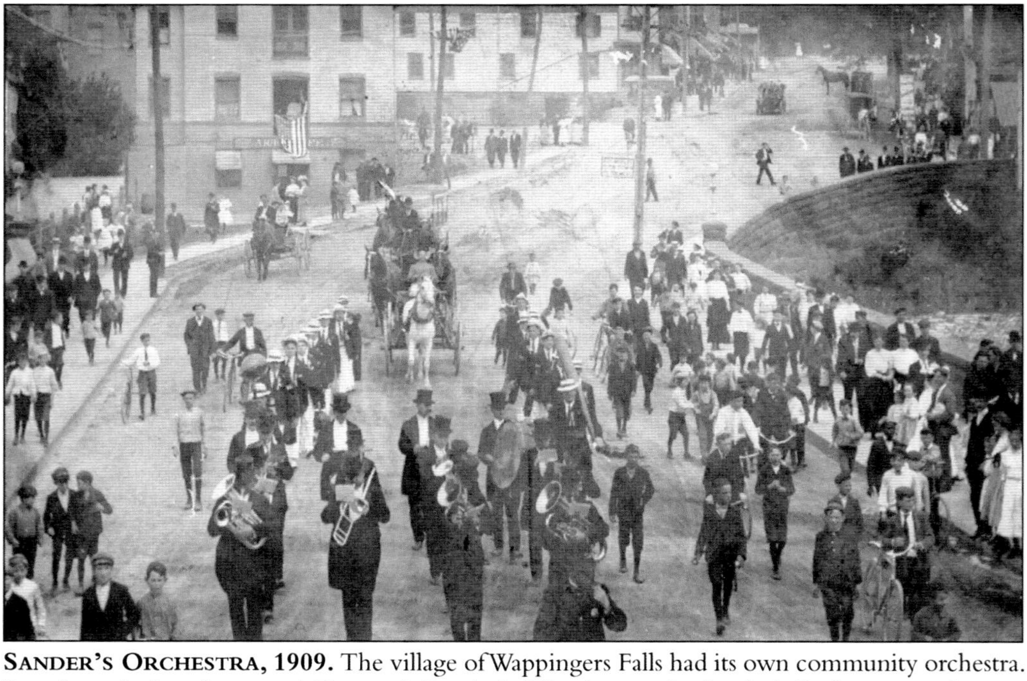

Sander's Orchestra, 1909. The village of Wappingers Falls had its own community orchestra. Seen here during the annual Firemen's Parade in Wappingers, the Sander's Orchestra was known for their theatrics. The members were mostly factory workers from the Garner Print Works who practiced for public events during their off time. (Courtesy of the Wappinger Historical Society.)

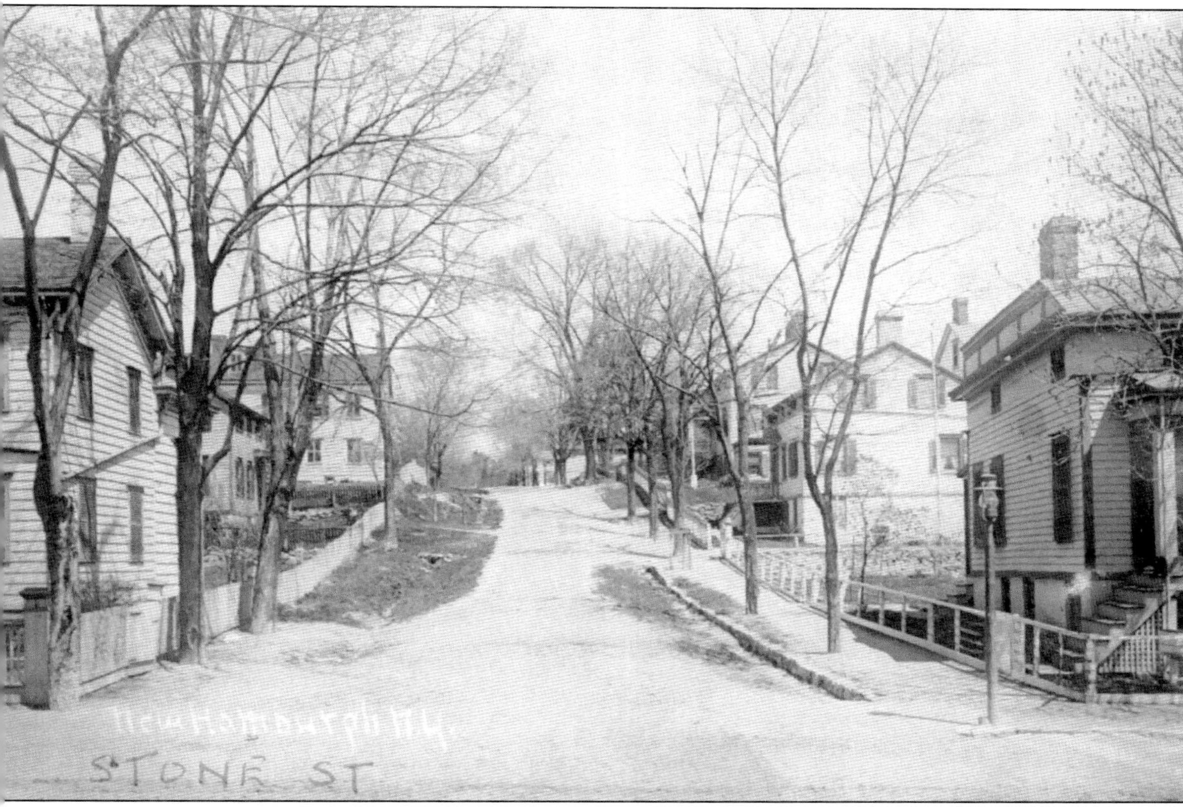

STONE STREET, C. 1908. Looking north from the post office on Main Street, Stone Street was once lined on both sides of the street with colonial-era homes. When the railroad cut was constructed, the homes shown here in the background were torn down for the extension of Bridge Street. Today, the foreground homes still stand with the section of street between them closed. (Courtesy of Lawson Edgar.)

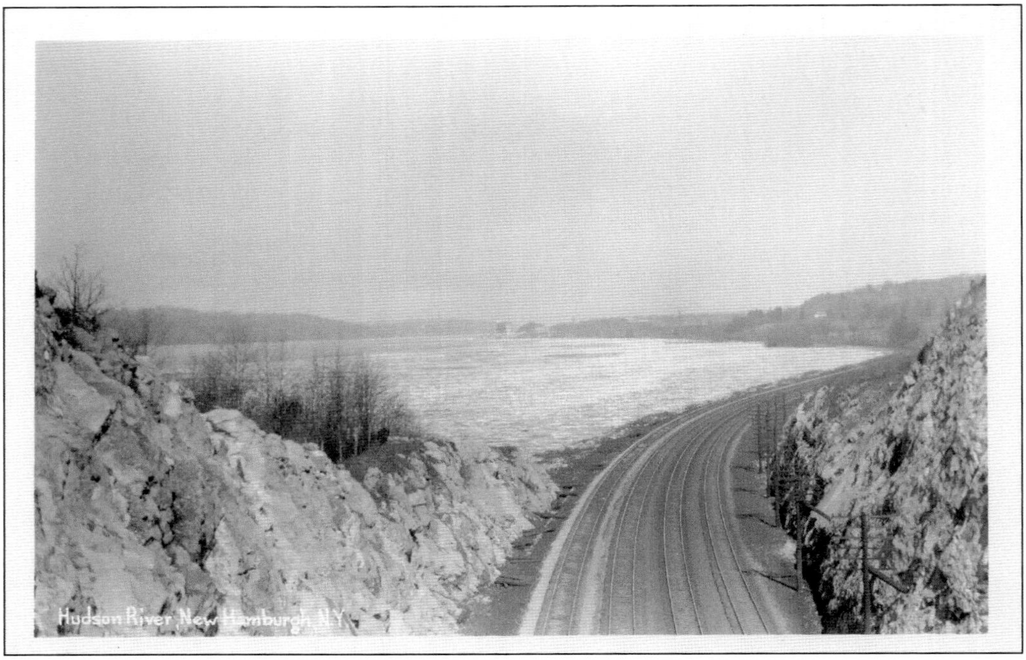

LOOKING UP THE HUDSON RIVER, C. 1930. Poughkeepsie was the next large railroad stop north of New Hamburgh. Two small hamlets lay between called Stoneco and Camelot. Both have since disappeared during the development of the IBM plant and the old Trap Rock Quarry. By the 1930s, the Hudson River Railroad expanded to three full service tracks to accommodate extra freight trains. This photograph was taken from the upper Point Street Bridge; this turn along the Hudson River Railroad was once the sharpest curve for railroad conductors between New York City and Chicago.

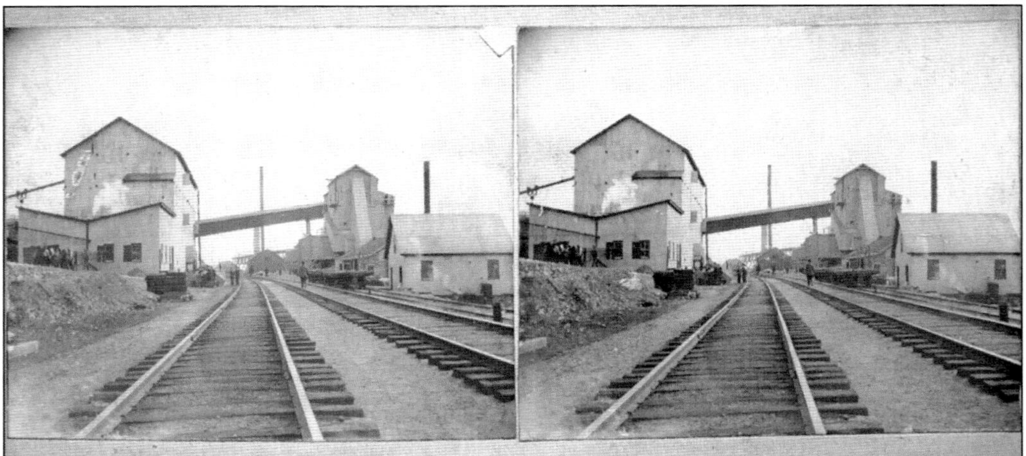

STONECO, C. 1890. The stone-crushing works at Stoneco near Clinton Point on the Hudson River was constructed around 1890. It provided track ballast for the New York Central and Hudson River Railroad Company. A major fire destroyed the works on the east side of the railroad tracks in 1895 and was subsequently rebuilt. These facilities existed until 1929, when a complete renovation took place. The original property was the home of George Clinton while he served as vice president of the United States from 1805 to 1812. The stone quarry is still in operation today. (Courtesy of the John DiDomizio.)

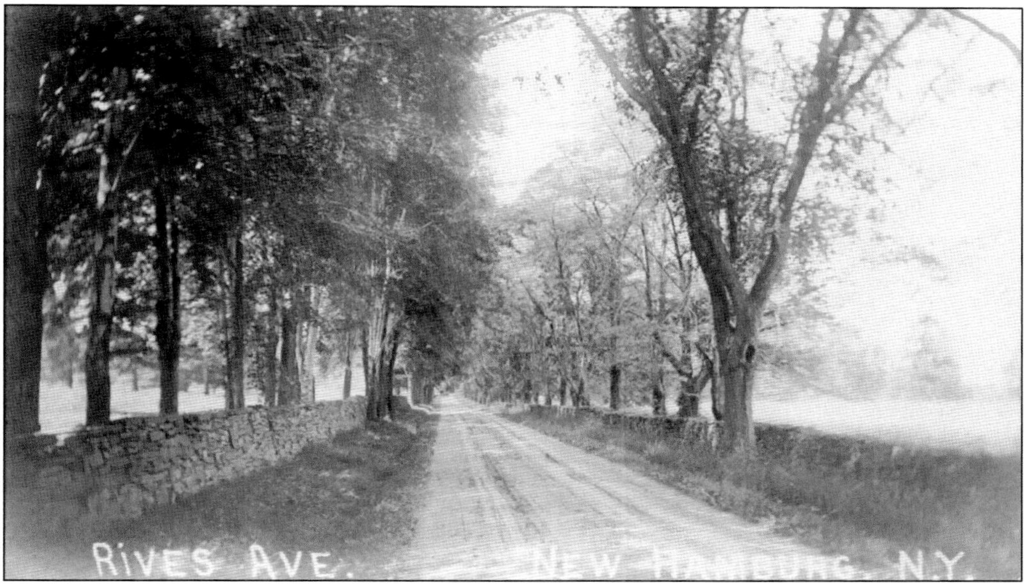

RIVES AVENUE, 1907. Today called Wheeler Hill Road, Rives Avenue led south from New Hamburgh Road towards Chelsea. On either side of the dirt road were large estates owned by local businessmen and wealthy New York City families. Beyond the large stone walls were open fields with a broad view of the river. Unlike the homes along Sheafe Road, many of these old houses still stand, now secluded by encroaching forests.

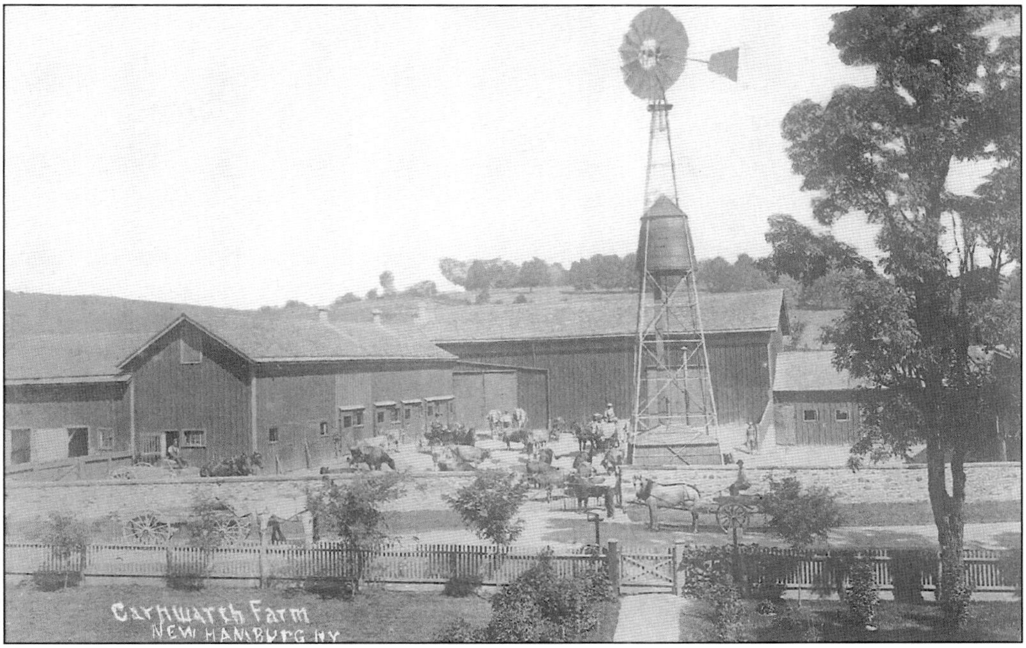

RIVES ESTATE, C. 1909. At the end of Rives Avenue along the Van Wyck Ridge, overlooking the Hudson River, is the Willis Estate, constructed in 1850. Sold to Francis Rives in 1870, he constructed a large gentleman's farm around an impressive Italianate mansion. The cow barn shown here was constructed in 1876, as Rives expanded the estate and named it Carnwarth Farms. After the death of Francis Rives, the farm was occupied by a convent. Now owned by the town of Wappinger, it houses the Sports Museum of Dutchess County. (Courtesy of George Lucas.)

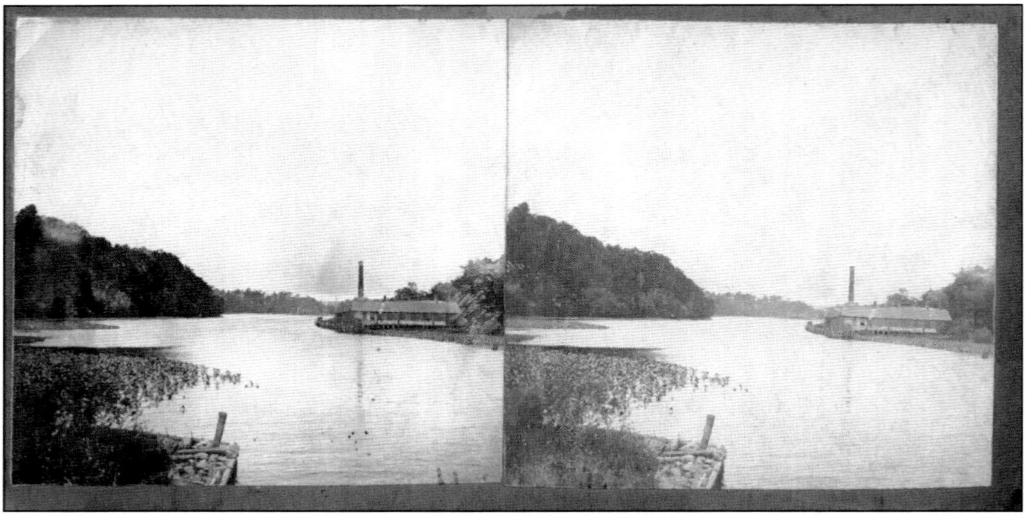

R.J. STUART FOUNDRY, C. 1890. Founded in 1852, the company was first known as the Eagle Foundry and was located on East Main Street in the village. When the building caught fire in 1873, it was so intense that many local residents thought the entire village would be consumed. Soon after, the business was sold to R.J. Stuart and was moved here to Creek Road near New Hamburgh. The foundry remained open until the 1920s, when it closed due to the poor health of the Stuart brothers.

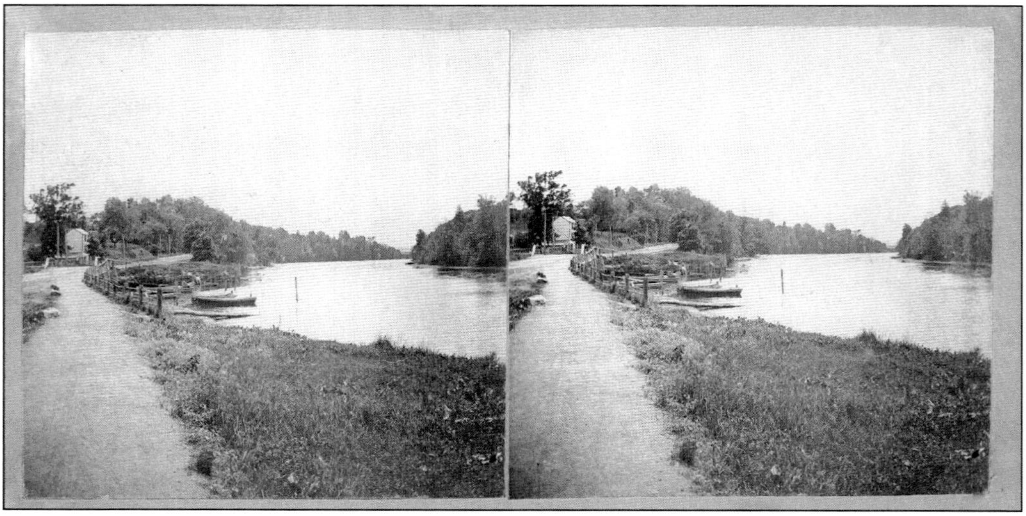

CREEK ROAD LOOKING SOUTH, C. 1890. Heading south from the Dutchess Print Works, Creek Road connected the village of Wappingers Falls to New Hamburgh. To the right is a small boat landing that was enlarged and still functions today as a boat slip for those wanting to explore Wappingers Creek.

Six

Wappingers Falls

An Industrial Village

The first mill constructed in Wappingers Falls was the old Yellow Mill, operated by the Brewer brothers and later Peter Mesier. Replacing the old wooden structure was the three-story Clintondale Mill, which provided lumber that constructed much of the housing along Mill and Spring Streets. On the other side of the stone bridge was the Franklindale Mill, which much like the Clintondale Mill, burned to the ground.

The Industrial Revolution during the 1860s would forever change the landscape of the village. Many factories began to sprout along the falls, including the Hyper Mill, Eagan Factory, Sweet Orr & Company, and the largest of them all, the Dutchess Print Works. Situated below the village along the Wappingers Creek, the factory was also known as the Garner Print Works. By the late 1800s, the factory complex employed a vast majority of village residents and consisted of dozens of buildings. In 1908, the factory was sold and renamed the Dutchess Bleachery. The new company began modernizing factory buildings and the entire village with a new hydroelectric plant. Although the factories are now gone, their impact and physical ruins can still be seen today.

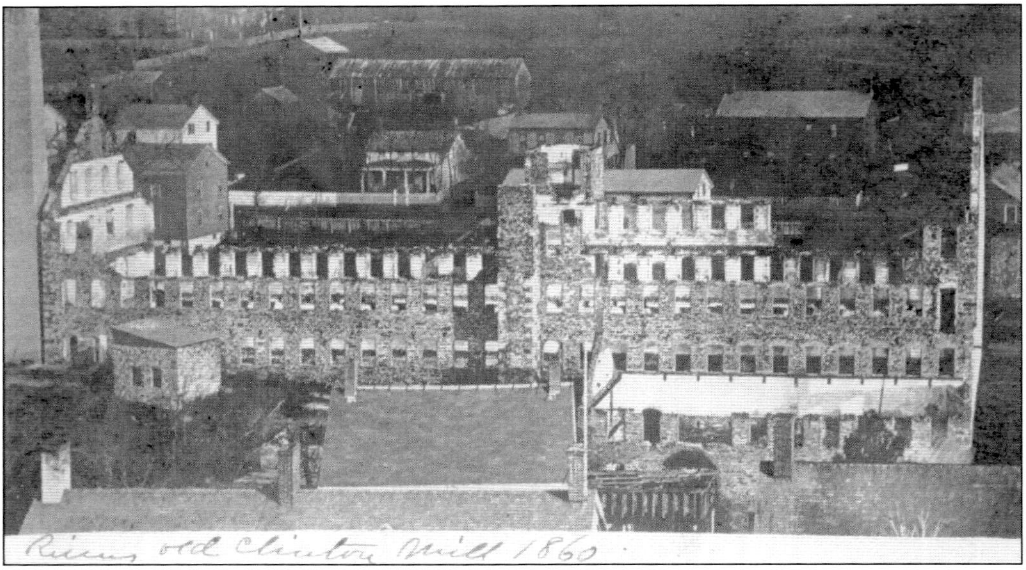

Clintondale Mill, 1860. By the time this photograph was taken, the Clintondale Mill was already a ruin. Constructed in 1846 by Benjamin Clapp, the factory was erected on the site of Peter Mesier's original Yellow Mill. The first floor housed a lumber mill while the upper three floors housed the Cook and Low Comb Manufacturing Company. On June 19, 1855, the factory was destroyed by an uncontrollable fire and never rebuilt. (Courtesy of the Wappingers Historical Society.)

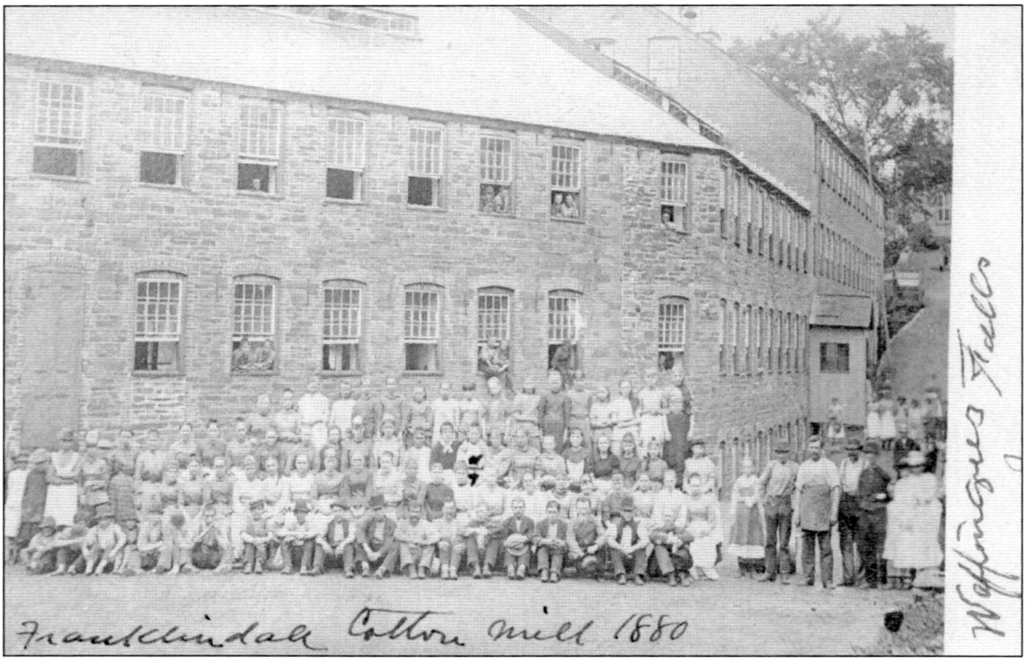

Franklindale Cotton Mill, 1880. Founded in 1844 by Benjamin Clapp, the mill was named after an old name used for the half of the village along the east side of the creek. The large five-story stone factory employed 200 people, mostly women and children, in the manufacturing of textiles. Women and children earned $6 and $1.50 a week, respectively. In what was called "the most spectacular fire to hit the village," the factory building burned in 1885.

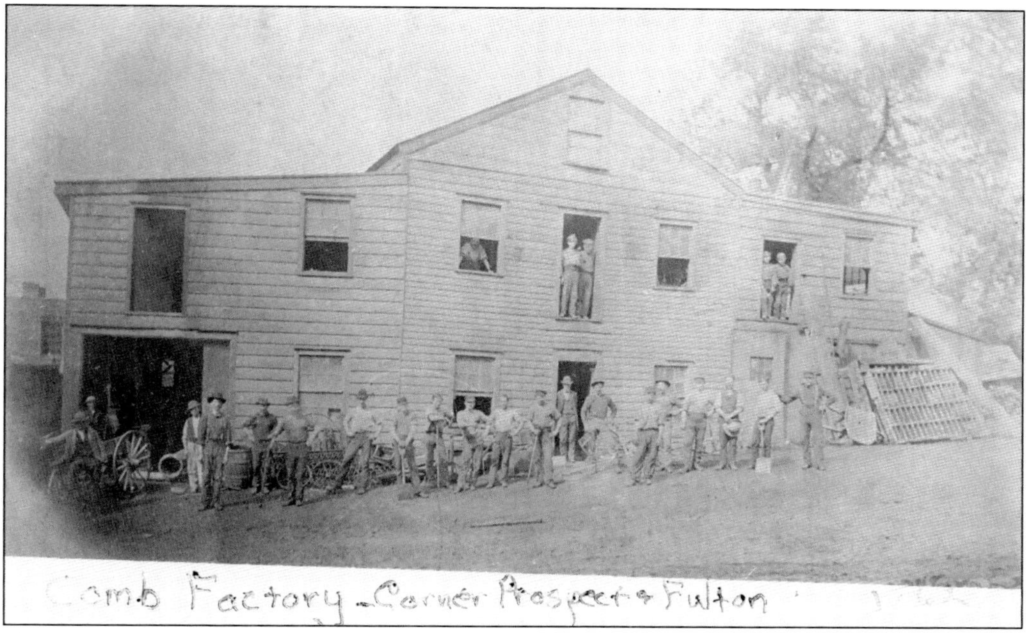

COMB FACTORY, C. 1862. Once housed in the Clintondale Mill, the Brown Comb Company split from its former partner and moved here on the corner of Prospect and Fulton Streets in 1856. The company manufactured decorative combs made of tortoise shell and mother of pearl, a luxury item mostly reserved for the wealthy. This building burned in the summer of 1868 and was replaced by a larger three-story building that still stands at this intersection.

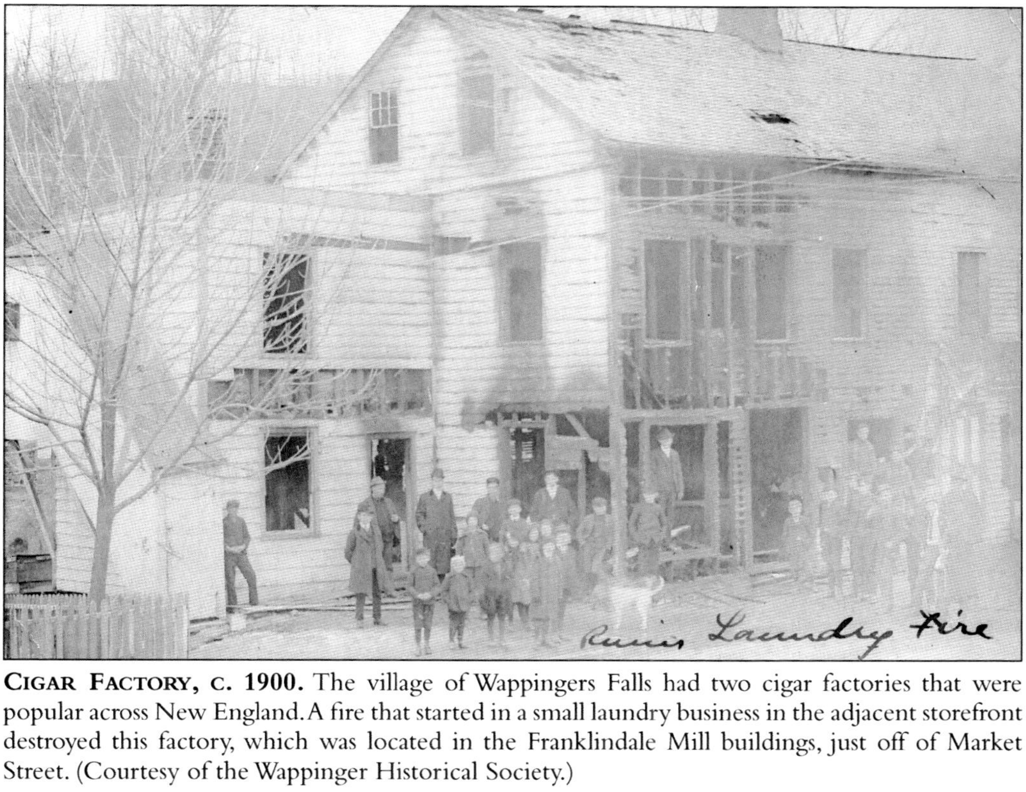

CIGAR FACTORY, C. 1900. The village of Wappingers Falls had two cigar factories that were popular across New England. A fire that started in a small laundry business in the adjacent storefront destroyed this factory, which was located in the Franklindale Mill buildings, just off of Market Street. (Courtesy of the Wappinger Historical Society.)

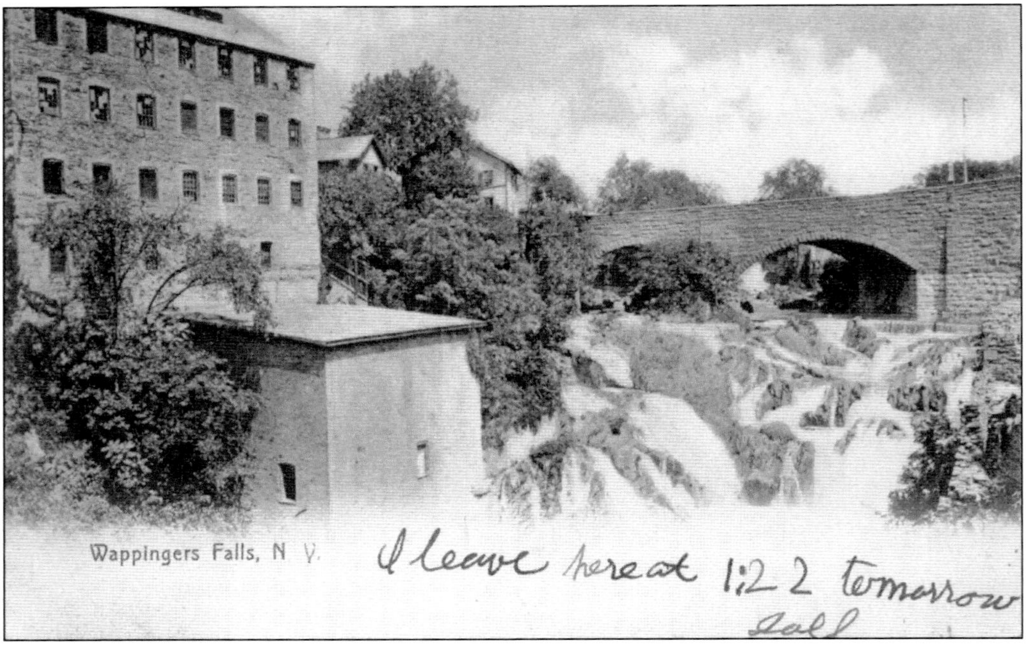

THE HYPER MILL, 1907. Along the west side of the creek below the stone bridge was the old Hyper Mill. Constructed by Henry Hughson in the late 1840s, the factory building housed the Hughson's floor mill on the first floor. The Nicholas and Shields Comb Factory, successors of the Cook and Lomb Factory, which was destroyed in the Clintondale Mill fire, used the upper floors. By the time this photograph was taken in 1907, the building was mostly vacant with the upper floor windows broken out.

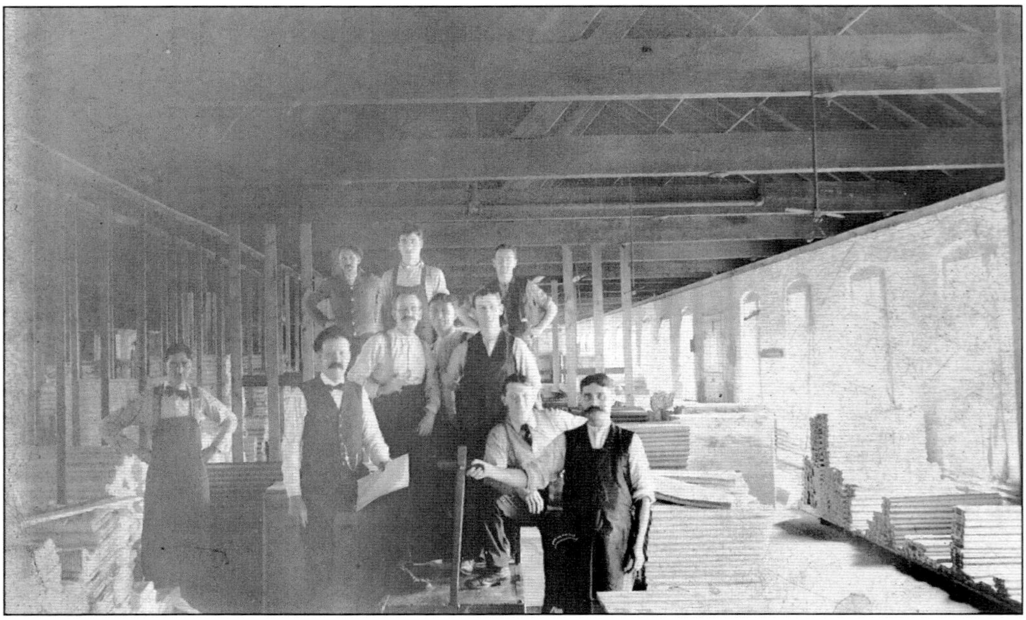

LUMBER COMPANY, C. 1904. During the early 1900s, a lumber company occupied the top floor of the Hyper Mill. The company had 10 employees, who are shown here in this group photograph. Large piles of lumber line the walls of the long factory floor behind them. (Courtesy of the Wappinger Historical Society.)

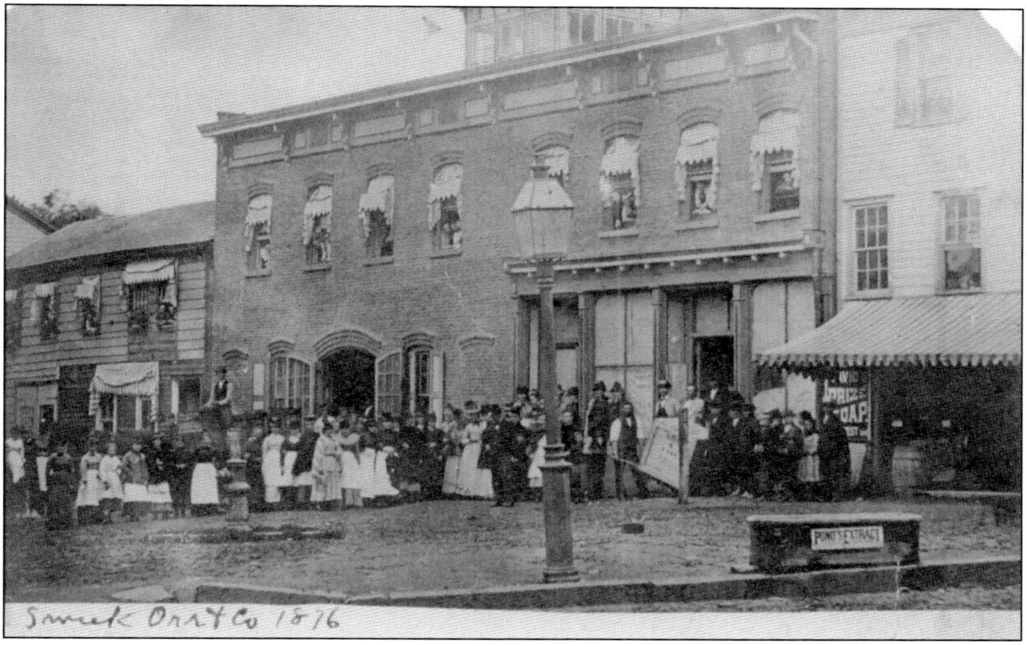

Sweet Orr Factory, 1876. James Orr and his two nephews Clinton and Clayton Sweet began producing denim overalls in their Mill Street factory in 1872. This photograph taken four years later shows the original two-story brick building with the wooden addition off to the left. The Sweet Orr & Company grew quickly and became very popular across the country, especially among railroad workers. (Courtesy of the Wappingers Historical Society.)

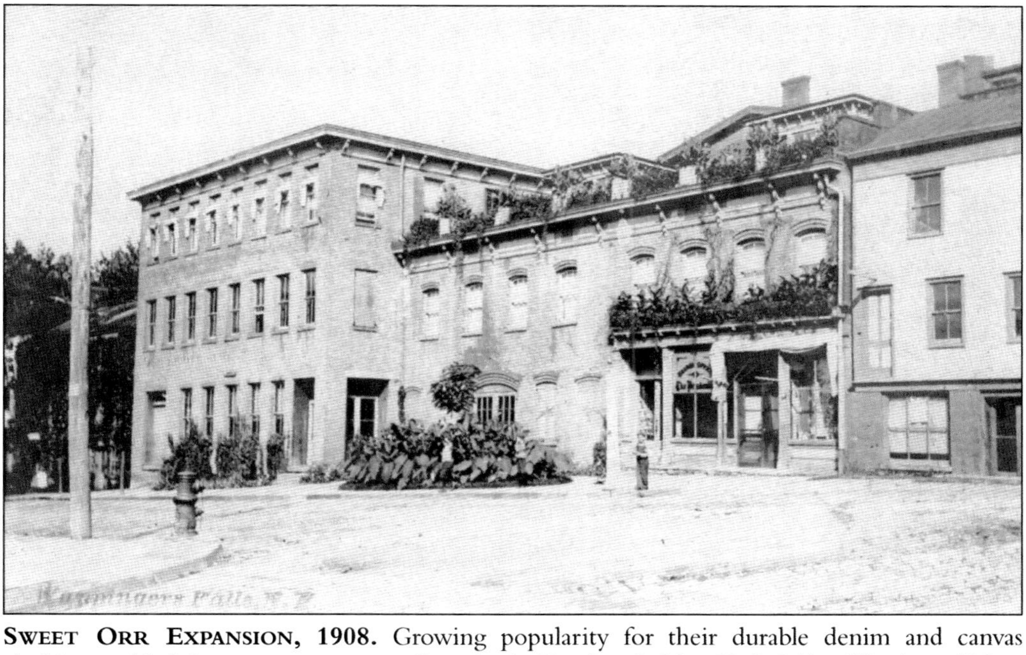

Sweet Orr Expansion, 1908. Growing popularity for their durable denim and canvas clothing enabled the company to open factories in Newburgh, New York; Juliet, Illinois; and New Orleans, Louisiana. Even the Wappingers factory expanded when a three-story brick structure was constructed on the north side of the original factory building. The company continued producing clothing in the village until 1958, when operations moved away.

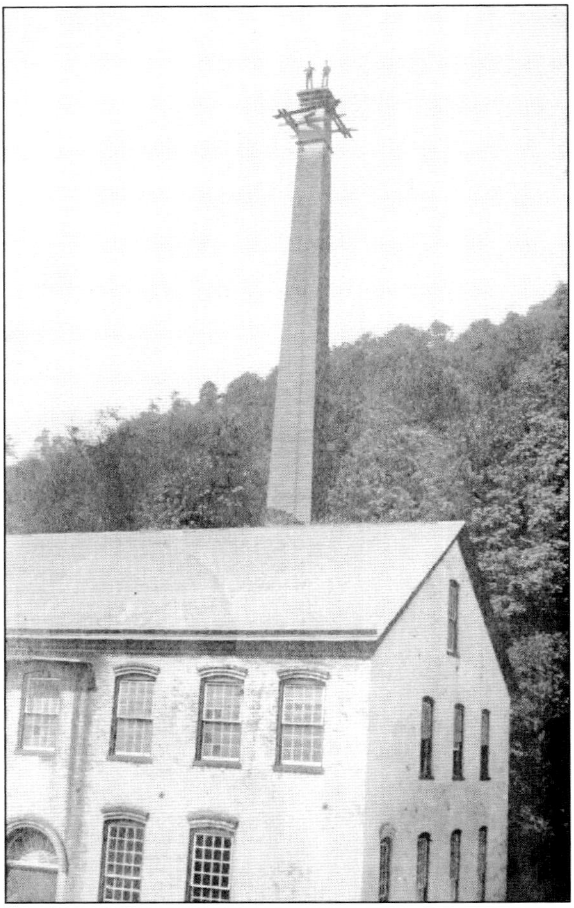

Tallest Smoke Stack Completion, 1885. In a display of bravery and engineering skill, a smoke stack rises behind one of the 1856 Dutchess Print Works buildings on the west side of the creek. At the top of the brick tower, two men stand overlooking the entire factory complex. Although called the tallest smoke stack in this 1885 photograph, it would soon be eclipsed during the factory's expansion.

View from Lower Falls, c. 1890. By the late 1800s, Wappingers Falls had already been established as a factory town. On the left are the Garner Print Works buildings and the Lower Falls. Just upstream is the Hyper Mill on the left and the old Stone Bridge. (Courtesy of the Wappinger Historical Society.)

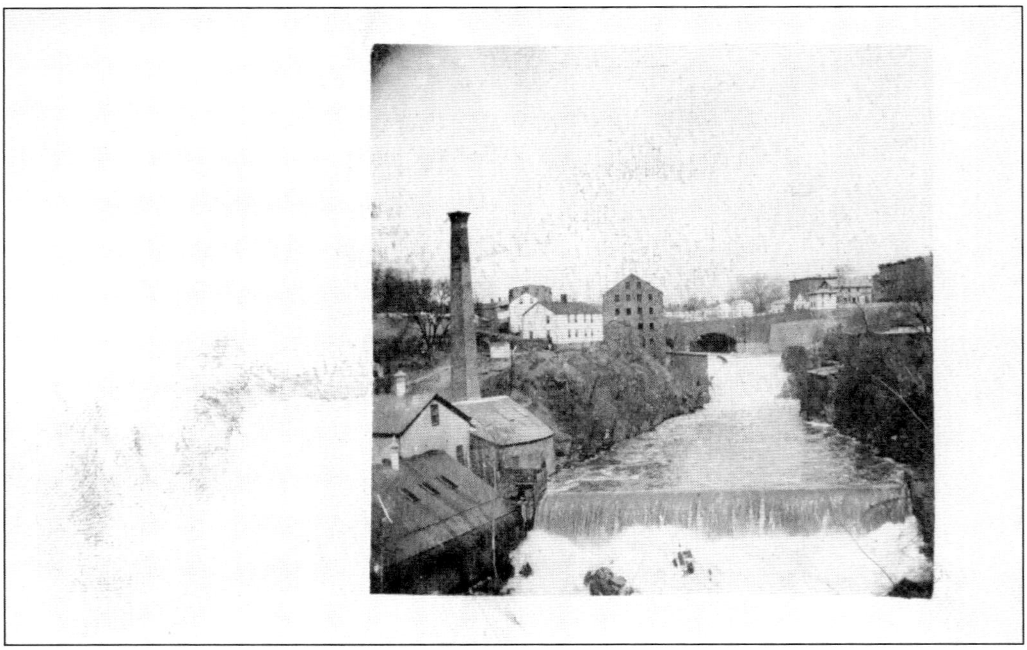

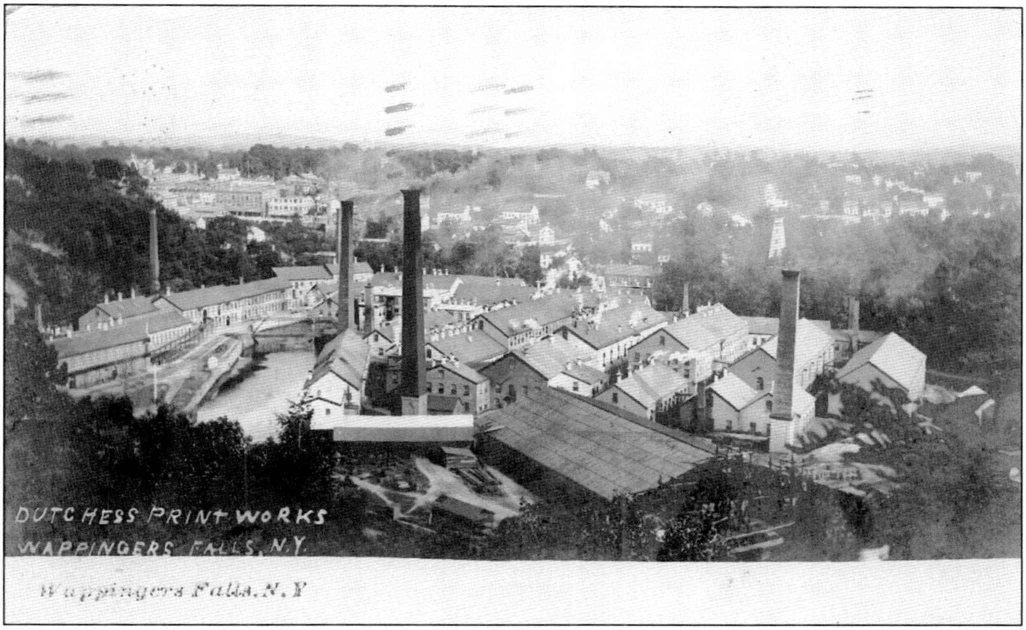

DUTCHESS/GARNER PRINT WORKS, 1906. The height of operation for the factory was between 1890 and 1915. The buildings along the creek to the left were primarily used for the manufacturing of acids and other chemicals used in the dyeing process. The buildings along the south shore of the creek is where the raw cotton cloth was cleaned, bleached, and dyed. Two years after this photograph was taken, the company was sold and renamed the Dutchess Bleachery. This new enterprise had ambitious plans to modernize and streamline the factory. One way the new owners wanted to improve operations was to update the means by which the factory obtained power.

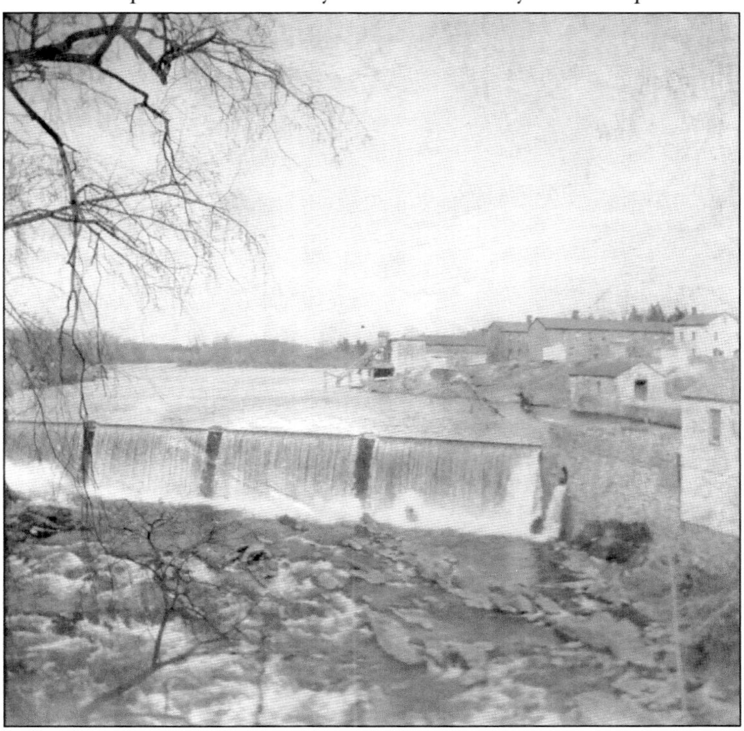

UPPER DAM AND FALLS, C. 1907. For decades prior to the Dutchess Bleachery, this dam at the mouth of Wappingers Lake was the only source of power for factories downstream. A bulkhead was constructed to the right of the dam so that a constant flow of water reached the factories along the gorge, even during the summer drought. (Courtesy of the Wappingers Historical Society.)

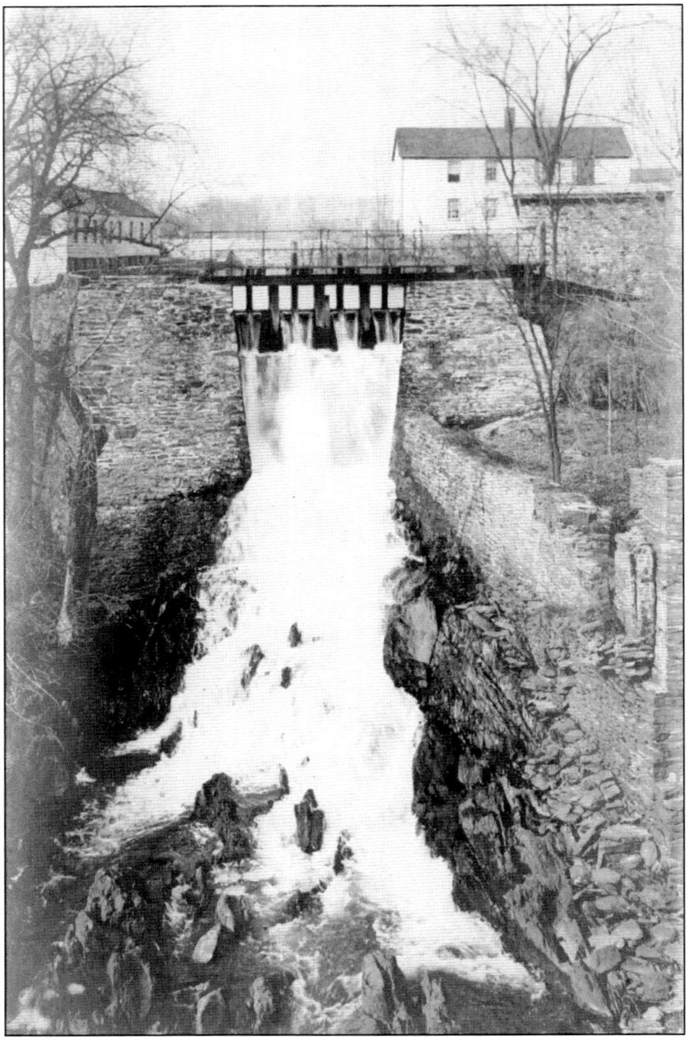

Bulkhead and Wappingers Lake Raceway, 1906. In 1909, the Garner Print Works replaced this old bulkhead with a new deeper gate to allow more water to flow downstream. The long building on the left was constructed on the island created between the dam and the raceway. For many years, it housed the carpentry shop owned by the print works to maintain their factory housing along Mill and Spring Streets.

Old Powerhouse, c. 1890. The old power plant located on Creek Road was powered by coal brought up the creek on barges from the river at New Hamburgh. The plant created enough energy to power the Garner Print Works just up the creek, but it failed to provide enough electricity for the entire community.

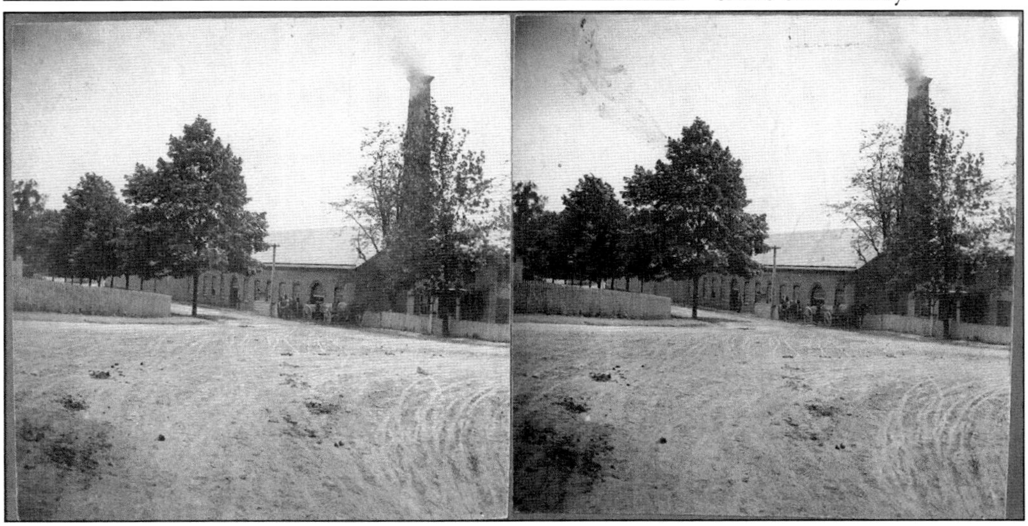

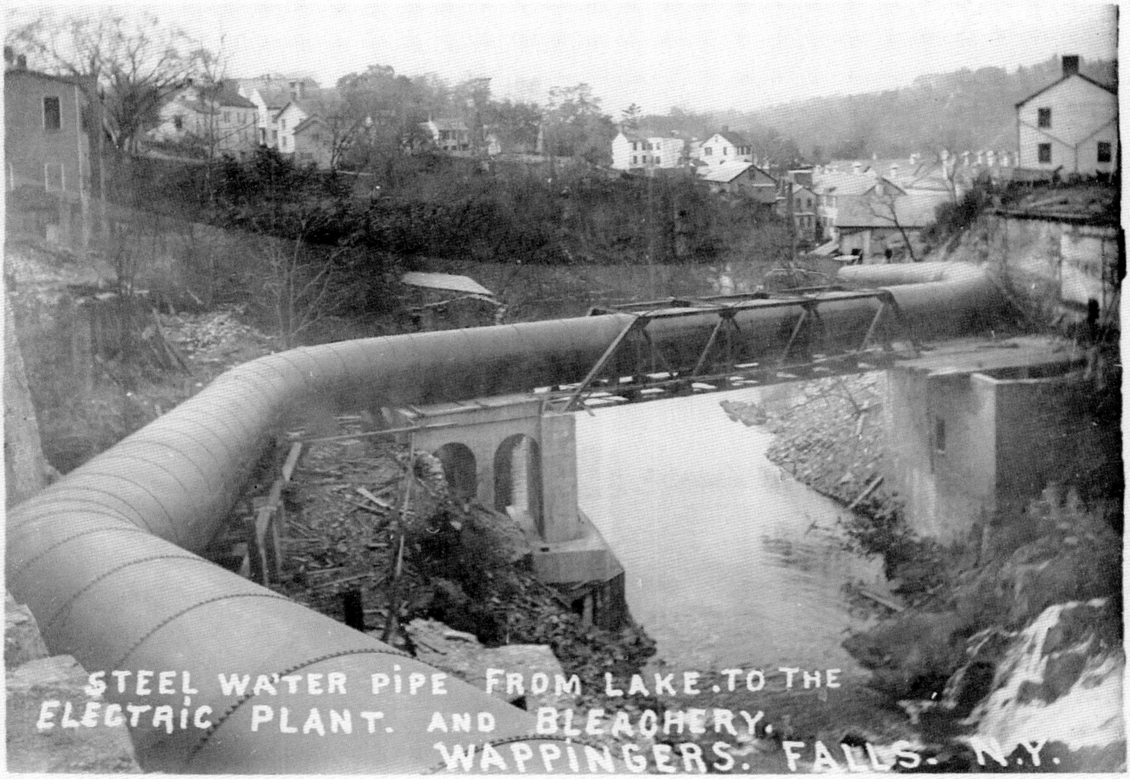

STEEL FLUME SOUTH OF STONE BRIDGE, 1910. Construction of the large steel pipe and its support columns were the largest engineering feet attempted in the village. As the pipe heads downhill from the stone bridge, it crosses the creek along a steel trestle. All concrete for the supports of the trestle was hauled by horse and cart and mixed on site. For the children of the village, the high steel bridge was a perfect diving spot when the water level was high enough.

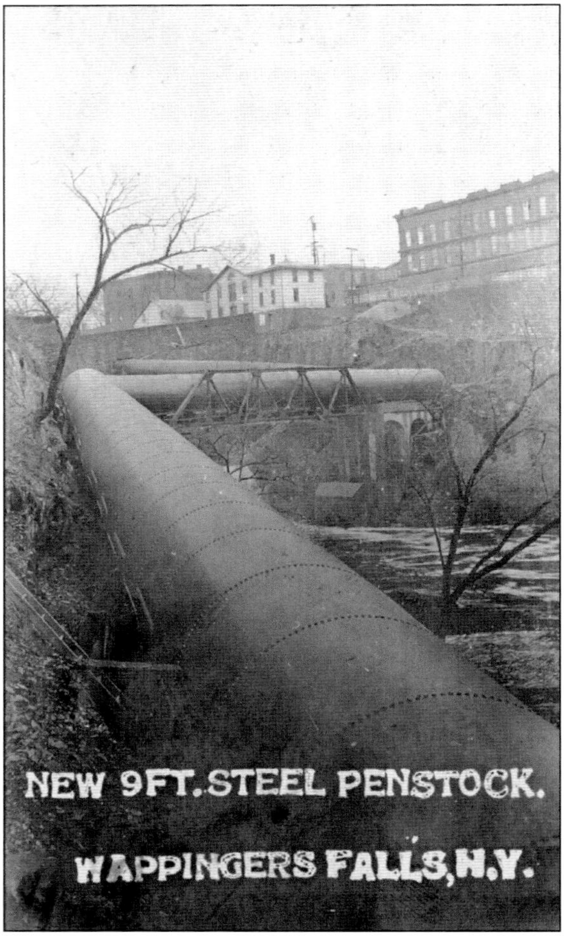

STEEL FLUME FROM POWER PLANT, 1911. Gravity brought the water downhill at a pressure of 27 pounds per square inch when it reached the turbines. This impressive amount of force created enough excess power that the entire village had 24-hour electricity. Electric power was finally available to the majority of homes and businesses that had formerly relied on kerosene lamps.

HYDROELECTRIC POWER PLANT, C. 1912. Completed in 1910, the new power plant at the northeasternmost portion of the Dutchess Bleachery was in continuous operation until 1970. After the bleachery closed, the community was already getting their power from other sources and no longer had a need for the plant. After being left abandoned for almost two decades, it was reopened in 1988.

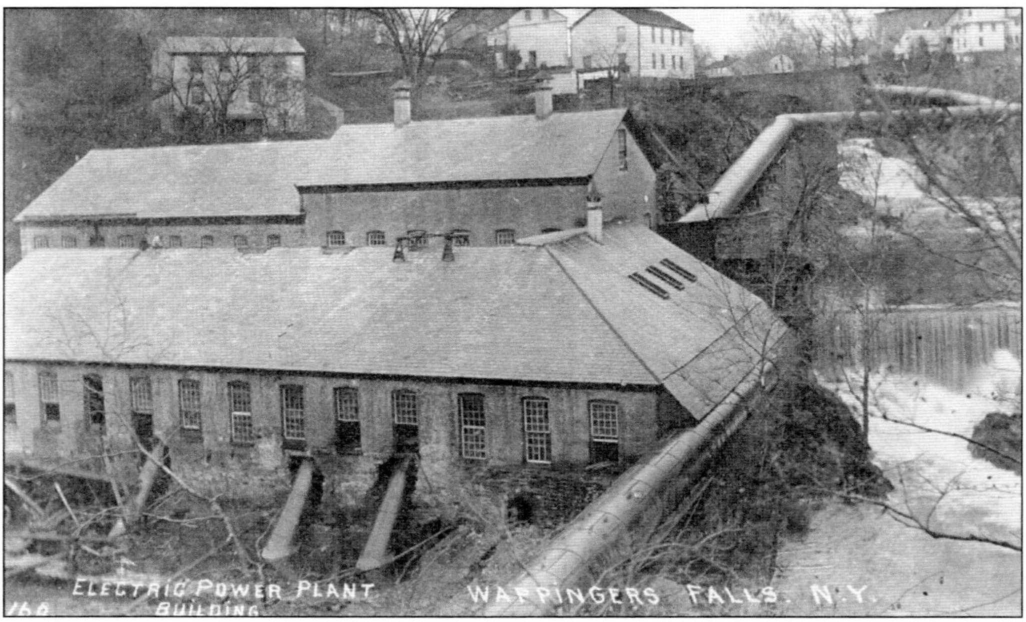

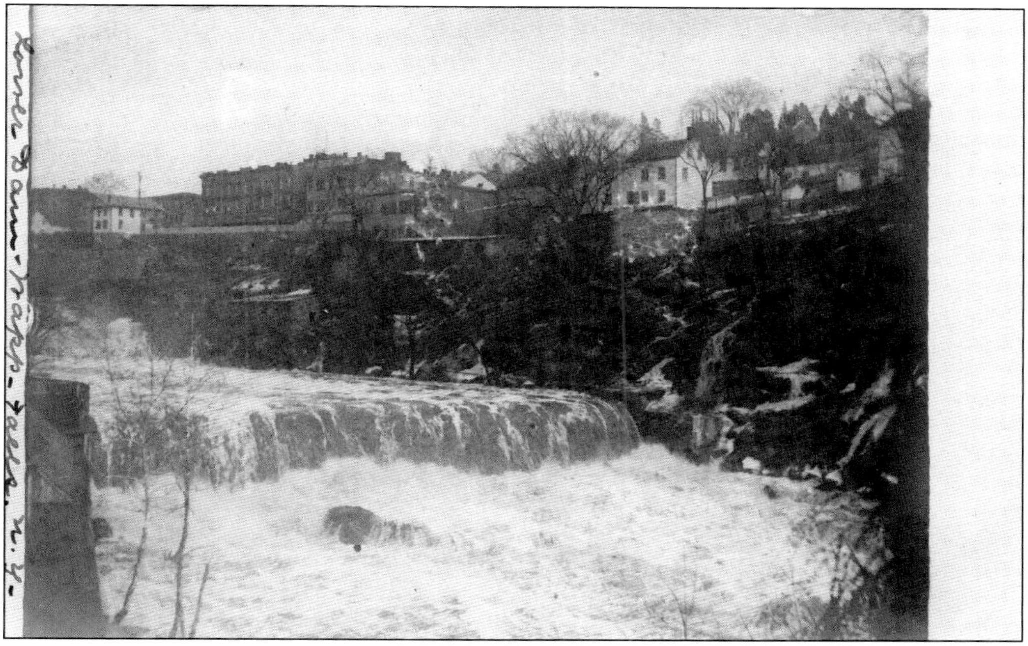

LOWER FALLS, C. 1906. Just beside the new powerhouse is the lower falls. In 1906, a strong spring flood would destroy many of the factory buildings in the Garner Print Works complex. On top of the bluff to the right are some of the factory houses constructed by the Franklindale Mill. This residential area was commonly referred to by locals as the hamlet of Franklindale even after the village was incorporated. (Courtesy of the Wappinger Historical Society.)

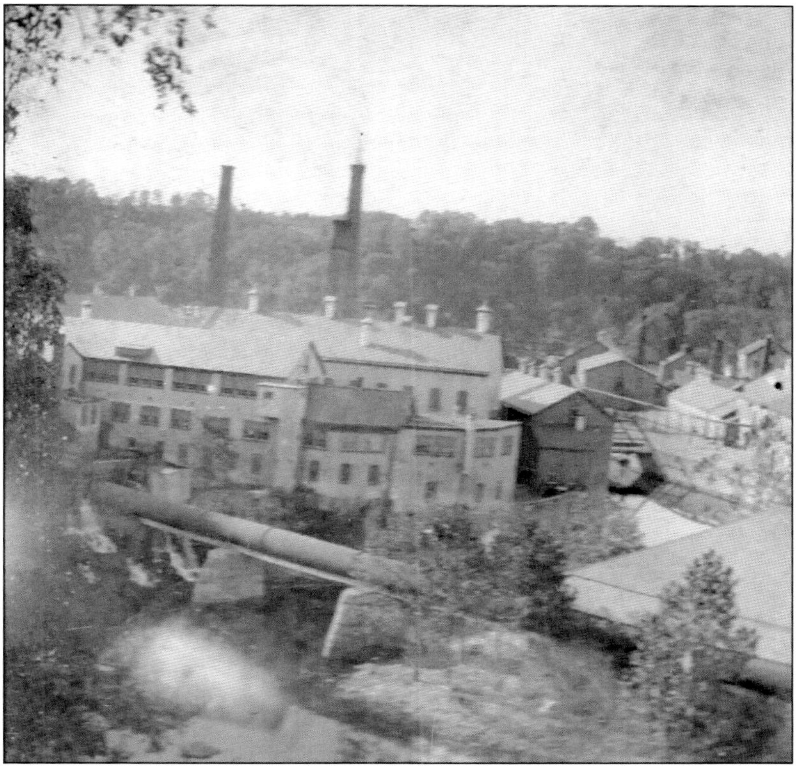

GARNER PRINT WORKS, C. 1890. After the factory was purchased, it was renamed the Dutchess Bleachery. These old buildings shown here were badly damaged during the 1906 flood, and it was decided that they would be torn down. In the next five years, the new company would raze many of the old buildings and modernize those that remained.

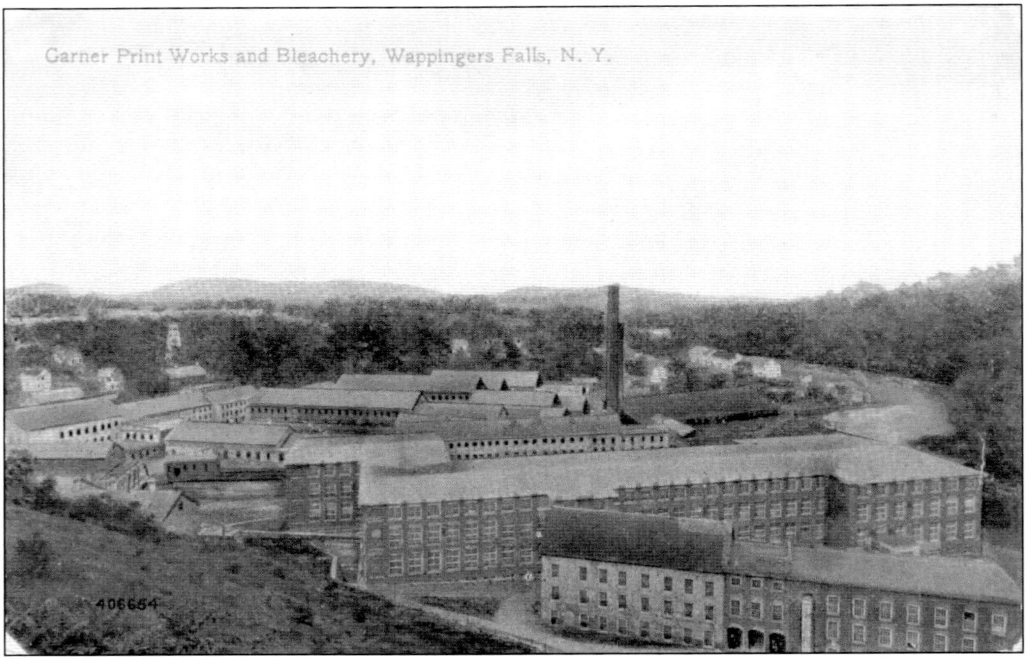

VIEW OF THE NEW DUTCHESS BLEACHERY, C. 1910. Looking south down Wappingers Creek, the new factory buildings of the Dutchess Bleachery spanned the entire valley. One of the most significant improvements was the addition of a modern sprinkler system throughout the factory. (Courtesy of the Wappinger Historical Society.)

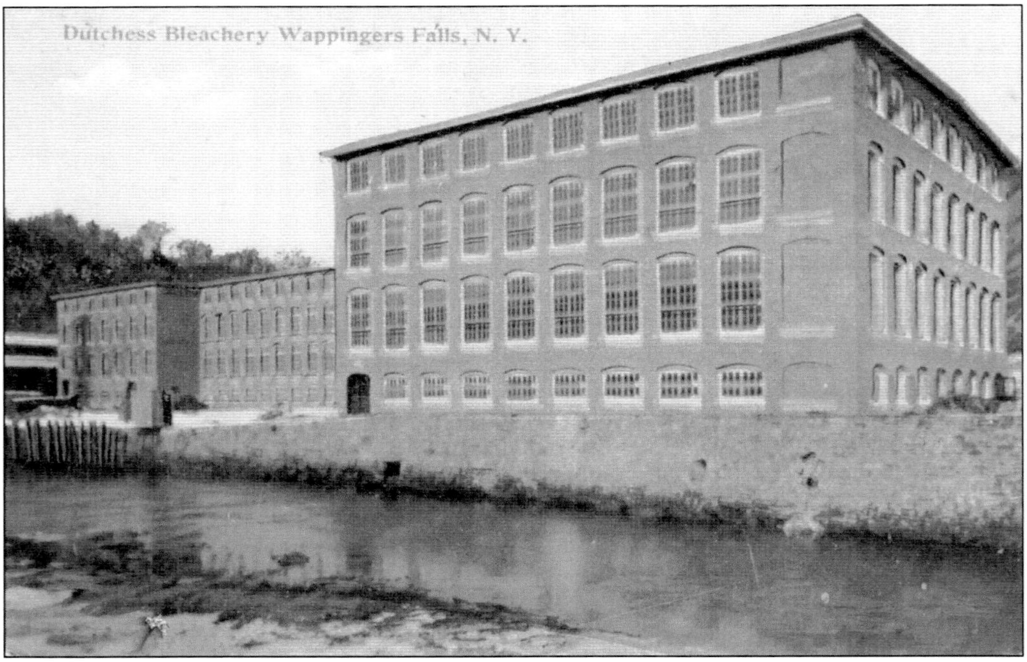

COMPLETION OF THE NEW DUTCHESS BLEACHERY BUILDING, 1910. Completed just after the hydroelectric plant, this four-story building was the largest ever constructed in the factory complex. The building housed a large portion of the manufacturing. Department 10, a successful division of the plant that made sheets and pillowcases, occupied the upper floors.

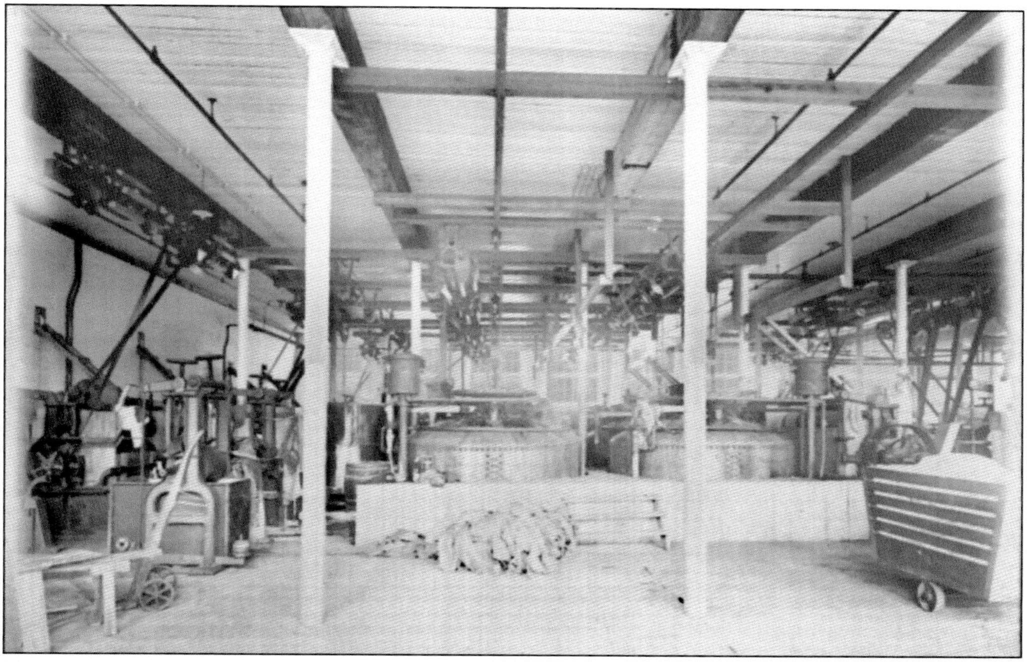

Processing Area, c. 1910. Large rolls of grey cotton, seen here on the floor, arrived from mills in New England. This unfinished fabric was then stretched and its ends were sewn together. One long sheet of fabric would stretch for hundreds of yards across the factory floor. Here, the cloth is being cleaned in large copper boilers. (Courtesy of the Wappingers Historical Society.)

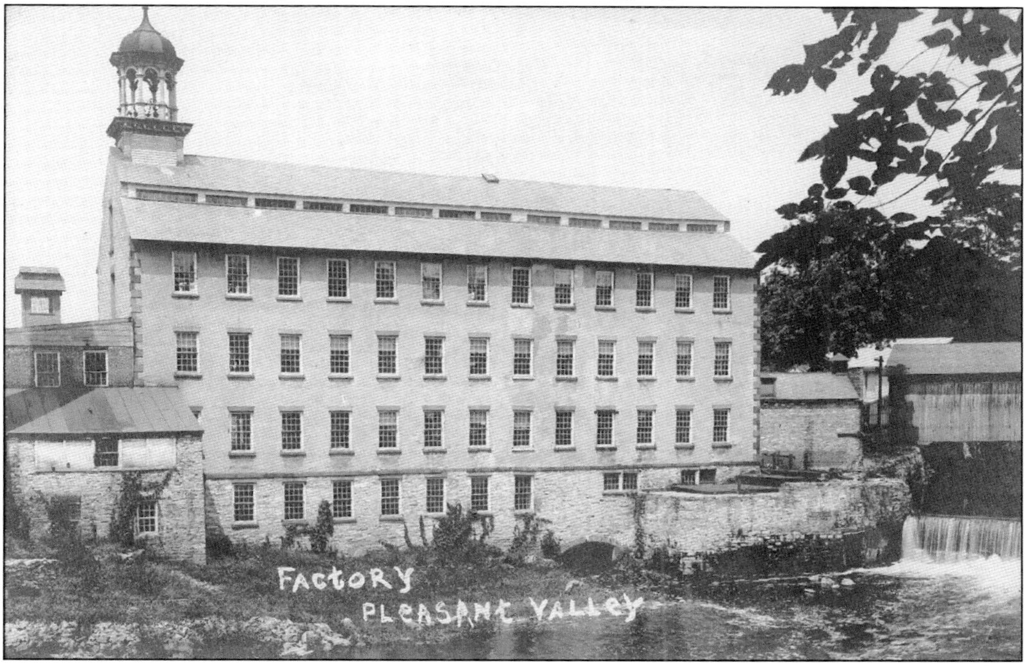

Pleasant Valley Cotton Mill, 1906. This factory along Wappingers Creek in Pleasant Valley was one of the many factories that purchased the raw white cotton fabric from the Dutchess Bleachery. The successful company continued operation well into the 1980s. In 1994, however, the large stone building was destroyed in a suspicious fire.

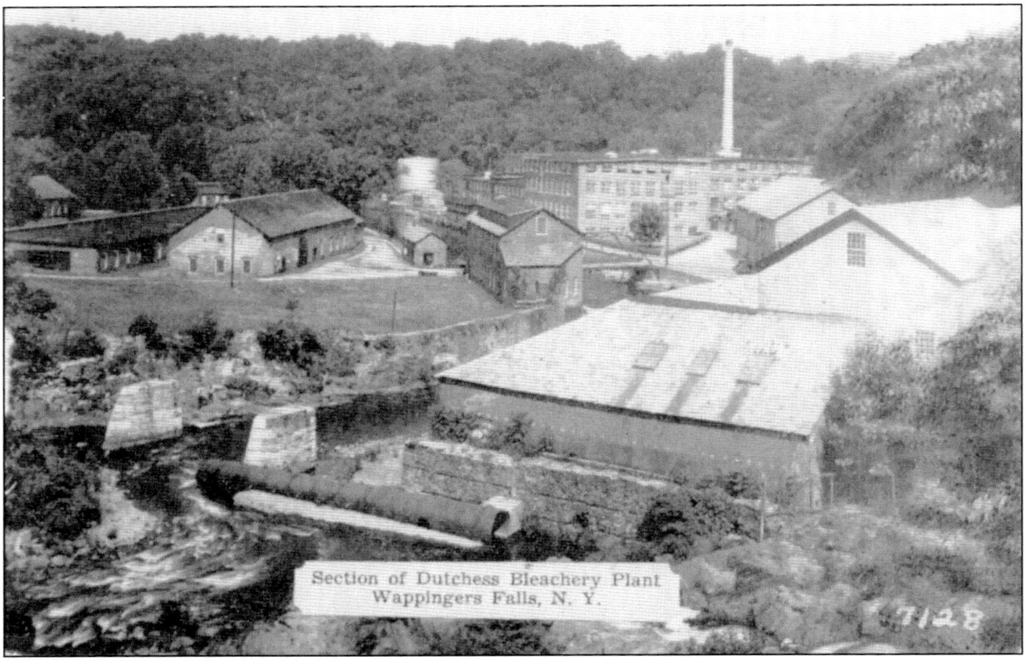

DUTCHESS BLEACHERY LOOKING WEST, C. 1930. By the 1930s, most of the buildings on the south side of the creek were torn down. Years later, in a move to cut costs, stockholders in the Lockwood Dutchess Company, the new owners of the Dutchess Bleachery, decided to liquidate the operation at Wappingers Falls. In the fall of 1955, the Dutchess Bleachery closed its doors, laying off over 700 local employees. Although almost all of the buildings along the south side of the creek are now gone, many of the factory buildings on the north side still stand and are rented out to various small companies.

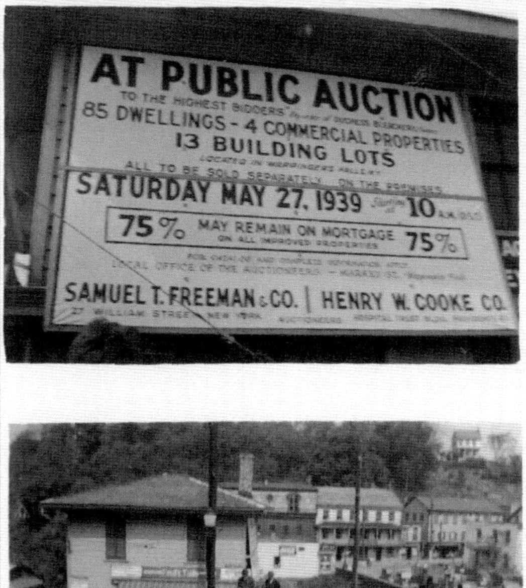

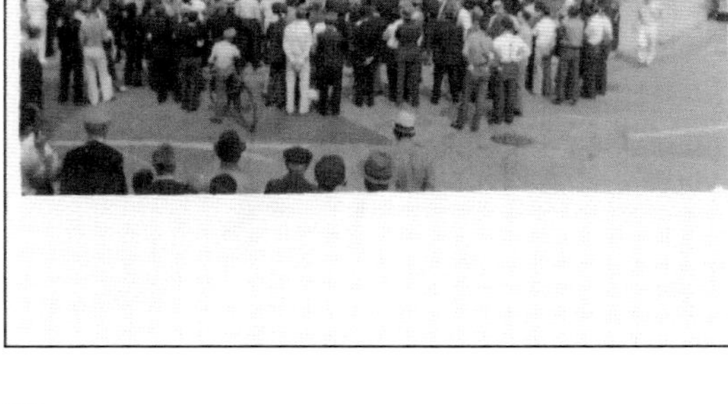

PUBLIC AUCTION, 1939. Before the bleachery closed in the 1955, the new owners were trying to raise capital to keep the factory afloat. This 1939 auction sold off many of the outbuildings, including numerous houses along Mill Street, Franklindale Avenue, Market Street, and Clapp Avenue. Over 80 homes, 4 commercial buildings, and 13 building lots were sold. The auction was held at the old Franklindale Office on the southeast corner of the stone bridge. (Courtesy of the Wappingers Historical Society.)

Seven

Wappingers Falls

East Main Street

For many early residents, the east side of Wappingers Falls was called Franklindale. Many places reflected the name, including the Franklindale Church, Franklindale Mill, and Franklindale Avenue. The first settlers constructed their homes on the gentle sloping land that would become the business center for the village. By the 1870s, East Main Street was lined by stores and included two large factories, Sweet Orr & Company on Mill Street and the Franklindale Mill on Market Street.

The east side of the falls also included many of the village's churches. The Zion Episcopal Church at the top of East Main is the oldest in the village, and its congregation includes many of the oldest and wealthiest in the community. This portion of the village saw some of the worst fires that would continue to reshape downtown. To fight these intense blazes, the village created two fire companies, W.T. Garner and S.W. Johnson. The annual Firemen's Parade was a county-wide event where bystanders packed the streets.

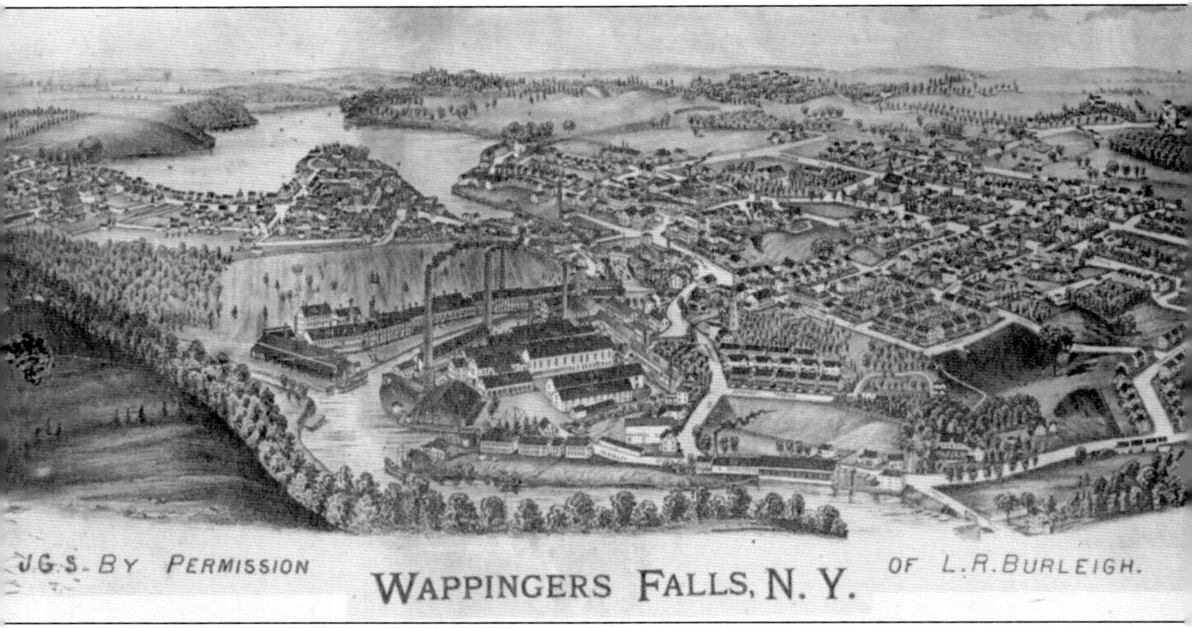

MAP OF WAPPINGERS FALLS, C. 1900. An interesting drawing shows an aerial view of the village during the turn of the century. On the right is the east side of the creek, once called Franklindale. On the left is the west side formerly called Ednamville and Channingville, which expanded along Wappingers Lake. In the center of the image is the Dutchess or Garner Print Works factory complex. (Courtesy of the Wappingers Historical Society.)

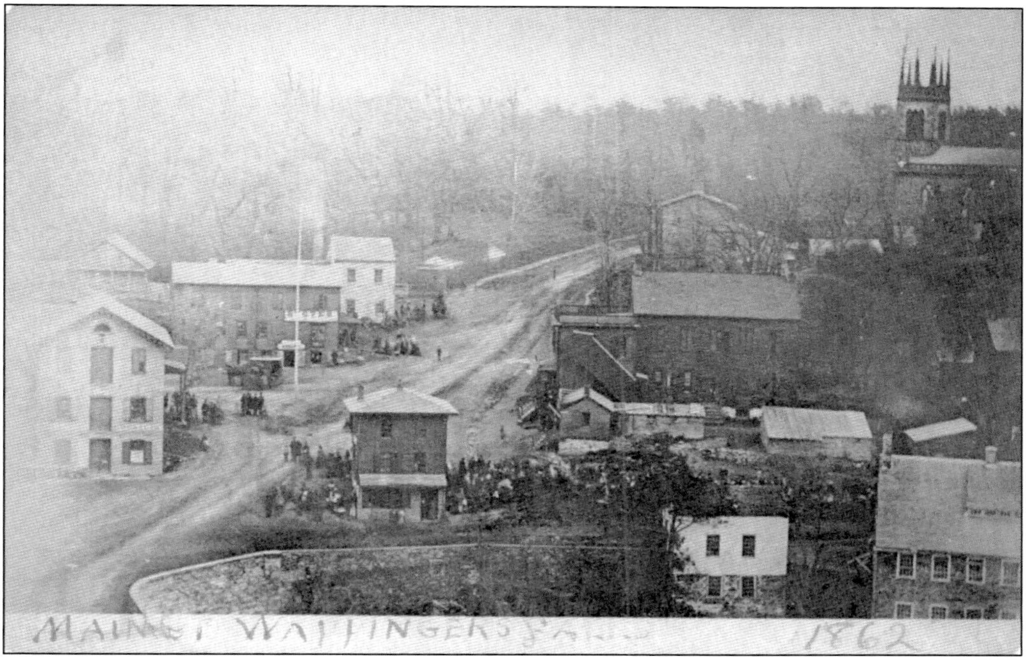

EAST MAIN STREET, 1862. This image is the earliest known photograph of the village of Wappingers Falls. In the lower right, one can see the old Franklindale Mill that was destroyed by an 1885 fire. Across Market Street is the old Brewer House, one of the first residences constructed in the village. The sparse scattering of buildings on Main Street was due to the town's small population at the time, numbering only 1,800 people. (Courtesy of the Wappingers Historical Society.)

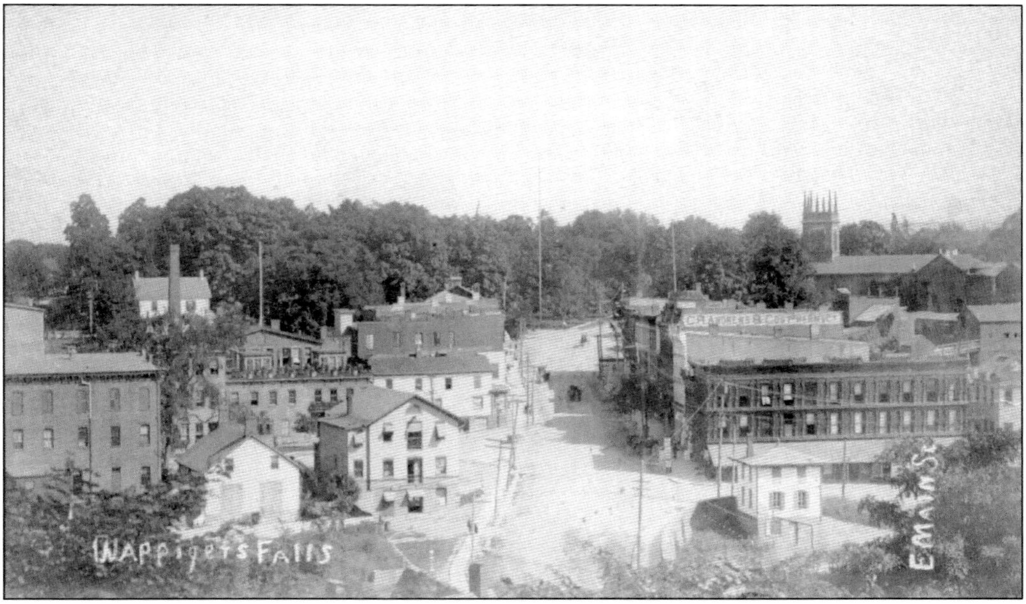

EAST MAIN STREET, 1900. By the turn of the century, East Main Street was lined on either side by large three-story brick buildings. Although three of the large factories constructed in the mid-1800s burned, the population of the town had grown to over 4,300 people. This large increase in population was due to the Sweet Orr factory and Garner Print Works that filled the void left by the other companies. (Courtesy of the Wappingers Historical Society.)

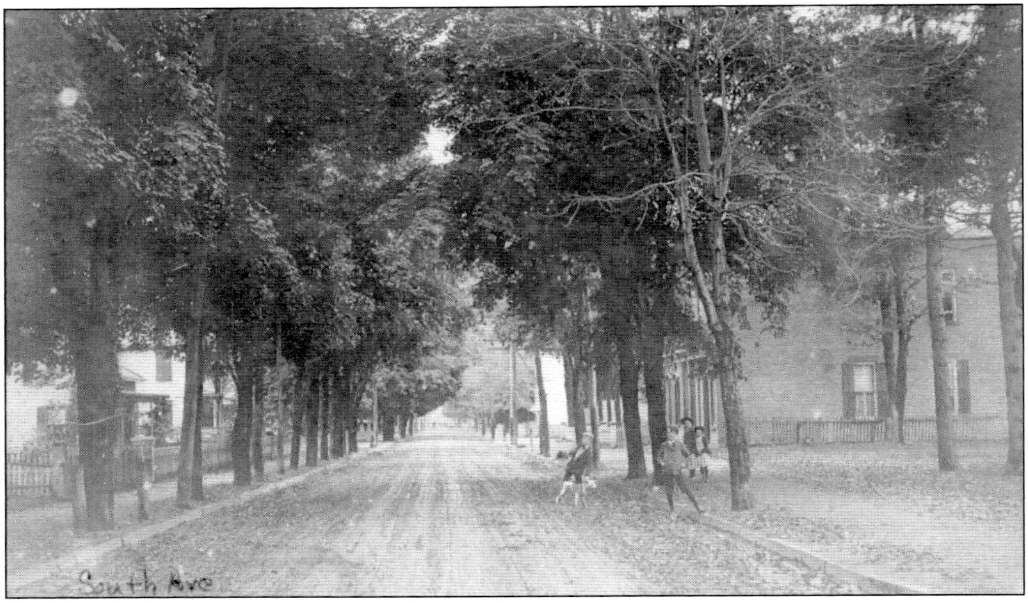

SOUTH AVENUE, C. 1908. Prior to the construction of Route 9 bypass, the main road into Wappingers Falls from Fishkill was South Avenue, today Route 9D. South Avenue, heavily shaded by maple trees, is where many merchants in town had their homes. One of the earliest inhabitants on the street was Benjamin Clapp, who constructed a large brick home on the corner of Henry Street in 1824. (Courtesy of the Wappingers Historical Society.)

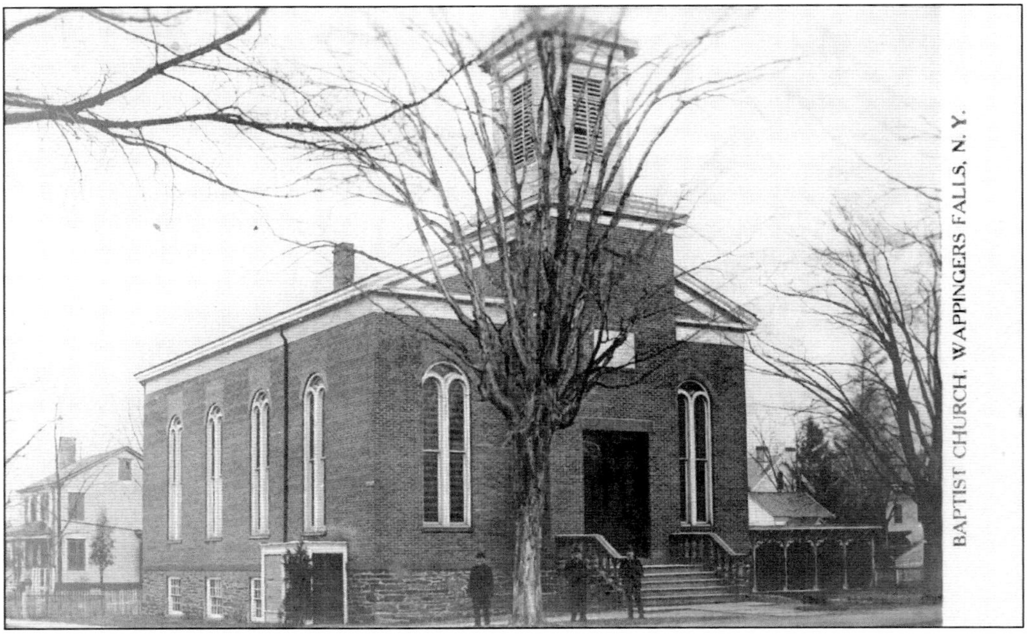

FRANKLINDALE BAPTIST CHURCH, C. 1906. Organized in 1843, the brick and stone Franklindale Church sat on the corner of South Avenue and Prospect Street. The man behind the project was Benjamin Clapp, who donated the land and money for the church's construction. After being closed in the 1920s due to a lack of a congregation, the church building sat dormant for decades. It was revived as the Bethel Baptist Church in 1967. In 2009, a larger church was constructed across the street to accommodate the growing congregation.

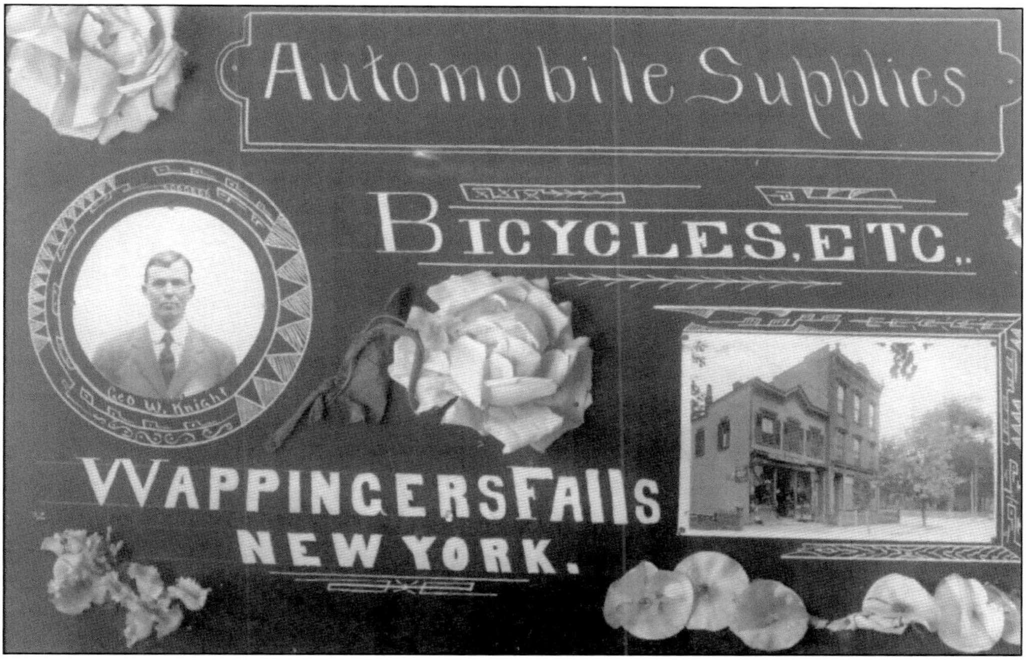

Bicycle Shop, c. 1915. Owned by George Knight, the bicycle shop on South Avenue was a popular place for local children. Expanding to auto parts during the early 1900s, George Knight's success was then passed down to his son, who operated a small car dealership in the village from the 1950s to the 1960s. Although his business is now gone, some of the old Knight family bicycles are still on display at the Mesier Homestead. (Courtesy of Ed Hogan.)

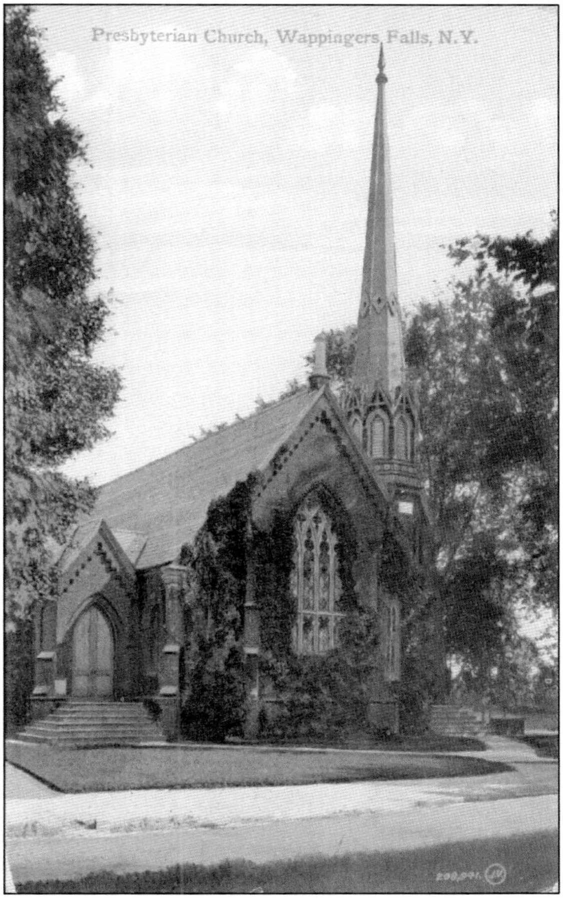

Presbyterian Church, c. 1910. The Sheafe family was instrumental in the organization of the first Presbyterian Church in 1848. A few decades later in 1872, enough money was raised for the construction of this large Gothic-style church on South Avenue. Even though extensive renovations occurred in the 1950s, the structure still retains its original styling. Today, the church congregation has grown since those early days and still stands near the southern entrance to the village.

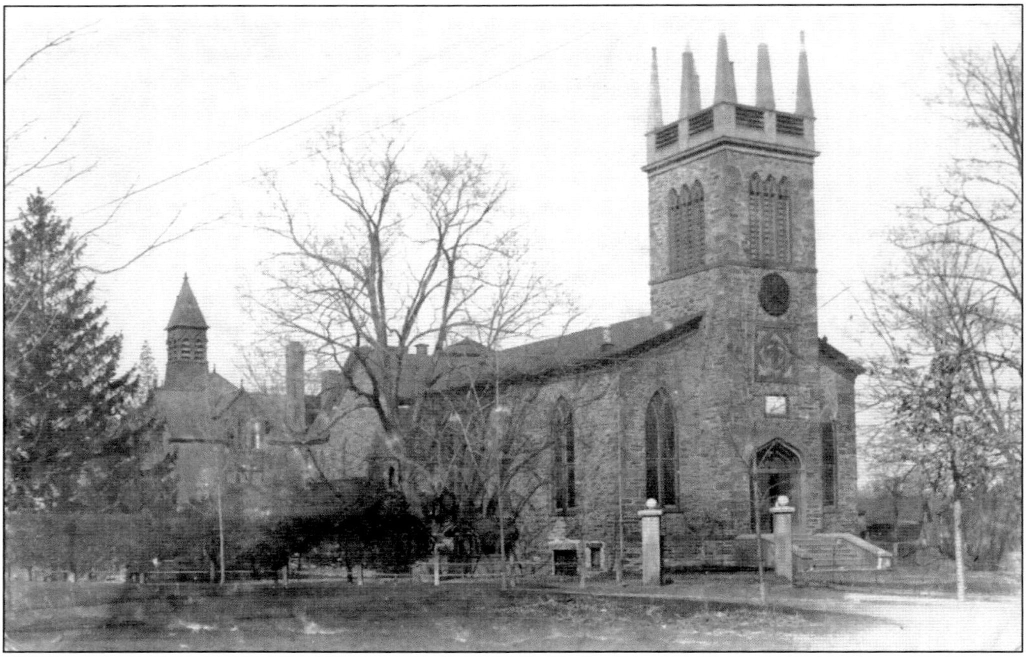

Zion Episcopal Church, c. 1910. Completed in 1836, the Gothic-style church was constructed on land donated by the Mesier family, whose home was across the street. The church, located near the top of East Main Street, was situated in front of the village's original cemetery and was established in 1747. The ornamental wooden spires shown here on top of the bell tower were removed in the mid-1900s.

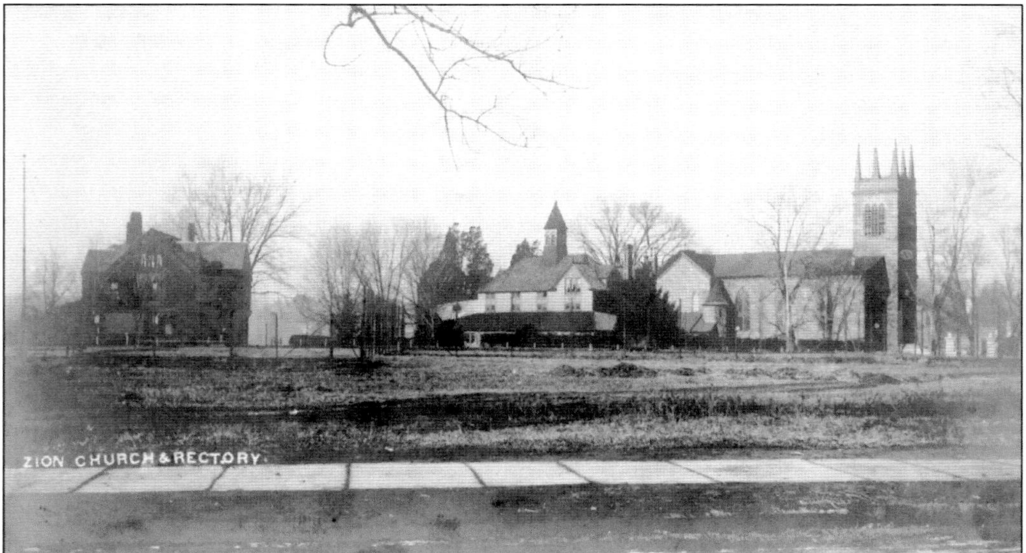

Zion Church Property, 1908. A view across Zion Park from South Avenue shows the Zion Church on the far right. Behind the church is the parish house, constructed in 1881, to accommodate an expanded Sunday school and to house various social activities. To the far left is the church rectory, which featured 18 rooms and eight fireplaces. It was constructed in 1886.

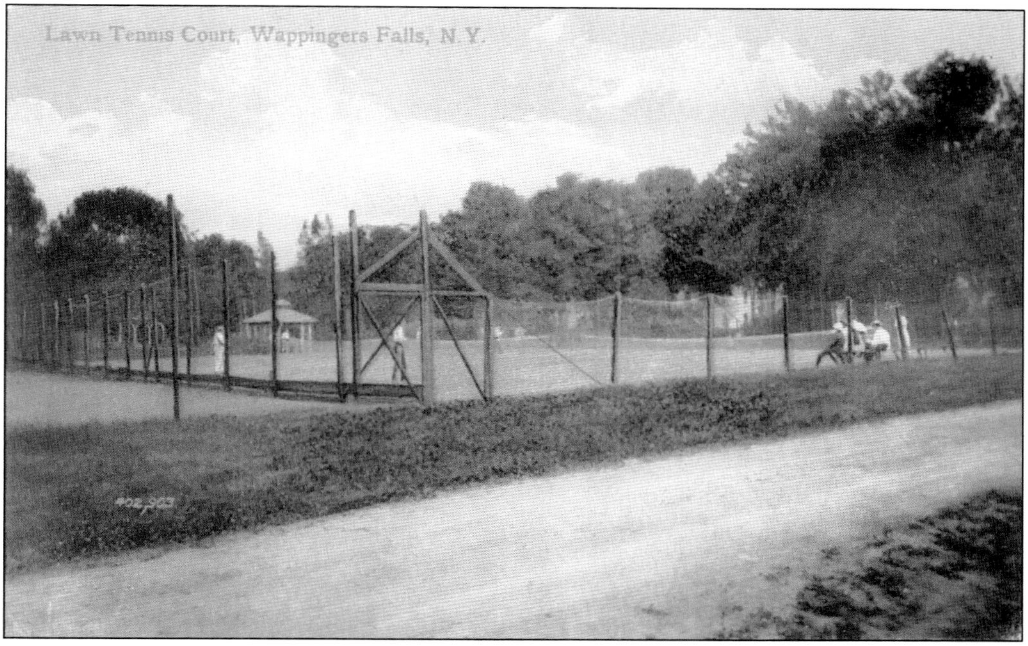

ZION PARK AND TENNIS COURTS, C. 1910. In the early 1900s, under the supervision of Dr. William Pott and the Zion Church, the vacant land just east of the church and parish house was improved with new landscaping and a pair of tennis courts. These dirt courts were very popular with the young adults in the village.

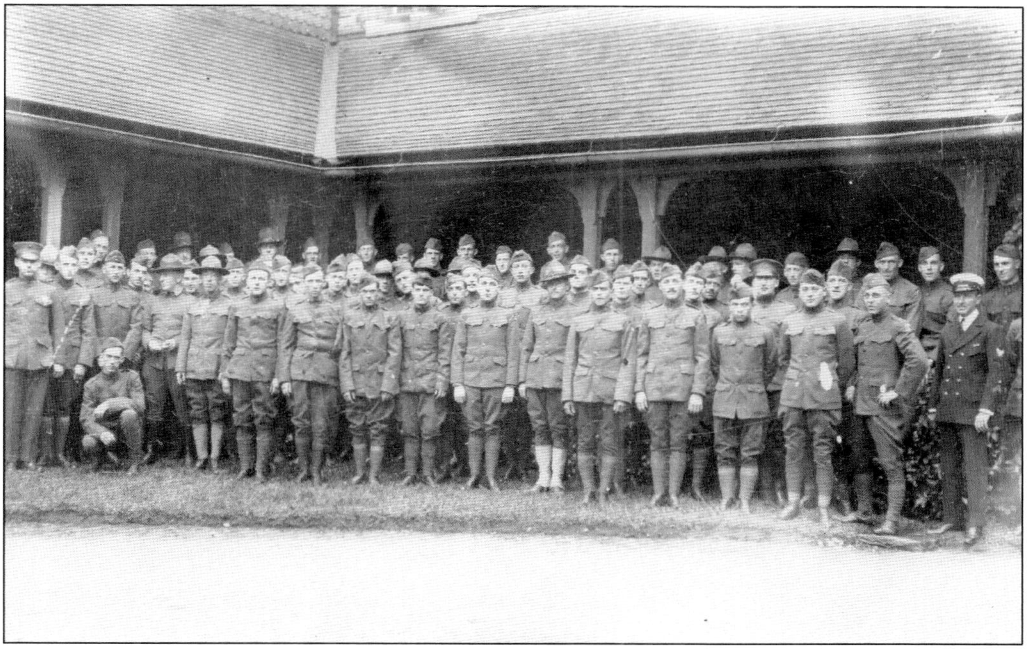

RETURNING WORLD WAR I TROOPS, 1918. Greeted with a hero's welcome, returning World War I soldiers met here at the Zion Parish House for a group photograph. Men from all over the town joined the ranks of the US Army, who returned in late 1918. Just after this photograph was taken, the troops participated in a parade in their honor. (Courtesy of the Wappingers Historical Society.)

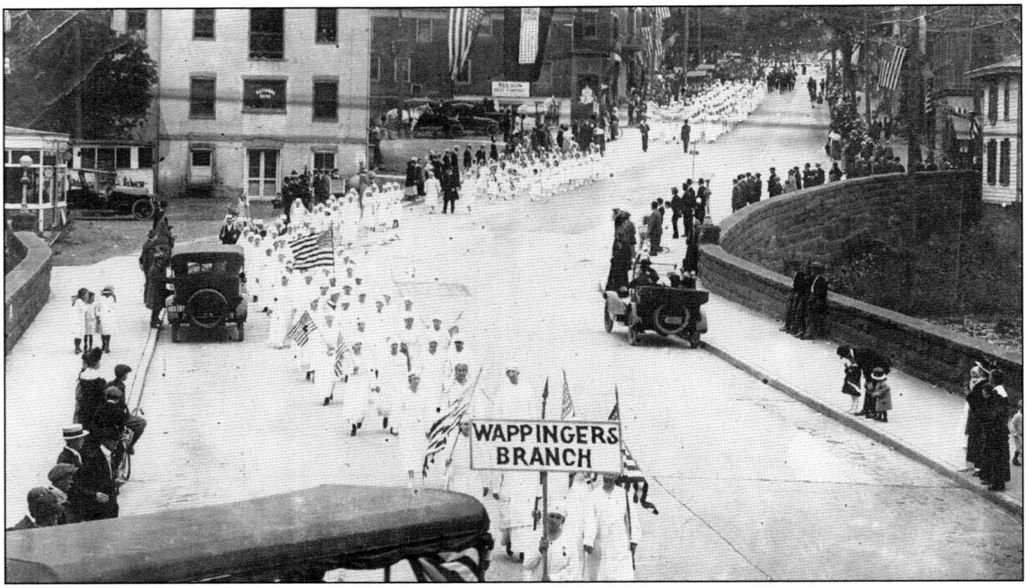

WAPPINGERS BRANCH OF THE RED CROSS, 1918. Women throughout the town also contributed much of their time to the war effort as well. This view shows the Wappingers Branch of the Red Cross walking down East Main Street during the World War I parade. Women on the home front were crucial in the sale of war bonds, sewing clothing and bandages for front line troops, and generally replacing jobs usually reserved for men.

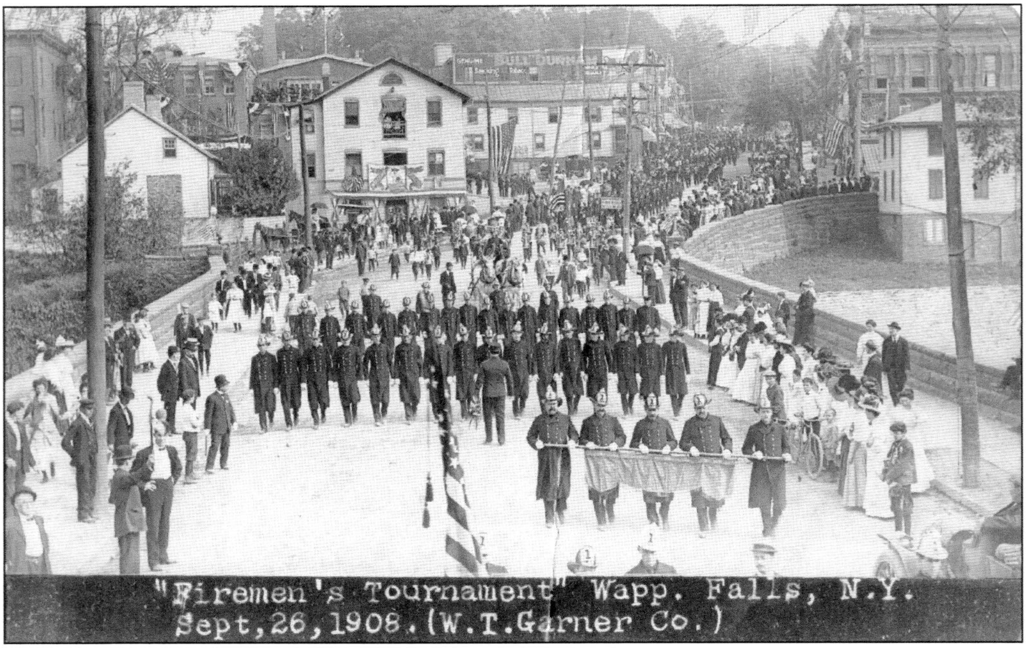

FIREMEN'S TOURNAMENT, 1908. Parades were a common occurrence in the village. Here, the W.T. Garner Fire Company walks across the stone bridge during the annual Firemen's Parade. Dressed in navy blue, the company was made up of mostly volunteers from the Garner Print Works. Fire companies from all over the region would attend the parade where crowds of well wishers packed the streets. (Courtesy of the Wappingers Historical Society.)

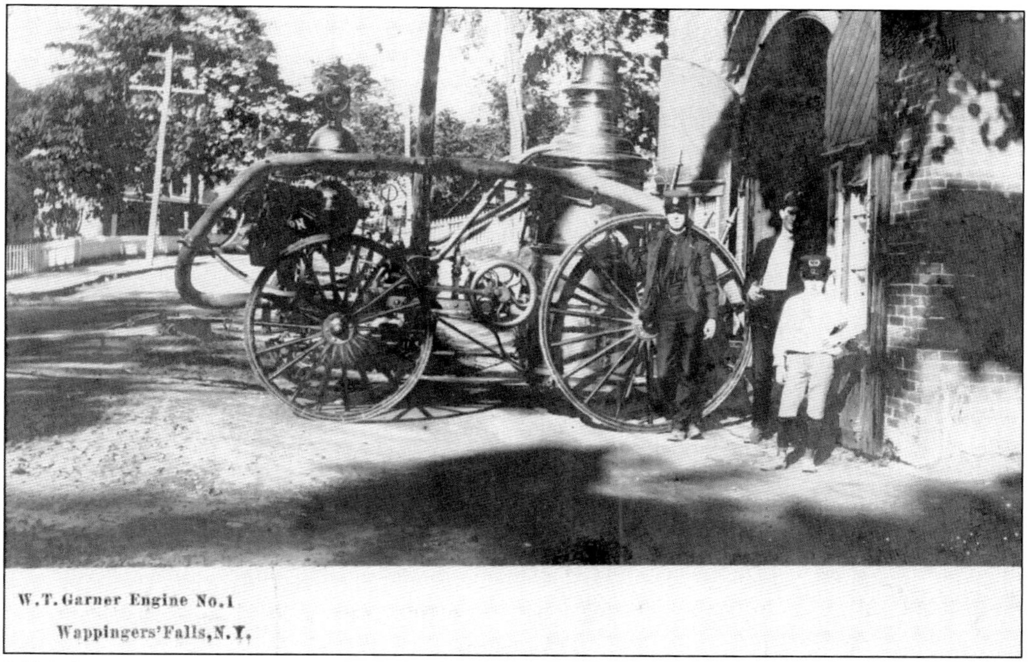

W.T. Garner Firehouse, c. 1900. The Garner Firehouse was located on Lower Market Street near the entrance to the Dutchess Print Work. The two-story building housed the engine on the bottom floor and a meeting room above. Shown here, the fire pumper was steam operated and pulled by a team of horses housed at the Print Works.

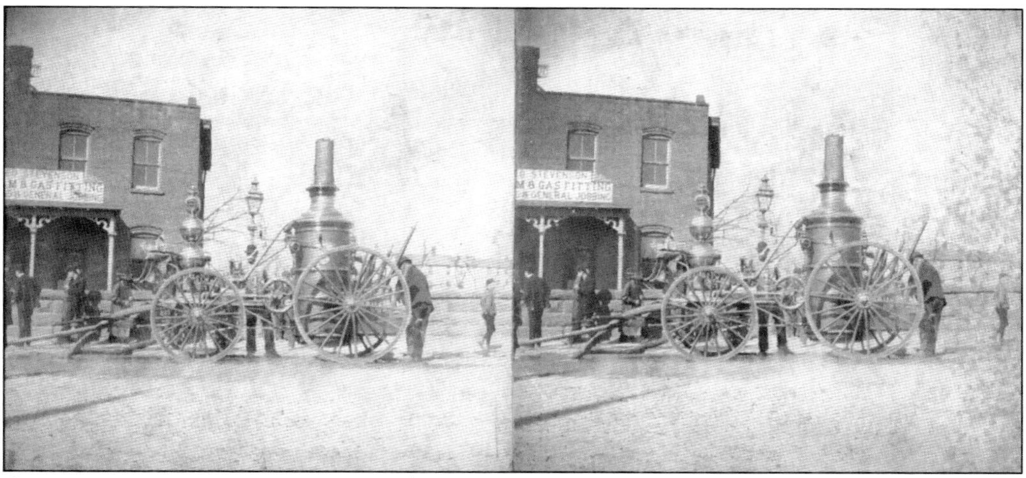

Garner Fire Engine, c. 1890. The steam-powered fire engine was a marvel of modern technology. Seen here at the west end of the stone bridge, the new engine was a curiosity to local residents. Donated by William Garner, owner of the Garner Print Works, the engine was used in many of the town's largest fires, including the New Hamburgh Train Wreck, Eagle Foundry Fire, and the Franklindale Mill fire.

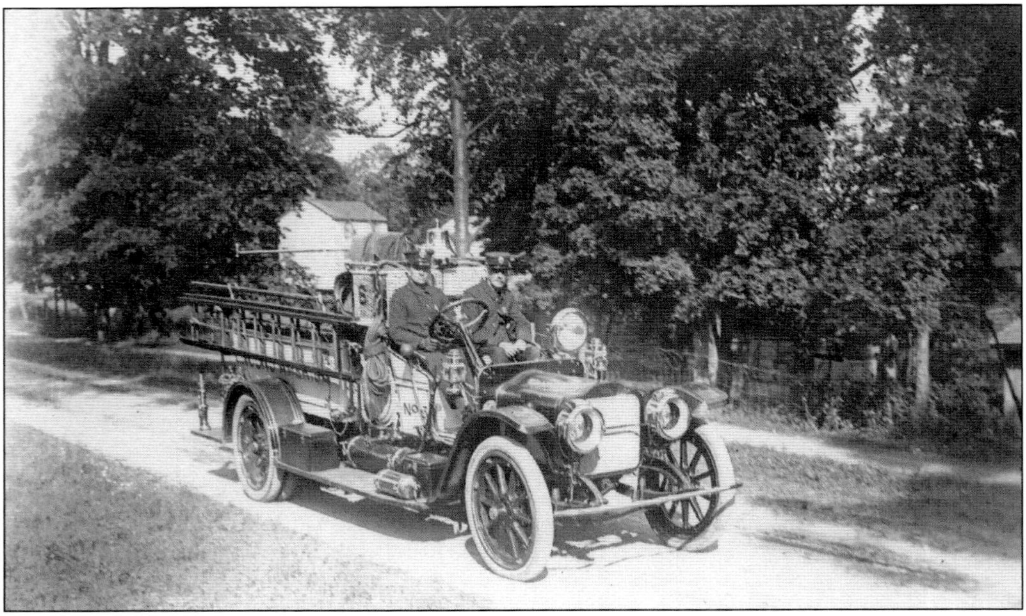

FIRST MOTORIZED ENGINE—W.T. GARNER, 1925. By 1920, the old horse-drawn steam engine was replaced by this motorized fire truck. Prior to this truck, separate support wagons with coal, water, and ladders were needed in addition to the horse-drawn pumper. With the addition of the new truck and fire hydrants around the village, the fire company could arrive at a fire faster and better prepared than at any time before. (Courtesy of the Wappingers Historical Society.)

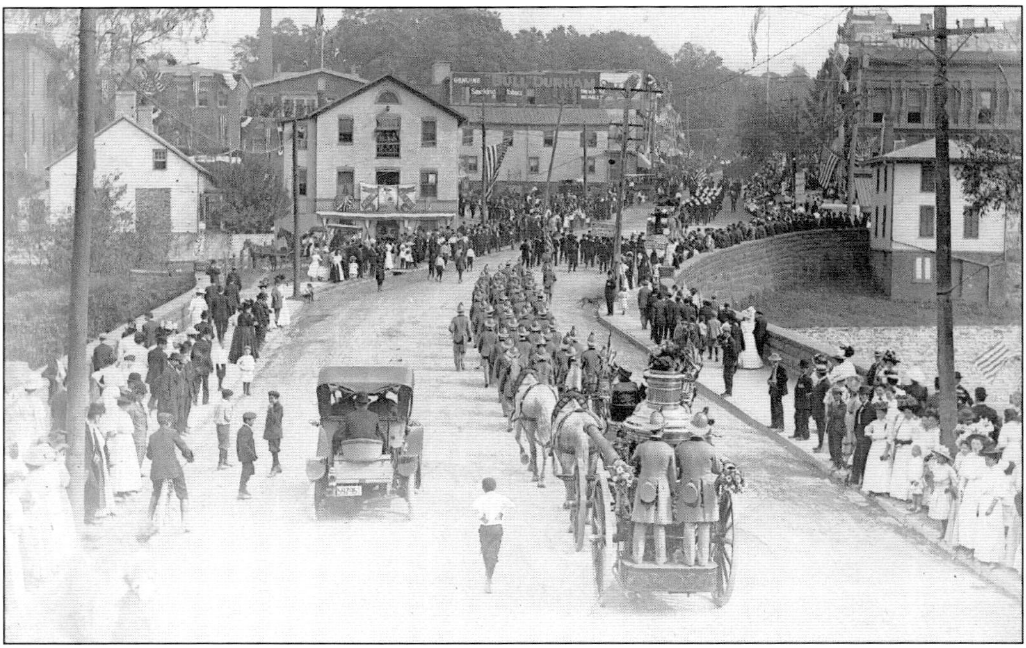

JOHNSON FIRE COMPANY—FIREMEN'S PARADE, 1908. As homes were constructed north along West Main Street, the village realized the need for an additional fire company. Shown here, the S.W. Johnson Engine Company walks across the stone bridge towards East Main Street. The fire pumper shown in the photograph was similar to the Garner Company's engine and was purchased by the village board at the cost of $4,000 in 1902.

JOHNSON FIREHOUSE, C. 1905. Located at the intersection of West Main Street and West Street, the three-story Temperance Hall Building was the headquarters for the S.W. Johnson Engine Company. Organized in 1872, the company was named after the manager at the Dutchess Print Works. The first floor of the building was occupied by the steam engine, while the upper floors were used as meeting rooms. (Courtesy of the Wappingers Historical Society.)

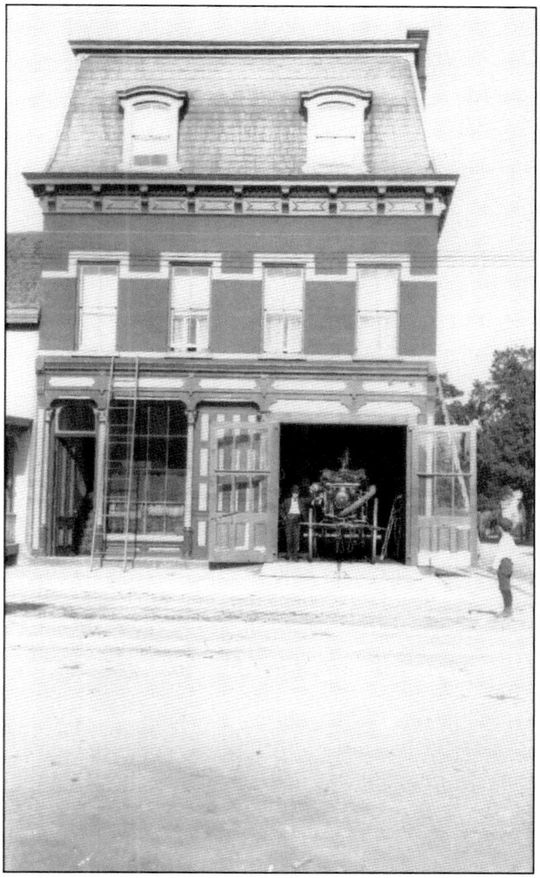

TEMPERANCE HALL FIRE, 1920. On March 15, 1920, in a show of irony, the Temperance Hall Building was destroyed by fire. The Johnson Fire Company's only engine was also destroyed in the blaze. After 10 years at a temporary facility on Givens Avenue, the town constructed a new firehouse on the corner of School Street and West Main in 1940. (Courtesy of the Wappingers Historical Society.)

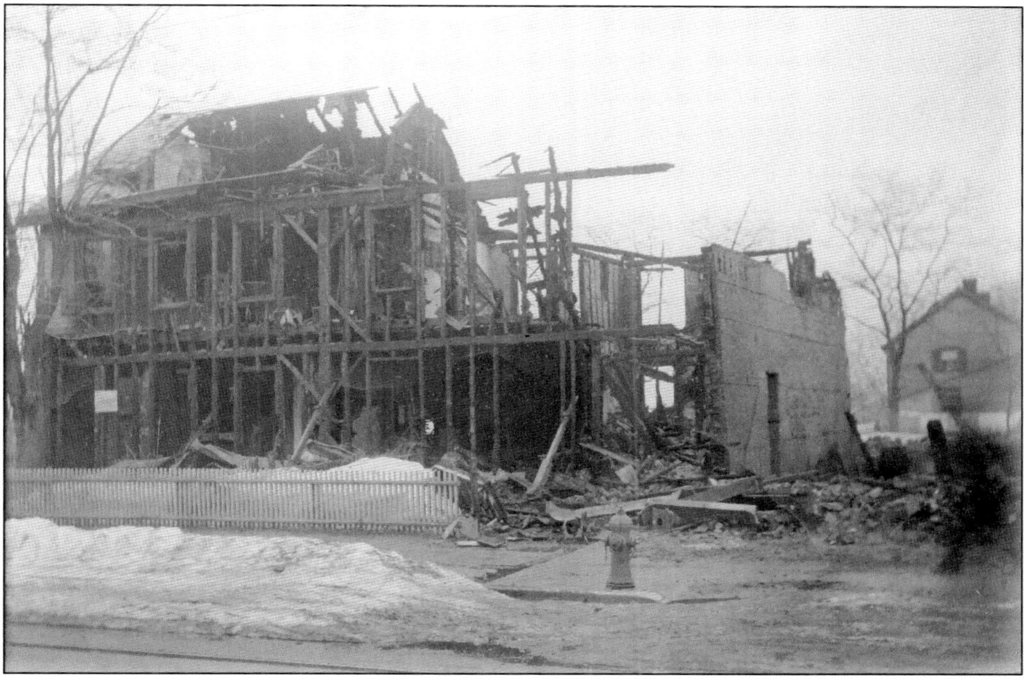

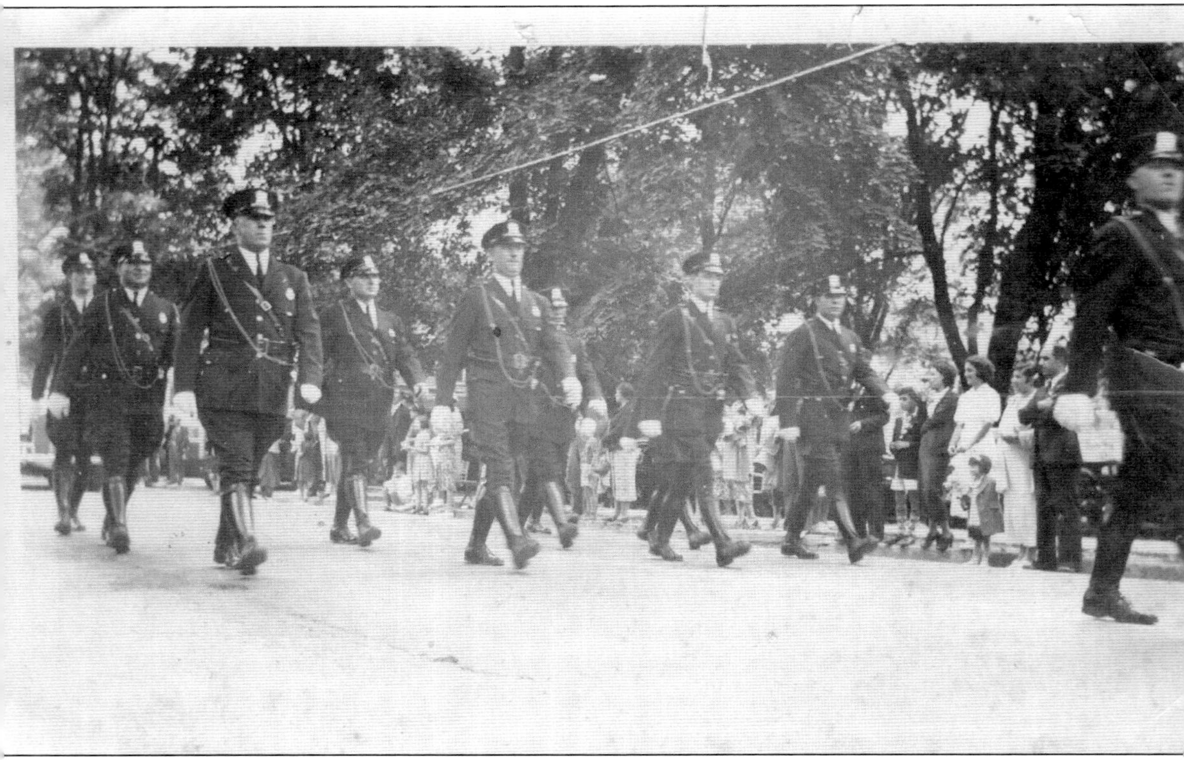

WAPPINGERS FALLS POLICE DEPARTMENT, C. 1918. Wearing their navy blue uniforms, the Wappingers Police Department marches during the World War I parade. Headquartered in the old Franklindale Office next to the stone bridge, the department lacked a car and telephone service. Police officers were a common sight in the village, spending much of their day walking the streets and talking to local residents. (Courtesy of the Wappingers Historical Society.)

LAFAYETTE LODGE, 1890. The four-story brick building at the end of South Avenue was constructed in 1877, as the headquarters of the Independent Order of Odd Fellows fraternal society. The impressive building had apartments on the first and second floors and a large hall on the third floor for the organization's meetings. Composed of local business leaders, the lodge was a social gathering place where many of the village's politicians emerged. (Courtesy of the Wappingers Historical Society.)

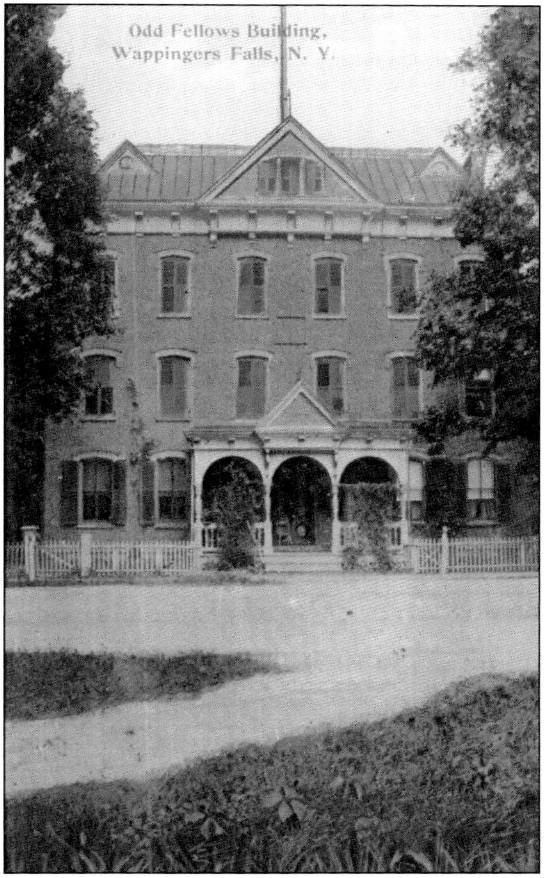

NEW POST OFFICE BUILDING, 1940. The post office building on the corner of South Avenue and East Main Street was the inspiration of Franklin D. Roosevelt. Constructed in a Dutch colonial style, the building was similar to other Franklin D. Roosevlet post offices in Rhinebeck, Hyde Park, and Beacon, New York. It was no surprise that the president would take interest in the area since he spent much of his life in Dutchess County. The Roosevelts were also good friends of the Grinnell and Howland families, which both had estates along Sheafe Road. (Courtesy of the Wappingers Historical Society.)

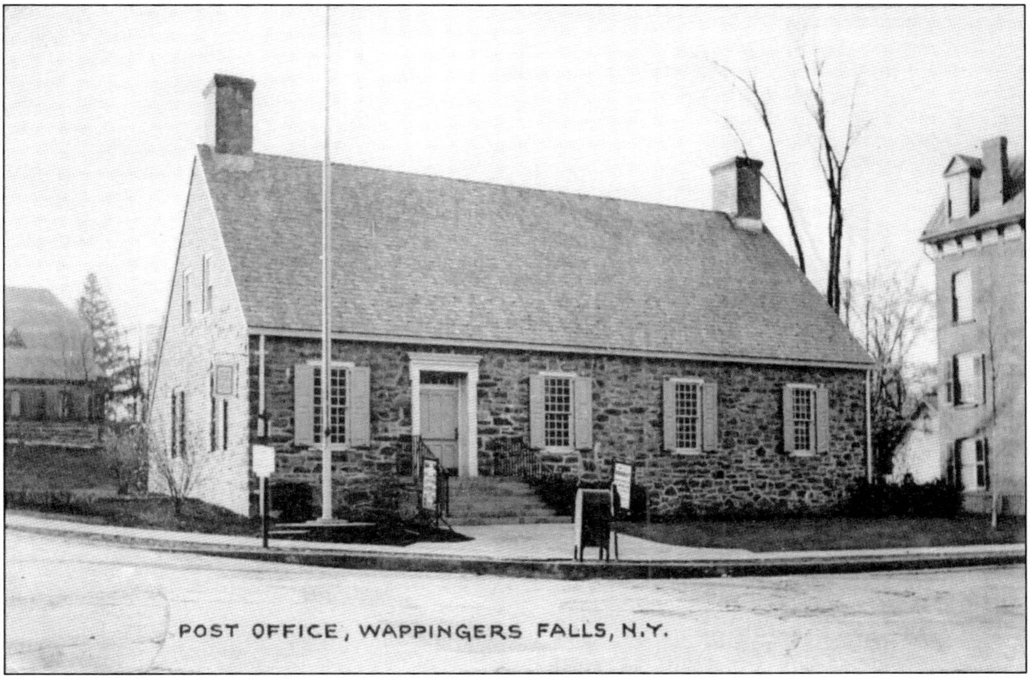

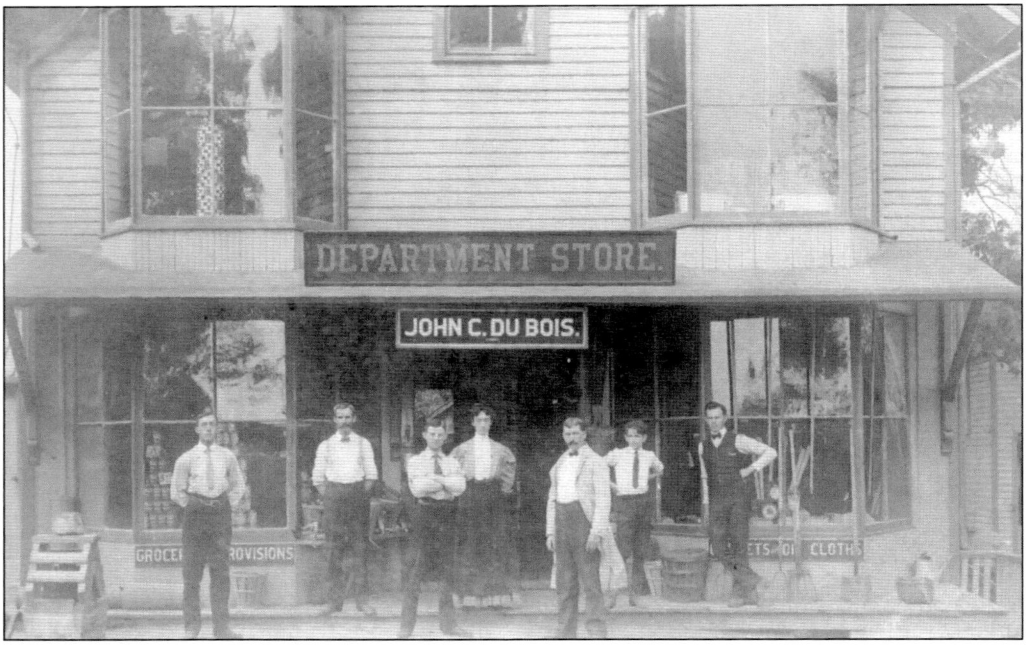

DuBois Department Store, c. 1906. John C. DuBois, seen here in the long coat, operated a successful hardware and grocery store on the corner of North Remsen Avenue and East Main Street. Standing beside him are his wife and son who lived in the house just behind the store on North Remsen. In 1909, John C. DuBois became the first president of the National Bank of Wappingers Falls. (Courtesy of the Wappingers Historical Society.)

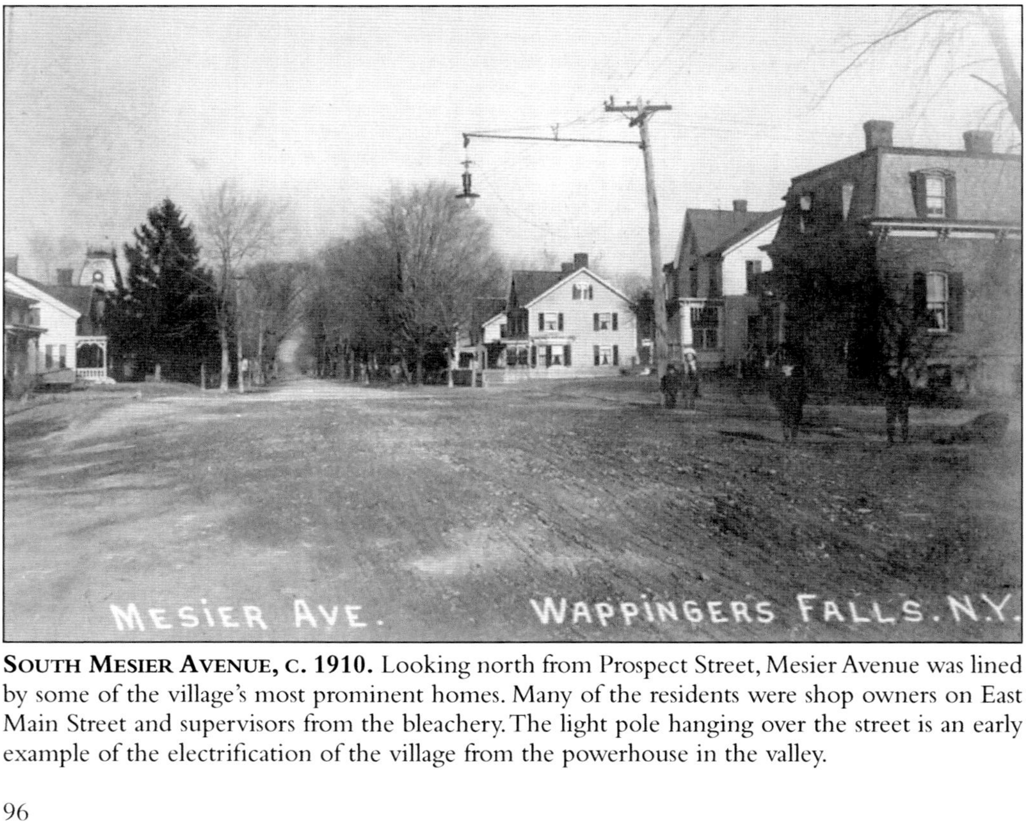

South Mesier Avenue, c. 1910. Looking north from Prospect Street, Mesier Avenue was lined by some of the village's most prominent homes. Many of the residents were shop owners on East Main Street and supervisors from the bleachery. The light pole hanging over the street is an early example of the electrification of the village from the powerhouse in the valley.

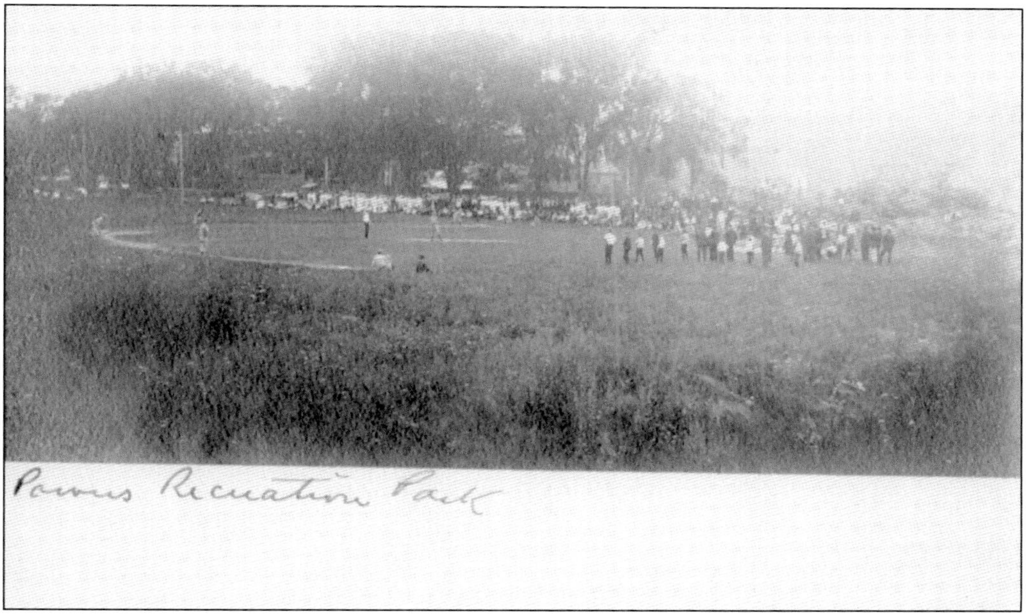

Baseball Fields, c. 1905. On the outskirts of the village, a small baseball park was erected for neighborhood children as shown here in this 1905 photograph. Baseball became a popular sport in the village partly due to a local star, Dan Brouthers, nicknamed Big Dan. Playing in the major league in Boston from 1894 to 1896, Brouthers was considered the first big slugger in major-league history. (Courtesy of the Wappingers Historical Society.)

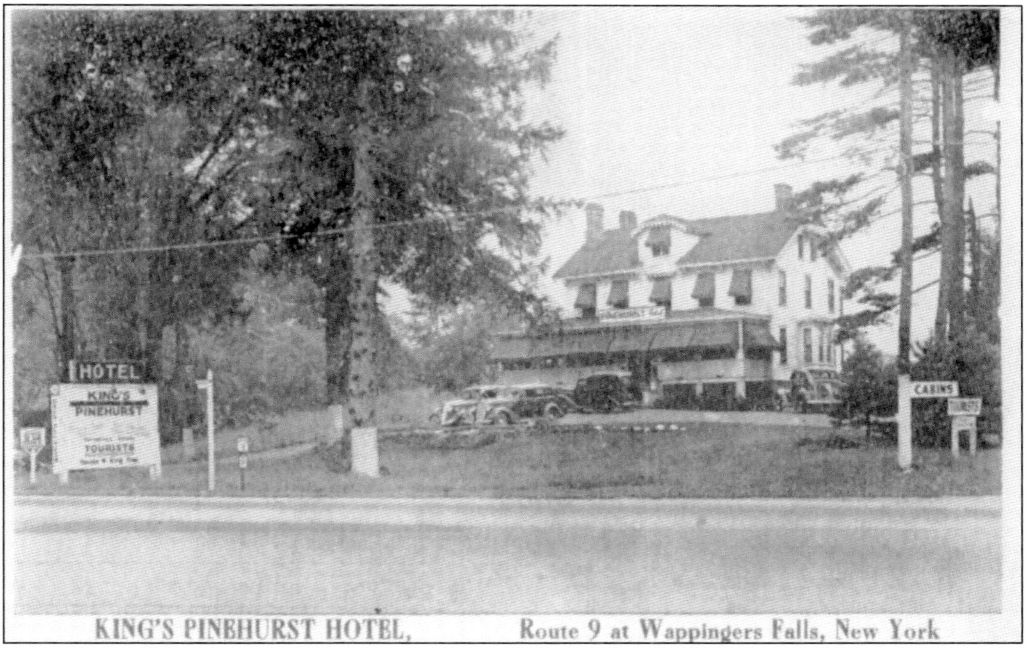

King's Pinehurst Hotel, c. 1930. During the 1930s, Route 9 became a popular route for travelers coming north from New York City. To accommodate all of these motorists, many of the old homes were converted into restaurants and hotels. The Pinehurst Hotel, once owned by Dr. Phinney as his personal residence, was torn down for the construction of Imperial Plaza. (Courtesy of Timothy Holls.)

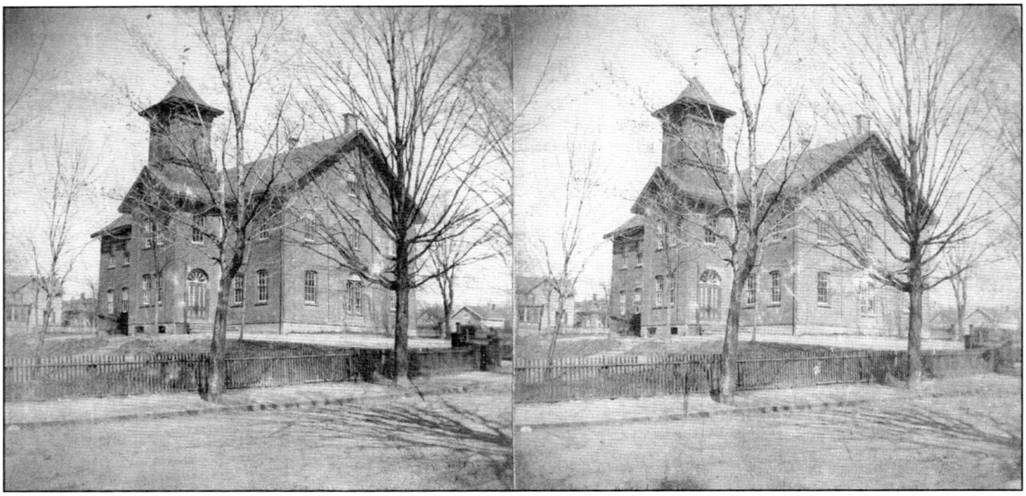

UNION FREE SCHOOL NO 2., C. 1890. On a small hill at the corner of East Academy Street and Mesier Avenue, a large two-story brick school was constructed. First called the Franklindale School, the building had eight classrooms and housed all grades up to high school. A large bell was installed to call students to class each morning in the early 1880s. (Courtesy of the Wappingers Historical Society.)

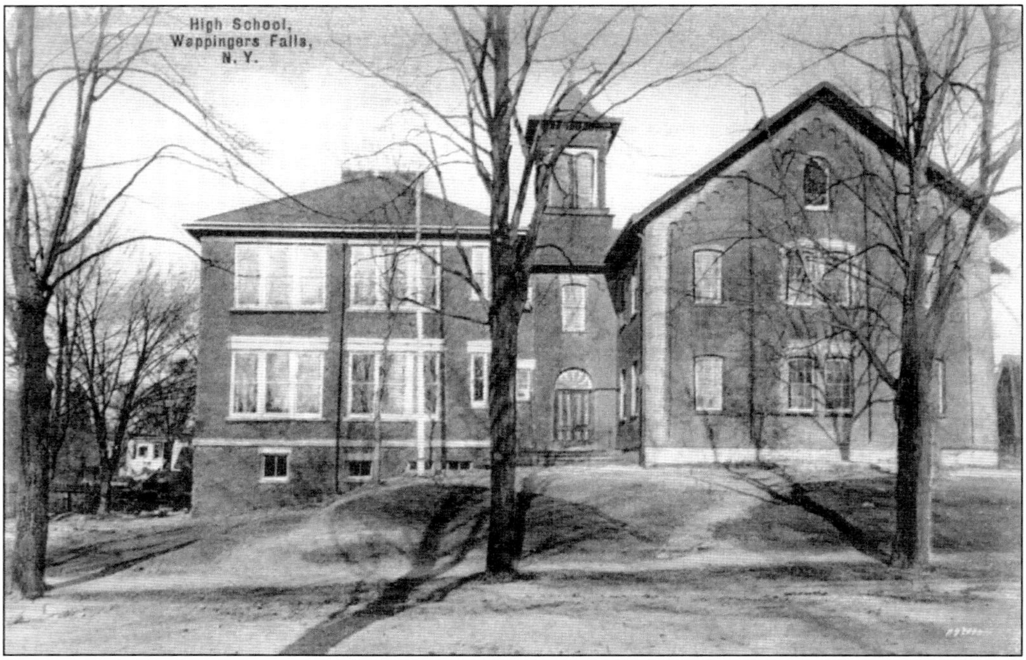

WAPPINGERS HIGH SCHOOL, 1910. School No. 2 on Mesier Avenue was later converted into the high school. In 1920, classrooms were added on the north end of the school along Mesier Avenue, while a large gymnasium and auditorium were constructed on the western side. When the large central school was constructed in 1940 at the end of Remsen Avenue, this school closed its doors. (Courtesy of the Wappingers Historical Society.)

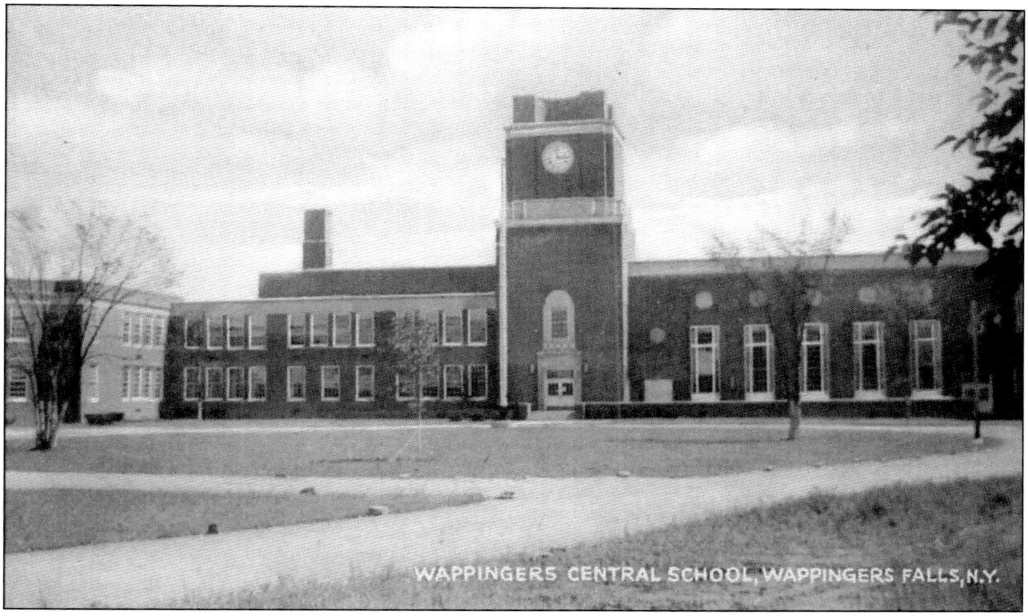

NEW CENTRAL SCHOOL, C. 1945. In 1940, the New York Education Department required all schools to be centralized with all classes from kindergarten to 12th grade in one building. At the end of Remsen Avenue, this large school was constructed to replace the two schools in the village and those in Hughsonville and New Hamburgh. (Courtesy of the Wappinger Historical Society.)

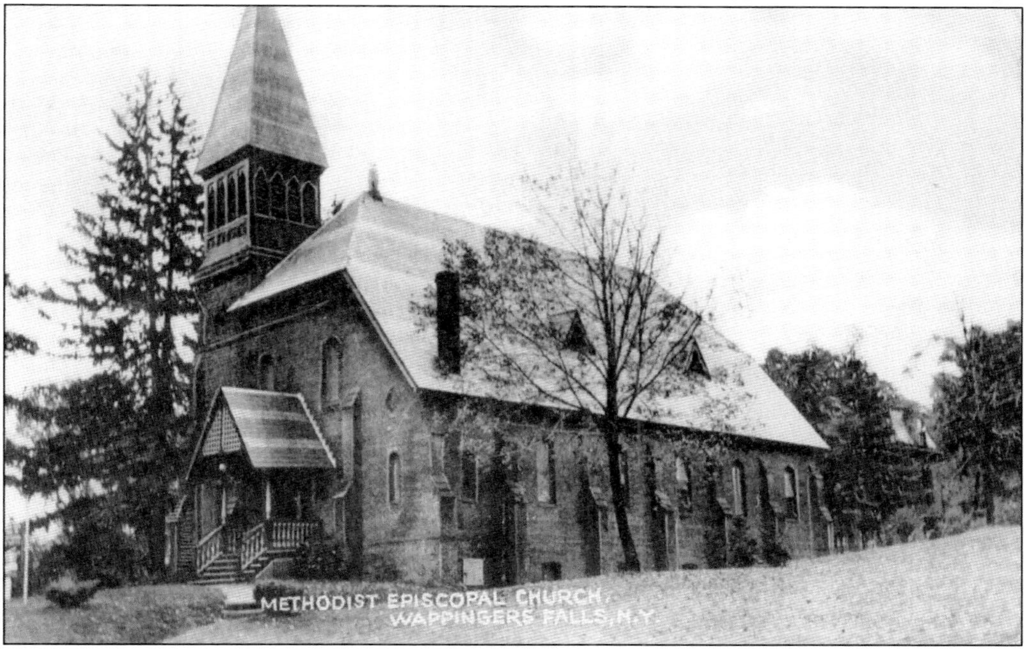

METHODIST CHURCH, 1890. Sitting on land donated from the Margaret Reese family, the Methodist Church on the corner of East Main and Mesier Avenue was erected in 1869. Built in the village on the east side of the creek, the church was a consolidation of two smaller chapels, one on West Main Street and the other on Middlebush Road. In 1871, a Sunday school was added by Reverend Mosehouse with 21 teachers and over 100 students. (Courtesy of the Wappingers Historical Society.)

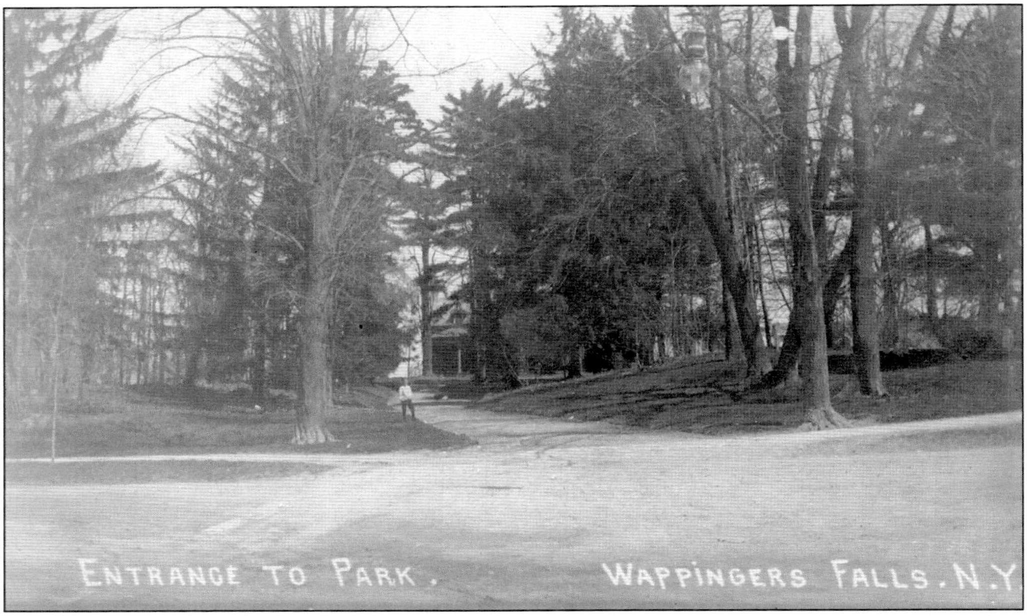

ENTRANCE TO MESIER PARK, 1906. At the intersection of East Main Street and South Avenue is Mesier Park, a five-acre remnant of a once large estate. First part of the 750-acre Brewer family estate, it was later sold to Peter Mesier in 1776. The Mesier family would occupy the property until 1891, when it was sold to the village with the understanding that it would forever be called Mesier Park and Homestead.

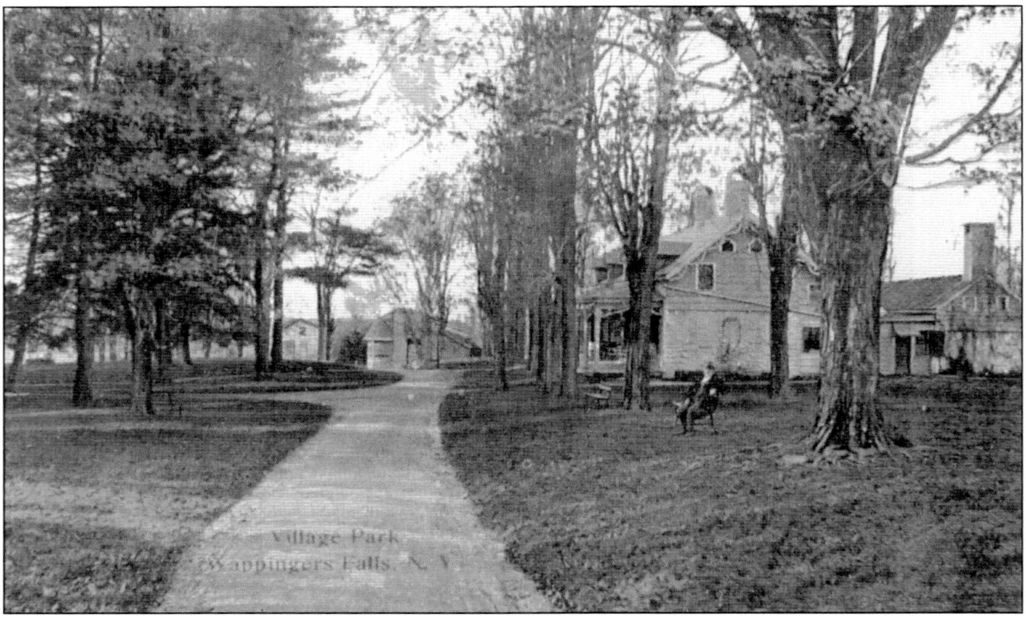

MESIER HOMESTEAD LOOKING TOWARDS SPRING STREET, C. 1910. In the center of Mesier Park is the Dutch homestead. To the far right, the Nicholas Brewer home, constructed in 1741, can be seen. The building visible from Main Street is the Mesier addition erected in 1777. After the homestead was sold to the village, it housed local government offices and the village police department. Today, it is occupied by the Wappingers Historical Society and serves as a museum of local history.

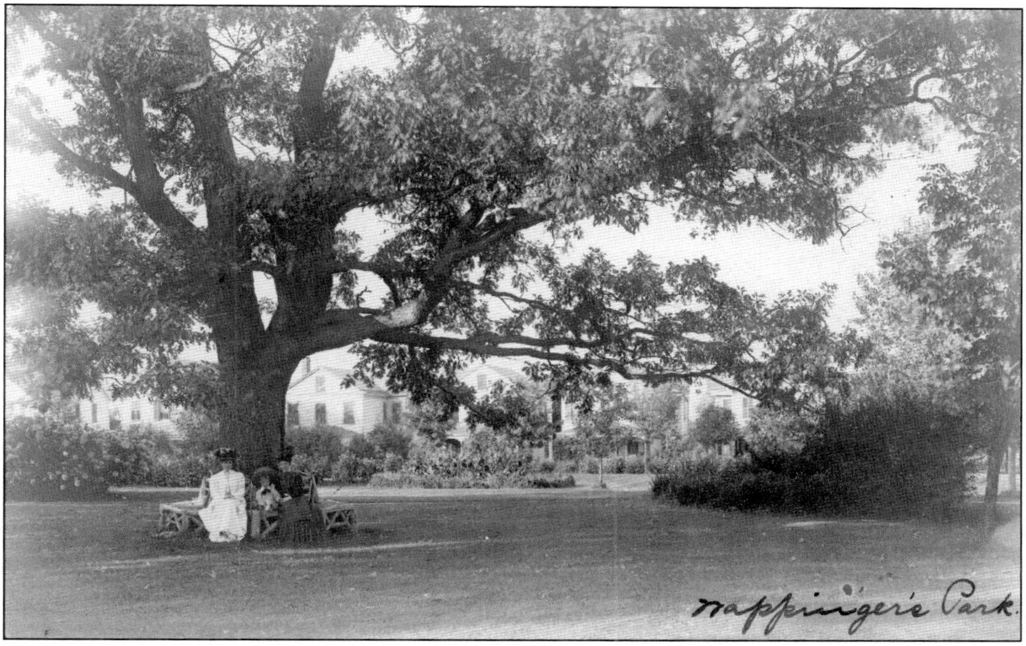

Mesier Park Looking North, c. 1905. Showing one of the wooden benches around an old maple tree, the park's creation was intended to be a gathering place for all residents to enjoy. A gazebo was placed near the entrance on East Main Street for lawn concerts. Longtime residents spoke of hearing the sounds of children echoing for blocks around the park during the summer. (Courtesy of the Wappingers Historical Society.)

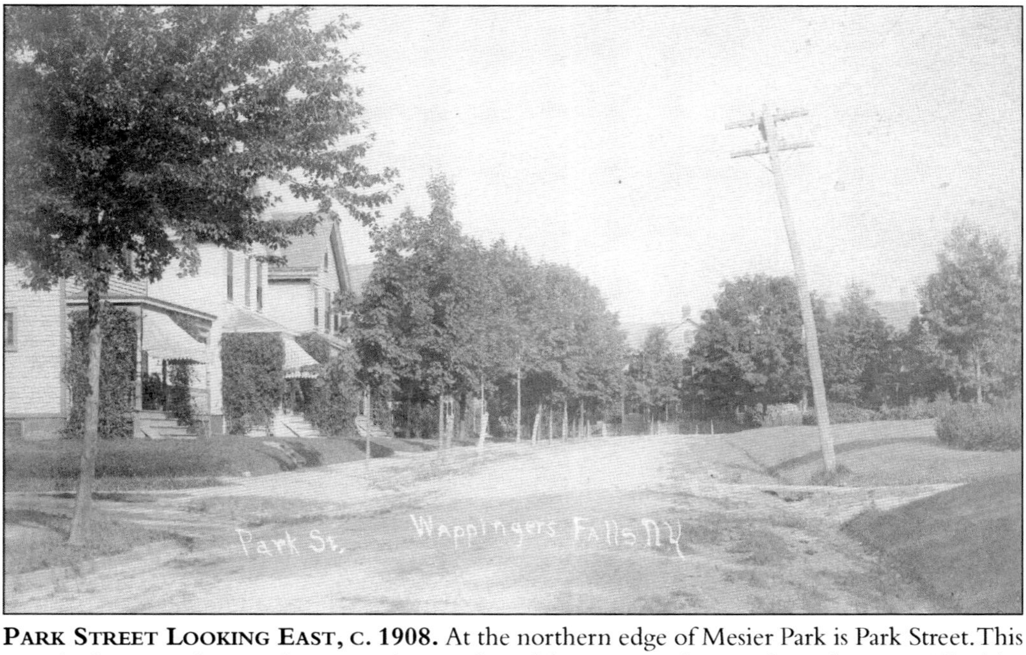

Park Street Looking East, c. 1908. At the northern edge of Mesier Park is Park Street. This view looking east from Park Avenue shows a few of the attractive homes along the street. All of the residences were almost identical in style with a large front porch facing the village park across the dirt road. A few of the homes were occupied by some the village's early doctors whose practices occupied the first floor.

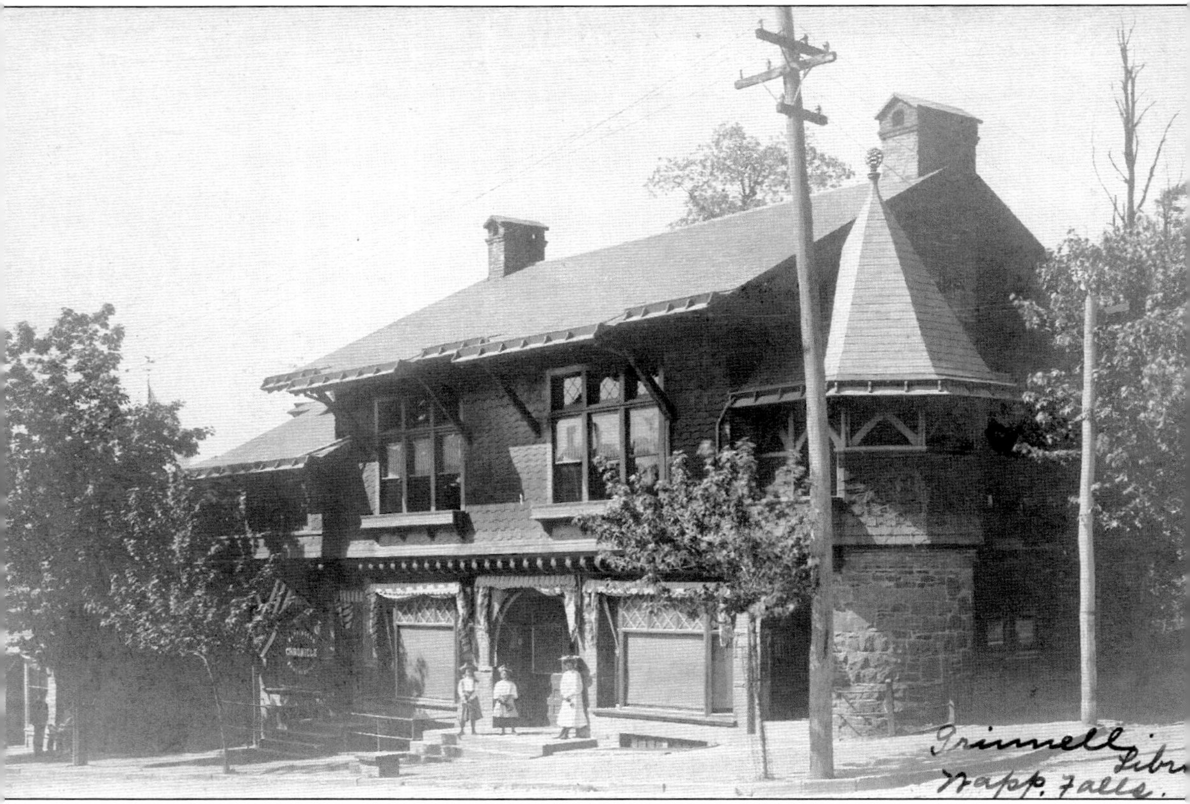

GRINNELL LIBRARY, 1907. Through the generosity of Irving Grinnell and help of the Zion Church, the village constructed this building in 1887, on the corner of Spring Street and East Main. Built in the Swiss-chalet style by architect Henry Congdon, the library occupied the second floor and was accessible from a spiral staircase on the east side of the building. The first floor housed the *Wappingers Chronicle* newspaper and the Simmons Jewelry Store. In 1967, the library expanded and now occupies the entire building. (Courtesy of the Wappingers Historical Society.)

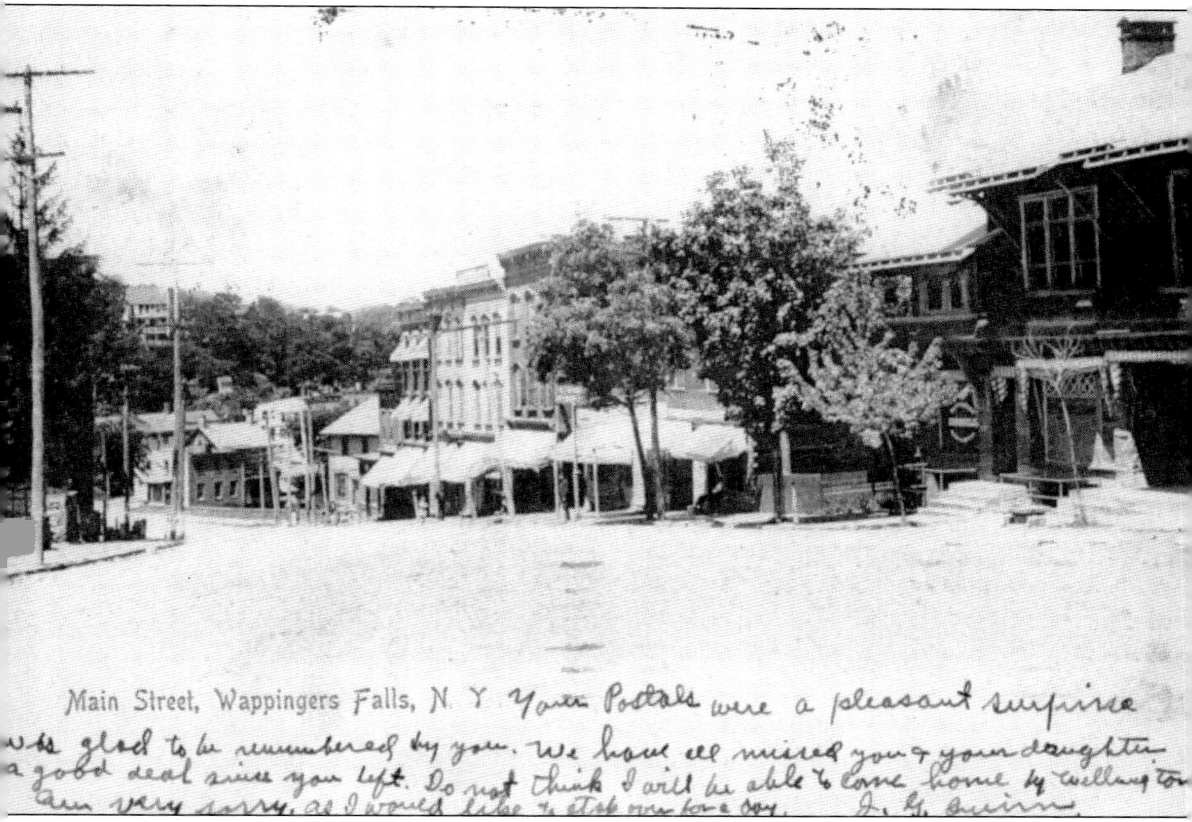

EAST MAIN STREET FROM SPRING STREET, C. 1900. The portion of Main Street below Mesier Park was the business center of the village. To the right is the Grinnell Library, followed by the two-story Roe Building. The four three-story buildings in the distance, constructed in the late 1870s, were occupied by a number of hotels. The most prominent was the Rush Hotel, which was popular with traveling salesmen. (Courtesy of the Wappingers Historical Society.)

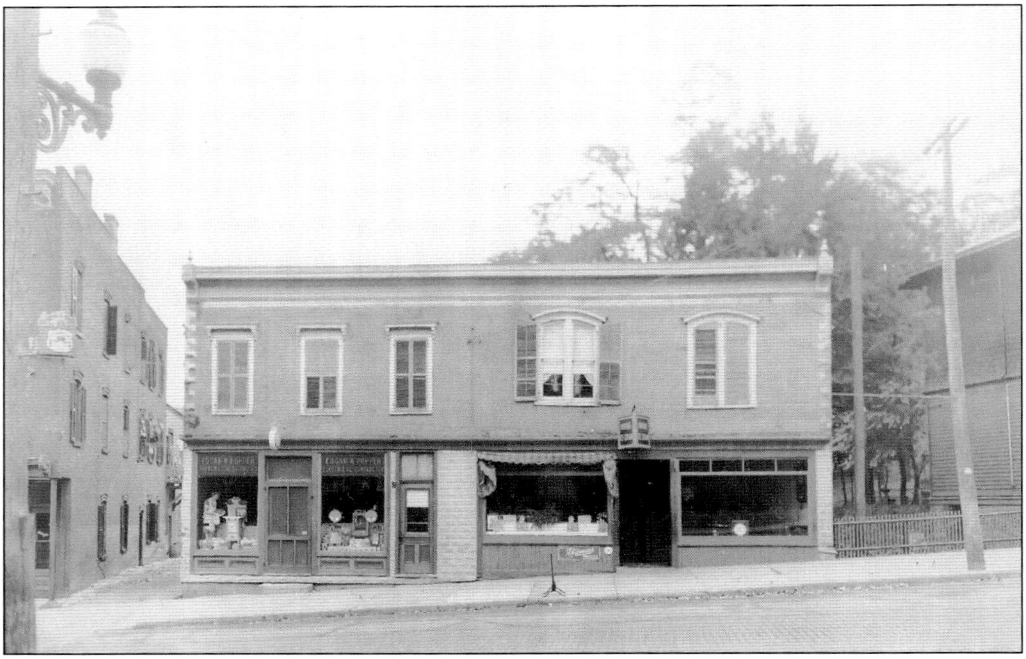

Roe Building, c. 1910. The Roe Building sat just below the Grinnell Library. The storefront on the left was occupied by an appliance store owned by Edgar A. Popper. On the right was a popular confectionery store run by Henry Pettit. In 1933, a fire started and spread throughout the building. The W.T. Garner Firehouse was able to keep the fire from spreading to nearby structures, but the Roe Building was destroyed. (Courtesy of the Wappingers Historical Society.)

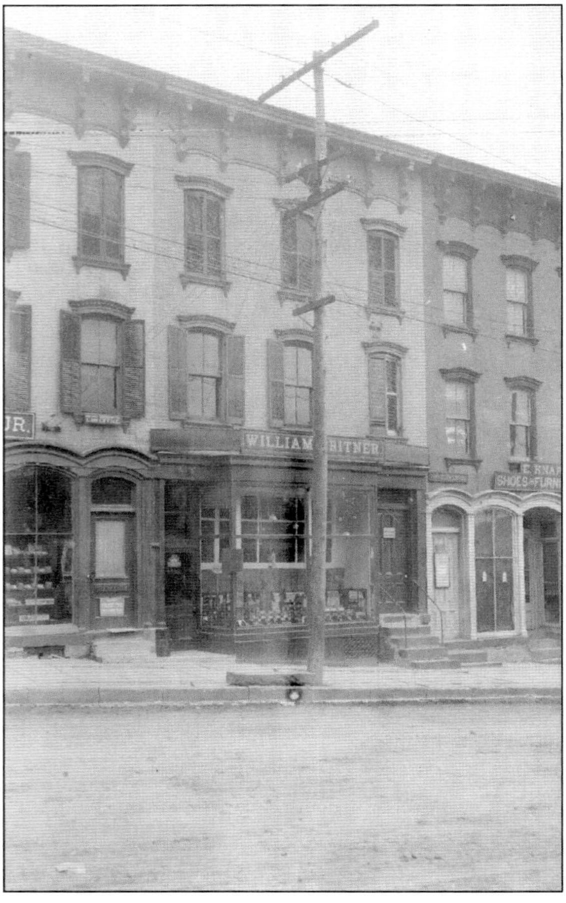

South Side of East Main Street, c. 1906. For most of the 19th century, the north side of East Main Street was an empty wood lot. Most of the industry in the village was centered around Mill and Market Streets. In the early 1870s, William Britner constructed the Britner Block, consisting of three identical three-story brick buildings with stores on the first floor and apartments above. William Britner ran a successful shoe store in the center building with a cigar store to the left and Knapps Furniture Store to the right. (Courtesy of the Wappingers Historical Society.)

Hunt Hardware Store, c. 1920. The corner store on East Main and Mill Street was Hunt's Tire and Supply Shop. This early store, operated by A. Seaman Hunt, sold automobile and bicycle parts alongside tools and fishing supplies. The basement store was operated by a Mr. Schaffer, who ran a popular butcher shop in his grocery store. In the early 1930s, a fire destroyed the old wooden structure, fueled by the oil soaked floors of Hunts Auto Supply store upstairs. (Courtesy of the Wappingers Historical Society.)

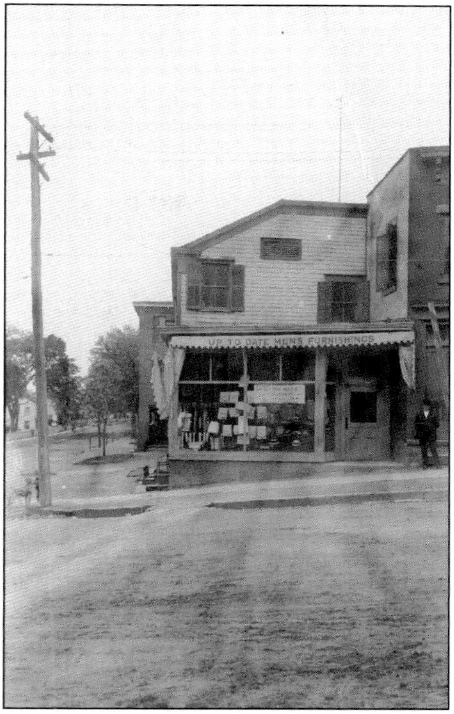

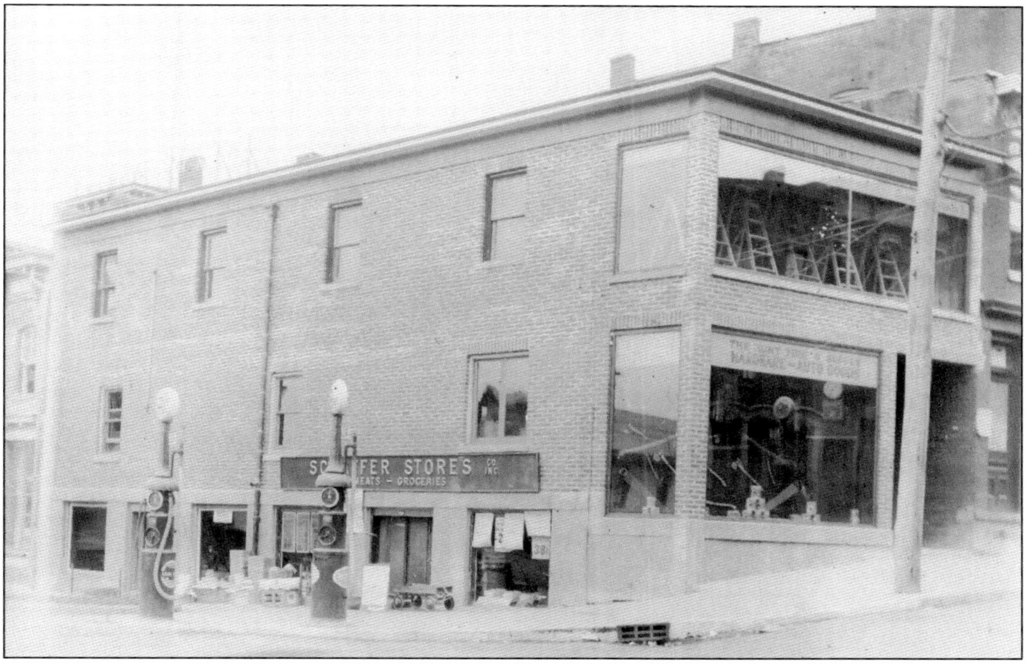

Hunt's Hardware Store, c. 1935. Soon after the fire, a new two-story brick building was constructed in its place. Hunt's Hardware still occupied the East Main Street storefront now expanding to the second floor. The Schaffer Grocery on Mill Street was also modernized with large windows and a second entrance. The corner grocery was a popular stopping point for factory workers going to work next door at the Sweet Orr factory. (Courtesy of the Wappingers Historical Society.)

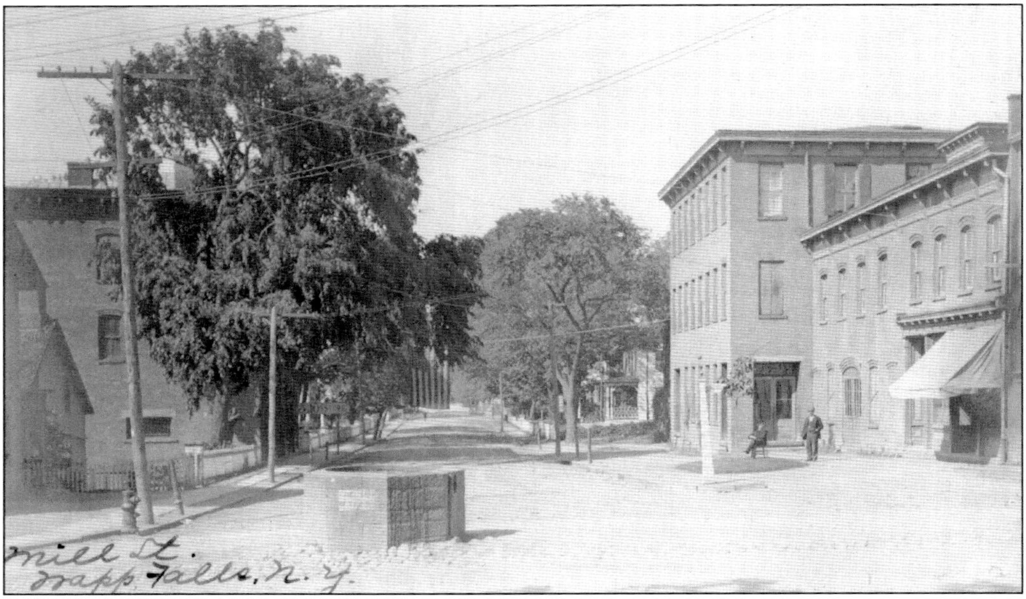

Mill Street Looking North, c. 1905. Running north towards Wappingers Lakes, Mill Street is one of the oldest streets in the village. To the right is the Sweet Orr factory building that burned in the early 1980s. The houses that line the street towards the lake were constructed by the Clintondale and Franklindale Mills for their workers and are some of the oldest homes in the village.

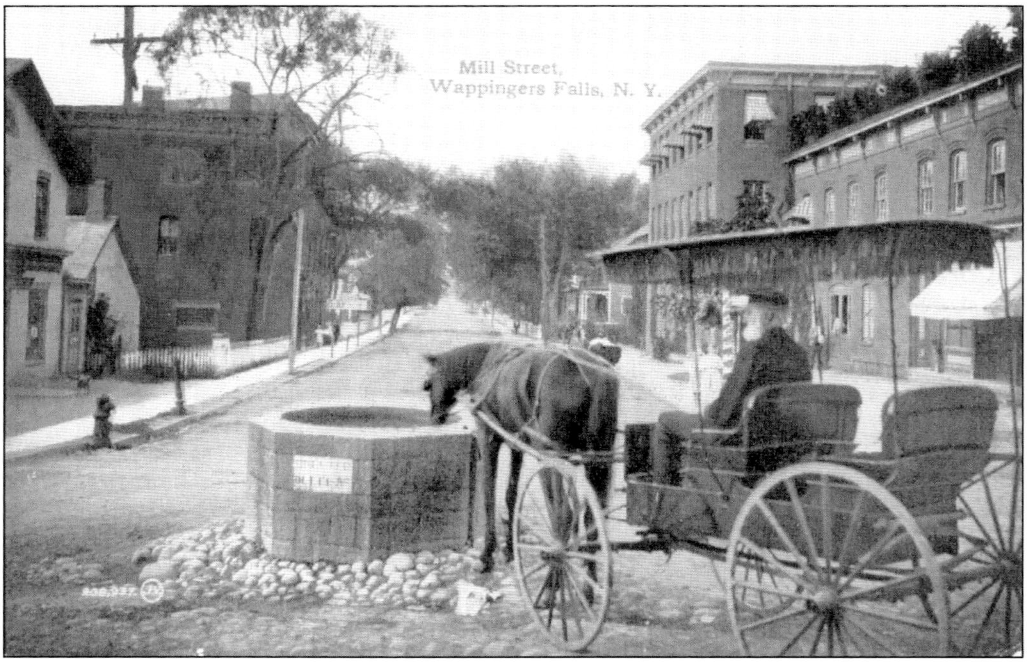

Mill Street Fountain, c. 1910. Albany Post Road was a direct route on the east side of the Hudson River that connected New York City to Albany. As the road entered the village, it was named South Avenue until it ended and was changed to East and West Main Street. This old postcard shows a weary horse and traveler stopping at a water fountain as they pass through the village.

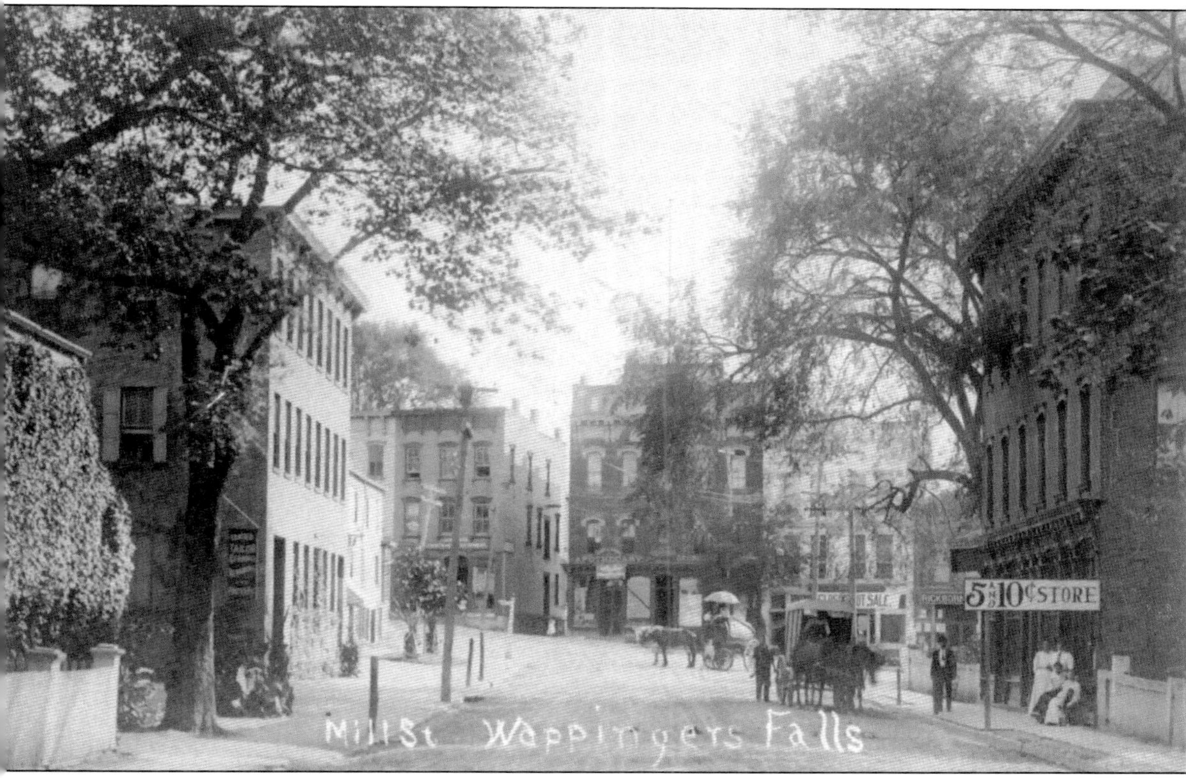

Mill Street Looking South, c. 1910. An early-morning scene shows delivery wagons bringing goods to the stores along East Main and Mill Streets. The large three-story brick building on the right was constructed by the Garner Print Works and housed the Wappingers Bank for many years. The building in the center of the photograph at 106 Main Street was the village pharmacy owned by C.R. Andrews. (Courtesy of the Wappingers Historical Society.)

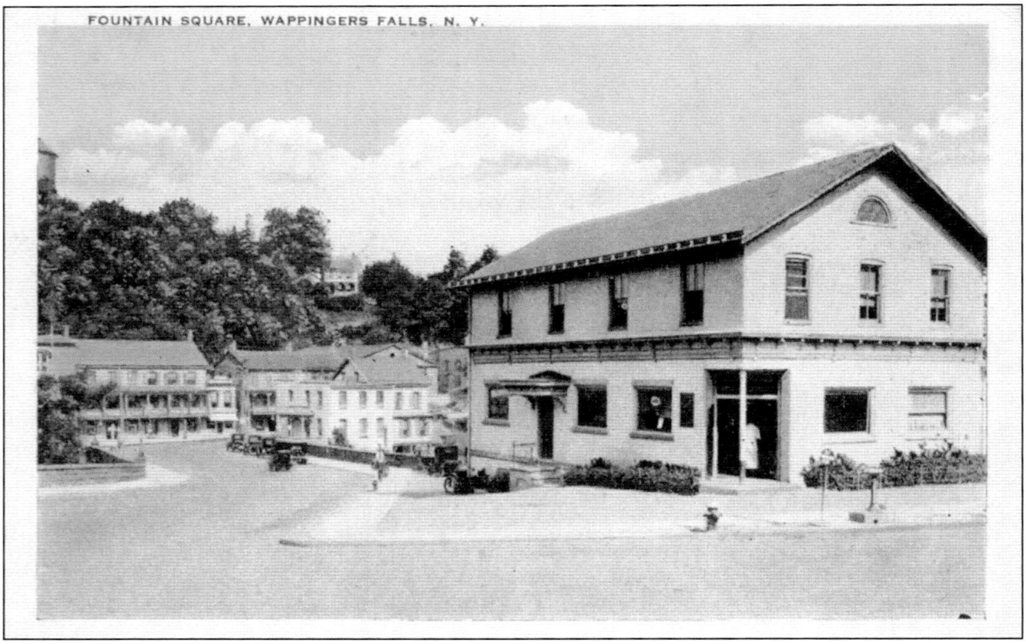

MANNING BUILDING, C. 1915. One of the earliest structures in the village, the Manning Building, at the corner of Mill and East Main Streets, was constructed in the 1850s. First operated as a general store, the building also housed the village's post office for many years. In 1915, the building housed the National Bank of Wappingers Falls on the first floor, the Baum Tavern in the basement, and the Fourth Ward Social Club on the top floor.

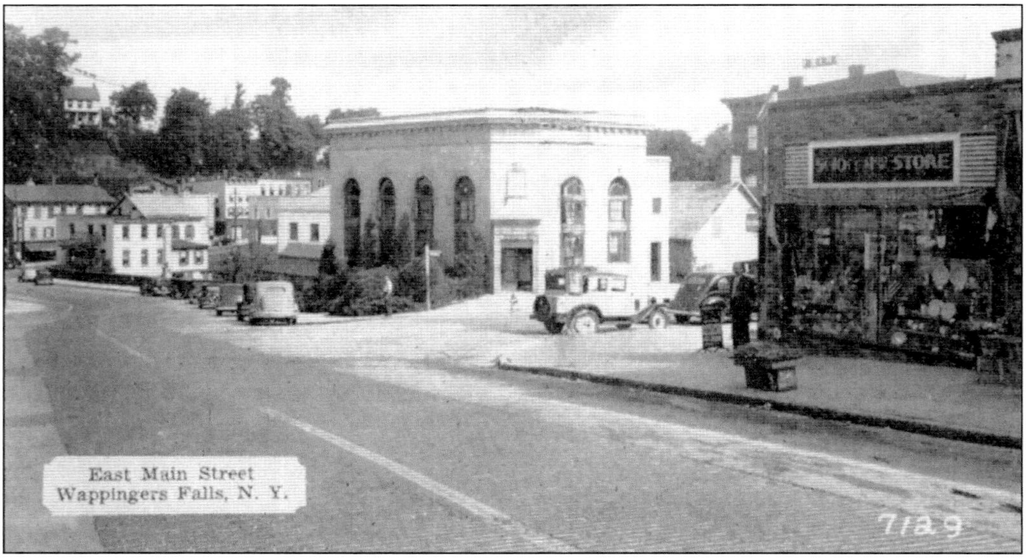

WAPPINGERS SAVINGS BANK, C. 1930. In 1928, the exterior of the Manning Building was renovated with a modern Art Deco design and was renamed the Marine Midland National Bank. The peaked roof was removed; the brick facade was covered with permastone masonry blocks, and new two-story windows were installed to allow more light to enter the bank. The change was seen as a great improvement for the center of the village. In 1916, Albany Post Road was paved through town as shown here, although many of the small side streets remained dirt streets well into the 1940s.

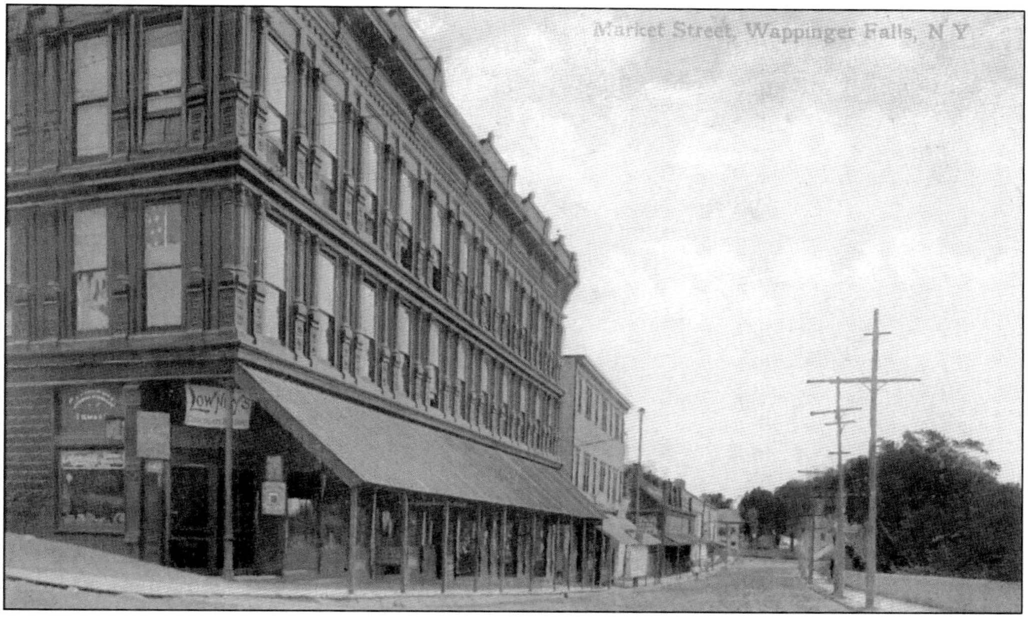

MARKET STREET FROM EAST MAIN, C. 1910. At this intersection during the 1740s, Nicholas Brewer constructed his home and a store. After the original Brewer Buildings burned in an 1892 fire, the three-story Smith Building was erected. The first floor contained the Smith Brothers Bakery and Store, Stripples Meat Market, and Knapps Furniture Store. The upper floors housed apartments that had some of the best views of the Wappingers Falls below.

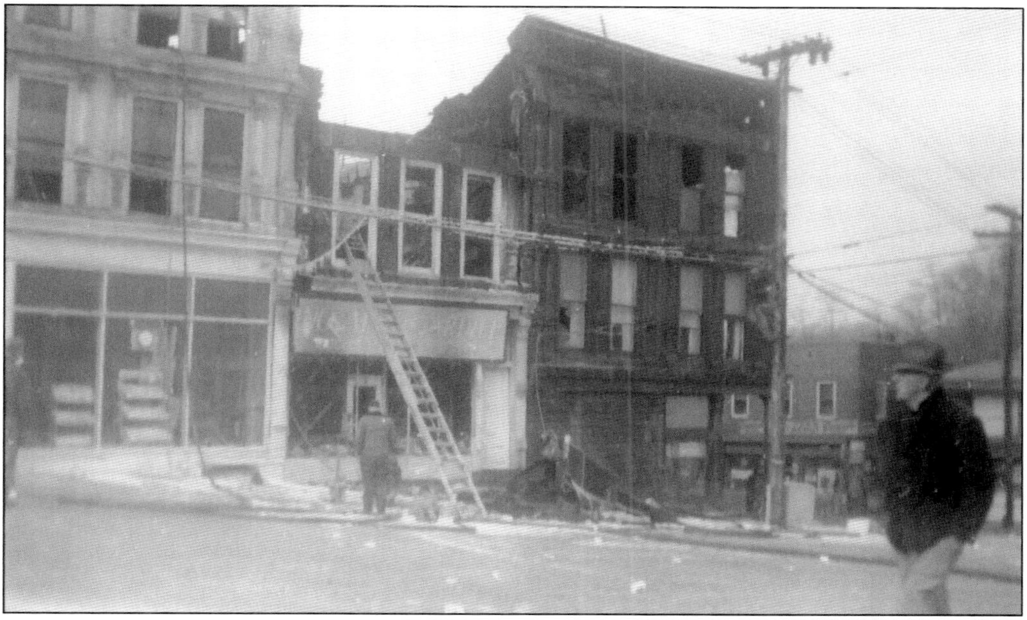

SMITH BUILDING FIRE, 1959. During the early hours of February 16, 1959, a fire broke out on the upper floors of the Smith Building. As the flames spread throughout the building, the intense heat began to melt the ornamental metal exterior. After the fire consumed the Tardiff's Jewelry Store next door, the fire was finally brought under control. Even though the buildings were destroyed, the hard work of the local fire companies ensured the rest of the village would be spared a similar fate. (Courtesy of the Wappingers Historical Society.)

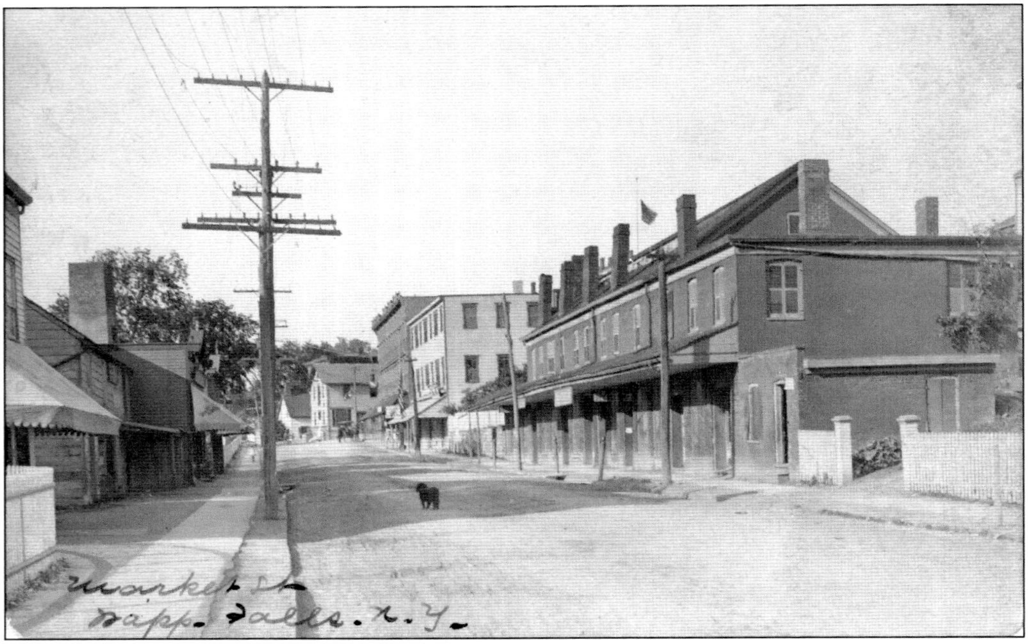

Market Street Looking North, c. 1905. Many of the residents of the village lived in factory-owned apartments. The small shacks on the left were constructed by the Franklindale Mill and housed a few of their workshops. Across the street, Garner Print Works erected the long wood frame building to house up to 12 families. Although rent was inexpensive, the apartments did not include running water or bathroom facilities. (Courtesy of the Wappingers Historical Society.)

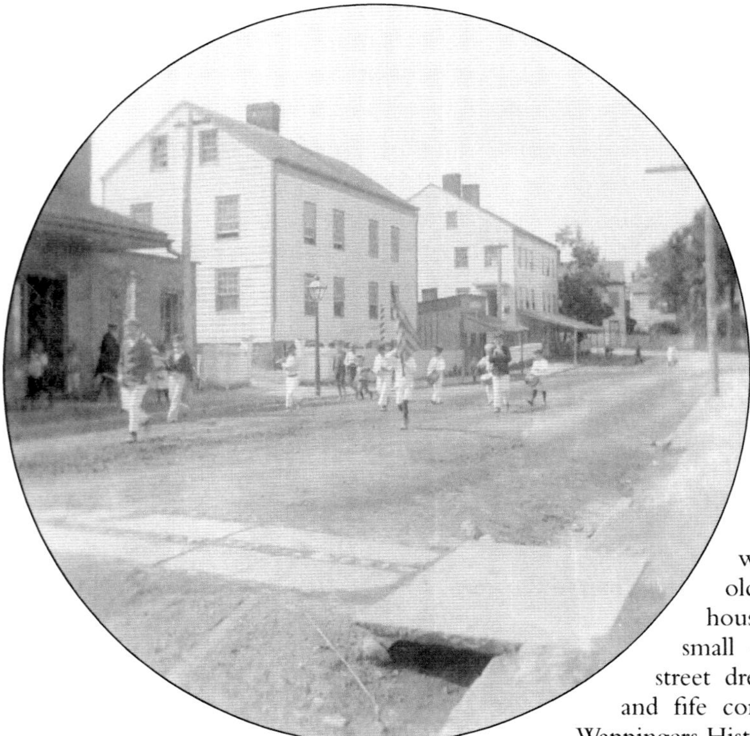

Market Street Looking South, c. 1900. The southern end of Market Street was lined by some of the old Franklindale apartment houses. Seen here, a group of small children walk down the street dressed as a colonial drum and fife company. (Courtesy of the Wappingers Historical Society.)

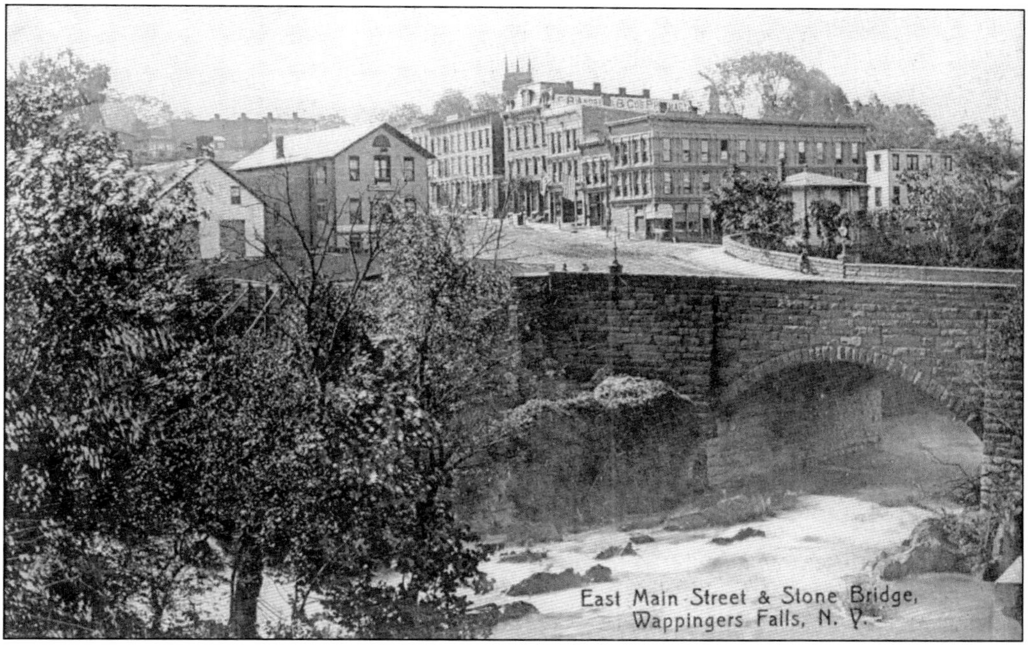

East Main Street and Stone Bridge, 1907. This old postcard shows East Main Street during a quiet afternoon. Taken from West Main Street, the view shows the business center of the village and the stone bridge across the Wappingers Creek. The village boom years, when both Sweet Orr and the Garner Print Works were at their height, occurred around this time in the early 1900s.

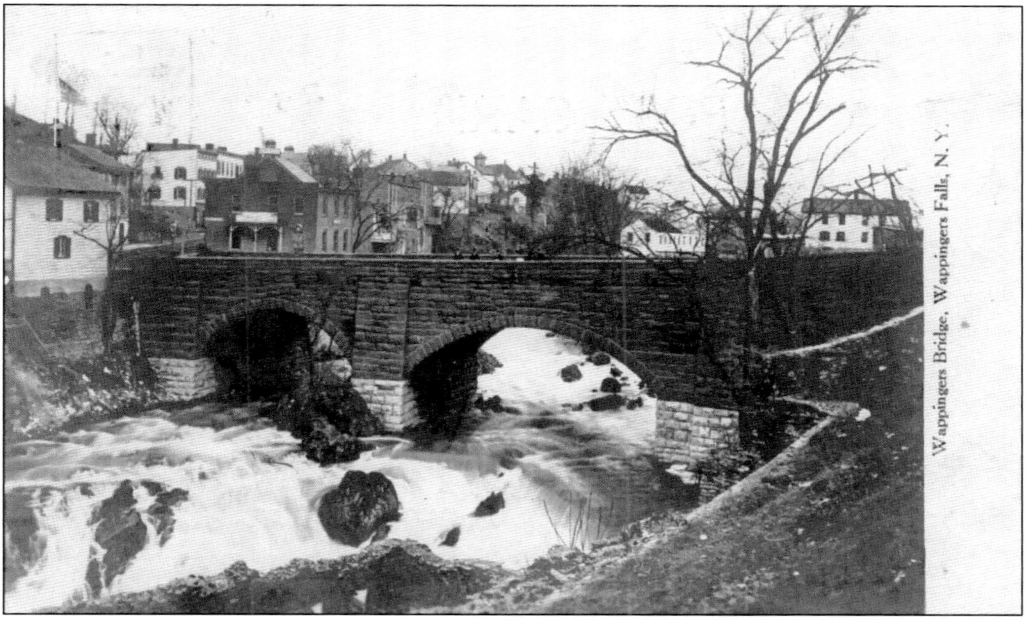

Stone Bridge over Wappingers Creek, 1906. Constructed of gray stone in 1852, the new stone bridge replaced a wooden covered bridge that was washed away the year before during a spring flood. The bridge was later ornamented with gas lanterns and widened in 1884. This dramatic view taken from the ruins of the Franklindale Mill shows the bridge before the steel pipe was constructed through it by the Dutchess Bleachery.

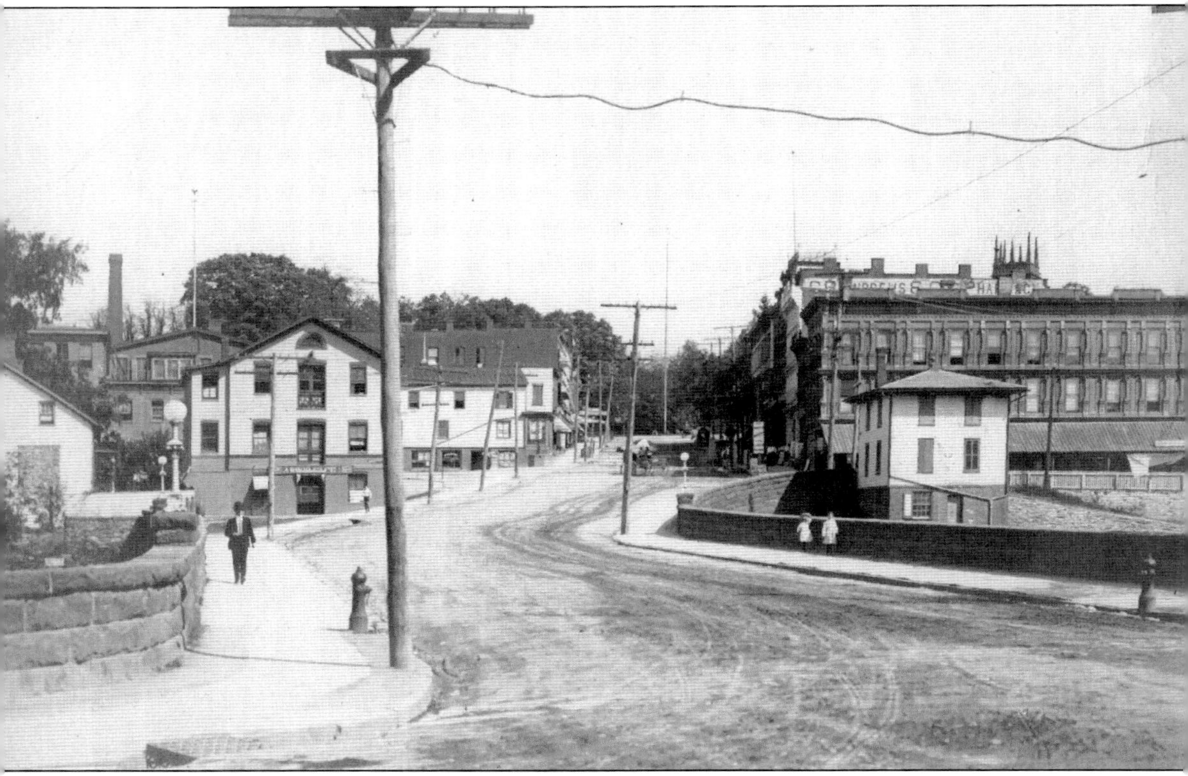

LOOKING EAST ACROSS STONE BRIDGE, C. 1910. Connecting the two halves of the village, the stone bridge was a vital link. The small white building on the right was the old Franklindale Factory office that survived the 1885 fire. During the 1890s, the building was used as a rental office for the many factory houses owned by the Garner Print Works and later by the Wappingers Police Department. (Courtesy of the Wappingers Historical Society.)

Eight

Wappingers Falls
West Main Street and Channingville

Only a few buildings stood on the west side of the creek during much of the 1800s. In 1844, John Givens constructed a few small buildings along the creek, naming the area Ednamville. As homes and businesses continued north along West Main Street, the area was called Channingville. Technically in the town of Poughkeepsie, the communities were incorporated into the village of Wappingers Falls in 1871.

Businesses and factories lined the west side of the creek around the old stone bridge. As one moved uphill, West Main Street became residential with many of the village's Irish immigrants settling along the side streets. At the center of community life was St. Mary's Church, which stood near the edge of the village. Farther west along Sheafe Road, wealthy village residents and prominent families in New York City constructed large mansions that overlooked the Hudson River. By the 1930s, many of these houses were abandoned and were either burned or were torn down.

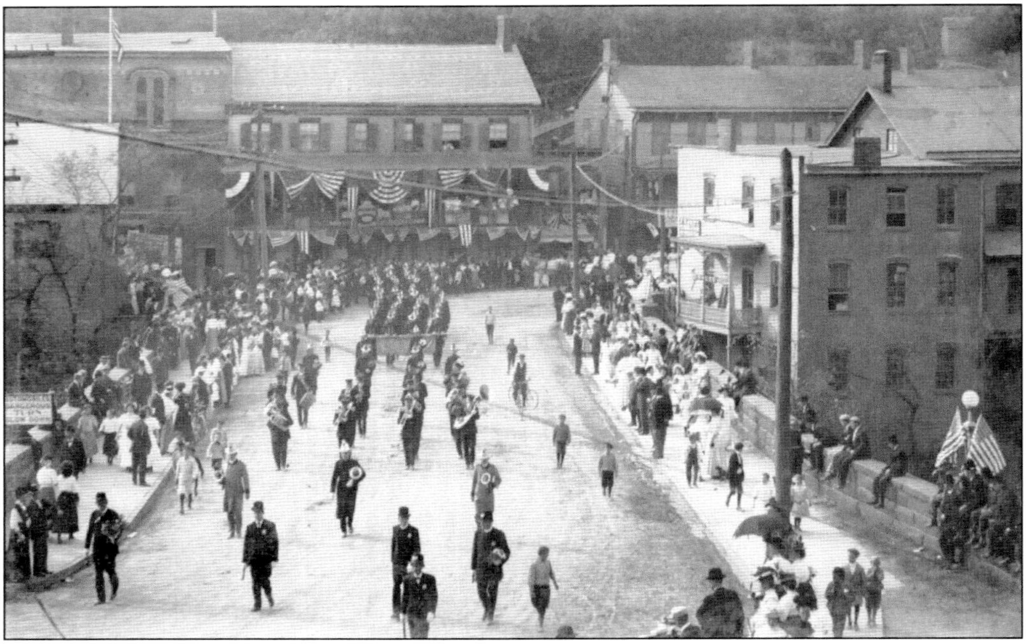

WEST MAIN STREET FROM BRIDGE, 1910. Shown here is a jubilant view of West Main Street at the end of the 1910 Firemen's Parade. The building in the center of the photograph is the old Farmers and Mechanics Hotel, later known as the Ryan Hotel. The building to the left of the hotel was known as the Eagen Building. The first floor contained Van Anden Flour Feed and Hay Company while the Eagen Overall Factory occupied the upper floors.

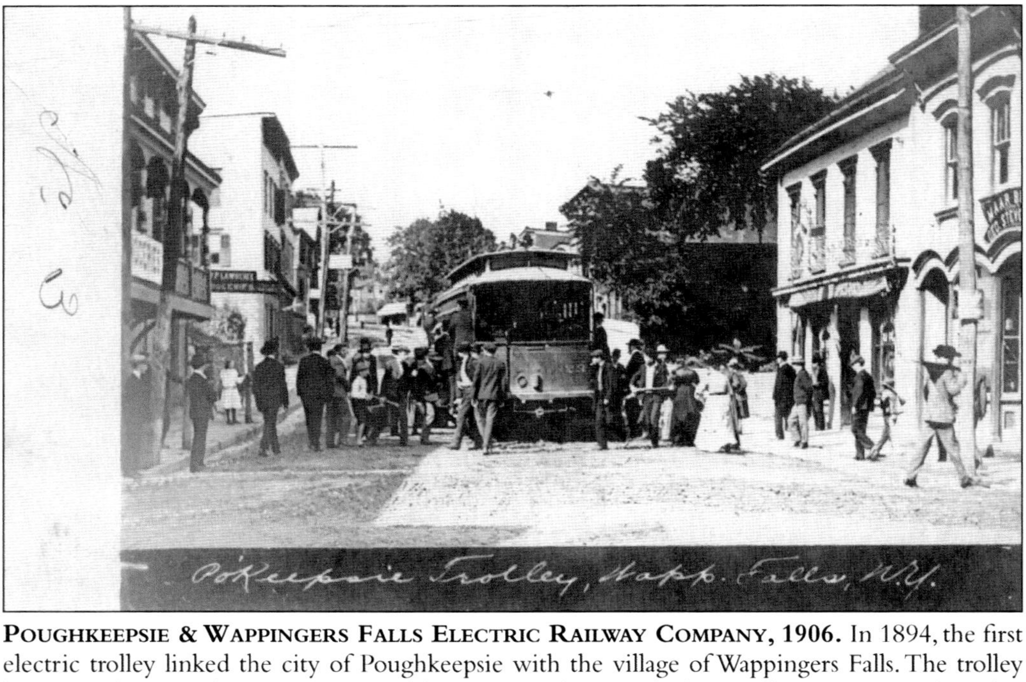

POUGHKEEPSIE & WAPPINGERS FALLS ELECTRIC RAILWAY COMPANY, 1906. In 1894, the first electric trolley linked the city of Poughkeepsie with the village of Wappingers Falls. The trolley line started on Market Street in Poughkeepsie, traveling south down Albany Post Road until it reached its terminus here on West Main Street next to the stone bridge. Shown in this photograph, a group of local residents wait to board a late afternoon trolley back to Poughkeepsie.

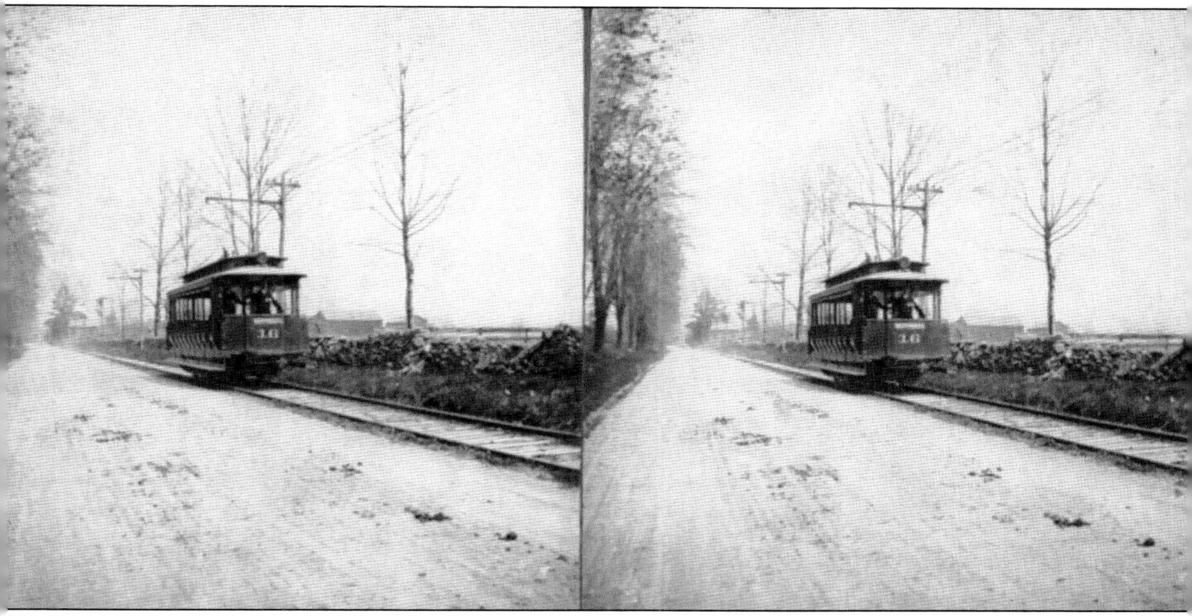

ALBANY POST ROAD NORTH, C. 1895. By 1928, the automobile had already replaced the need for the trolley line. Facing the dropping number of riders and the rising expense to maintain the trolley cars and track, the company sold its right-of-way on Albany Post Road. A bus soon replaced the old trolley route, and the tracks were paved over when Albany Post Road, now Route 9, was widened.

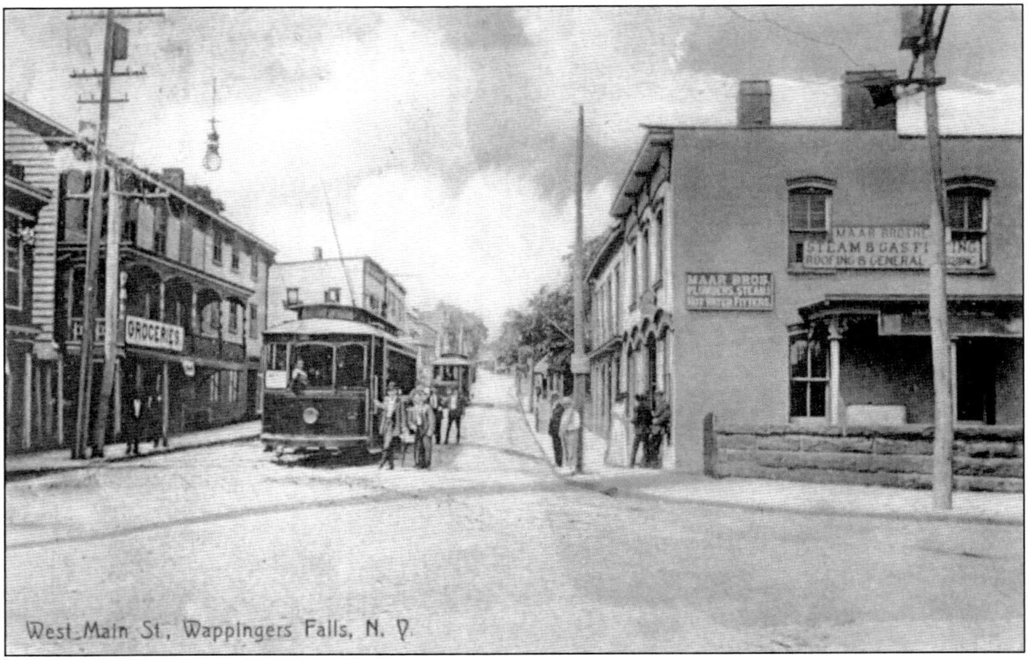

WEST MAIN STREET, 1911. To the right of the trolley stop was the Maar Brothers Plumbing and Heating Store. In 1871, the top floor housed the fledgling Sweet Orr & Company before they moved to a larger building on Mill Street. The buildings across the street were both grocery and dry goods stores established for the growing population of garment workers employed just down the hill.

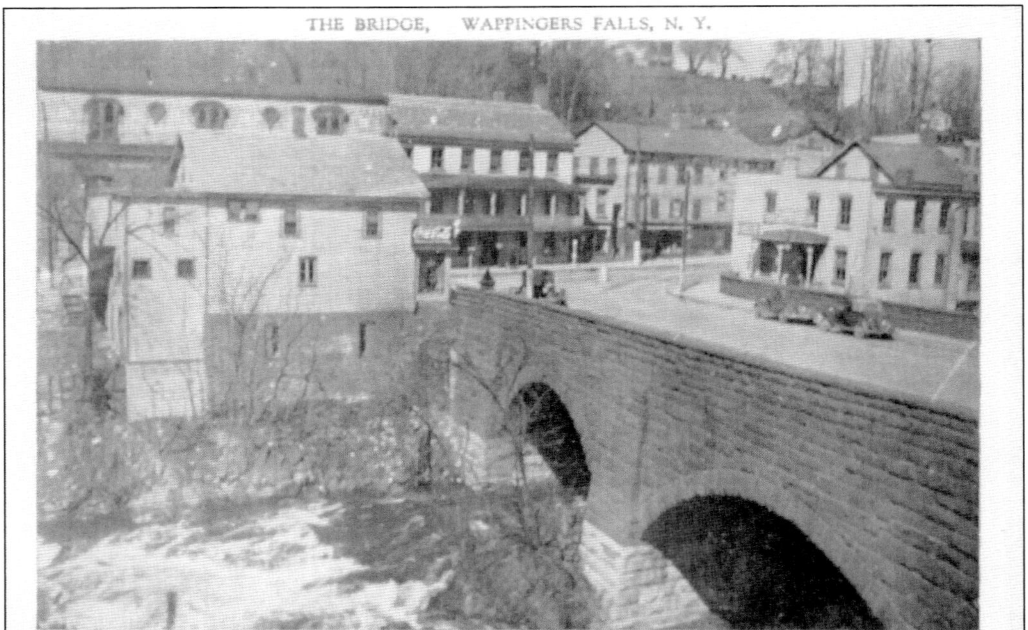

WEST MAIN STREET, C. 1920. This old postcard shows a broad view of the intersection of West Main Street and the stone bridge. To the left is the Roy Drug Store built in 1824; the building's foundation had to be lifted three times over the decades to meet the road next to the bridge.

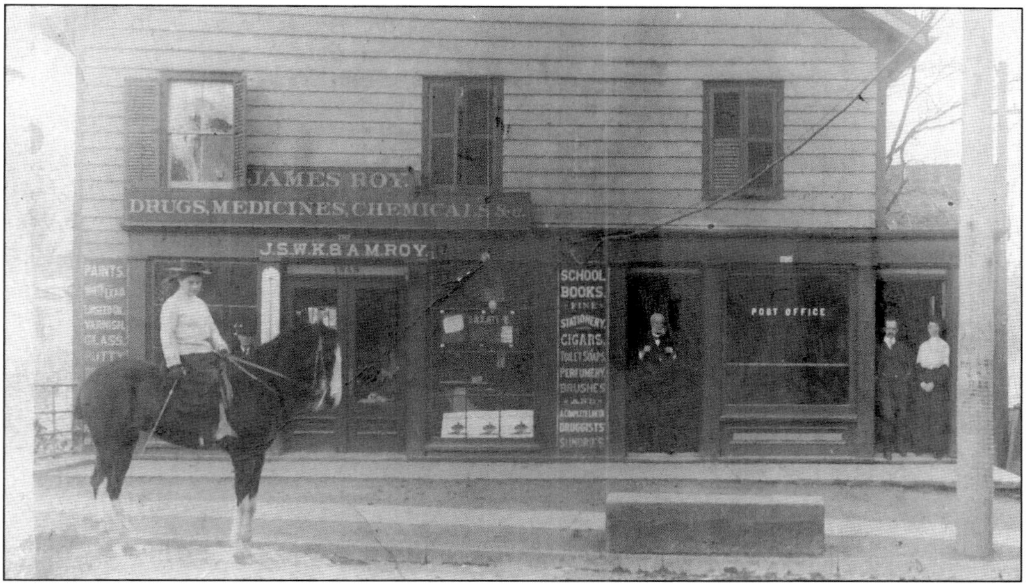

James Roy Drug Store, 1907. The two-story wood frame building on the southwest corner of the stone bridge was constructed in 1824. The first floor had two storefronts. On the left was the Roy Drug Store, which sold everything from paints, wine, cigars, school books, and groceries. From 1900 to 1910, as shown here, the Wappingers Post Office occupied the storefront on the right. A few years after this photograph was taken, the first gas pumps in the village were installed in front of the store. (Courtesy of the Wappingers Historical Society.)

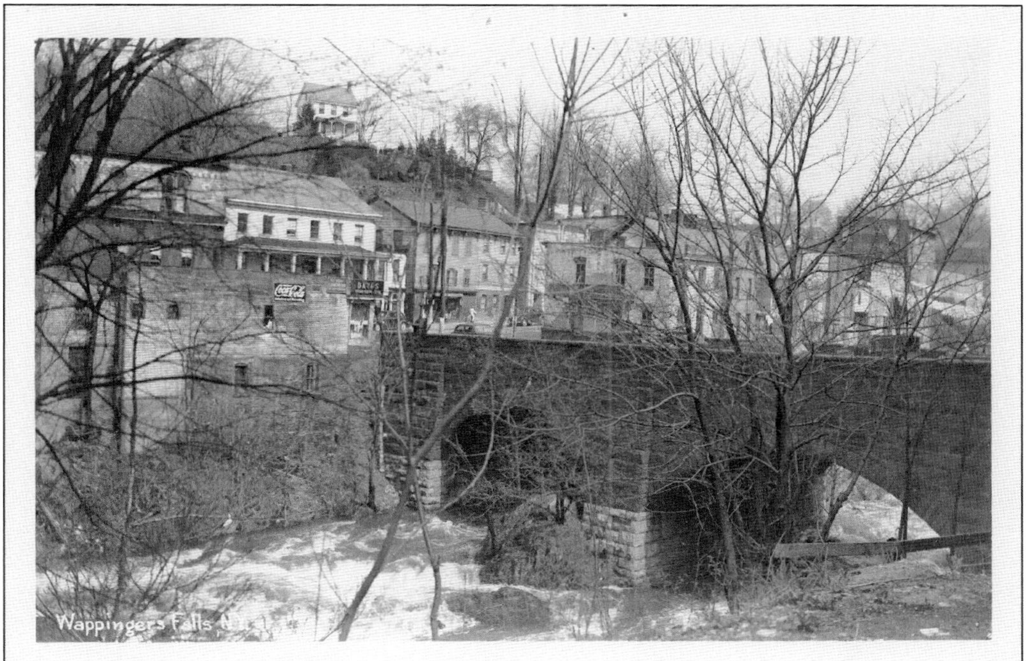

View from Market Street, c. 1925. By the time this photograph was taken, the Roy Drug Store had burned. Situated on the far left, a small fire spread throughout the building, leveling the structure. Today, a new one-story building has taken its place, constructed on the same foundation as the original store. (Courtesy of the Wappinger Historical Society.)

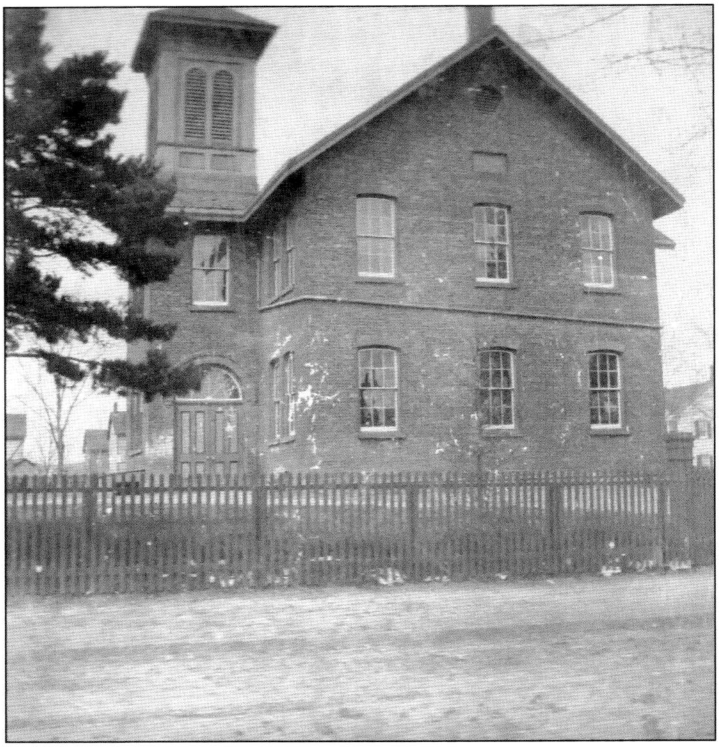

WAPPINGERS SCHOOL DISTRICT NO. 1, 1890. Every morning, a loud bell could be heard coming from this impressive building, calling the neighborhood children to class. Constructed in 1866, the Channingville School was one of the largest in the county. Sitting on the corner of School Street and Roy Avenue, it was constructed in the same style as its counterpart across the creek.

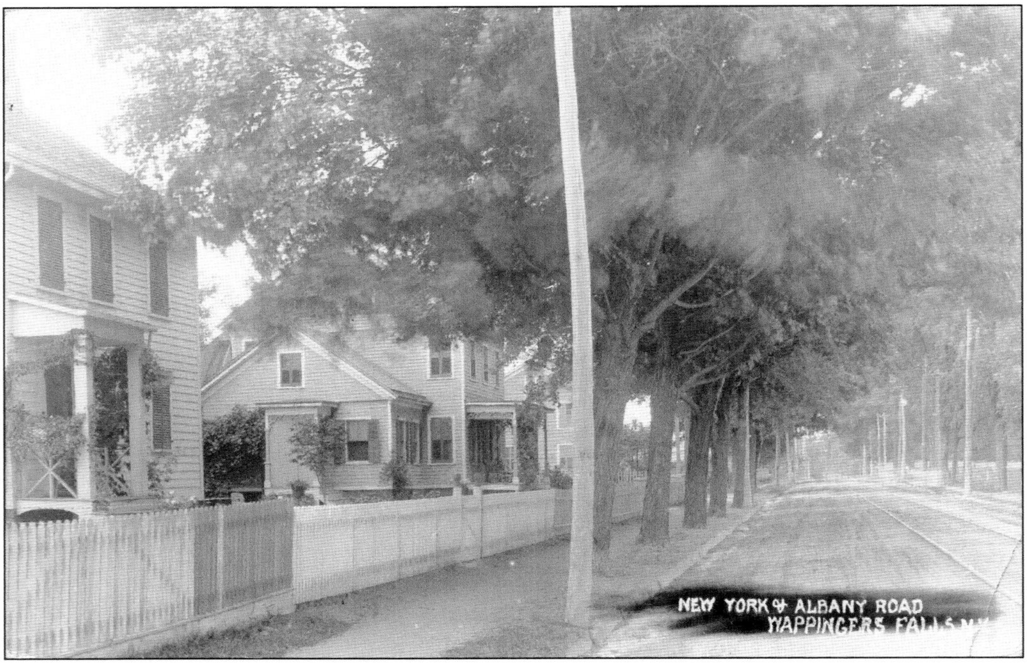

NEW YORK & ALBANY POST ROAD, 1910. Today called West Main Street, the upper part of the road grew rapidly after being incorporated into the village of Wappingers Falls. West Street, Clinton Street, North Street, and Cross Street, later named Delavergne Avenue, were all developed for the growing number of predominantly Irish factory workers from the Franklindale Mill and the Dutchess Bleachery.

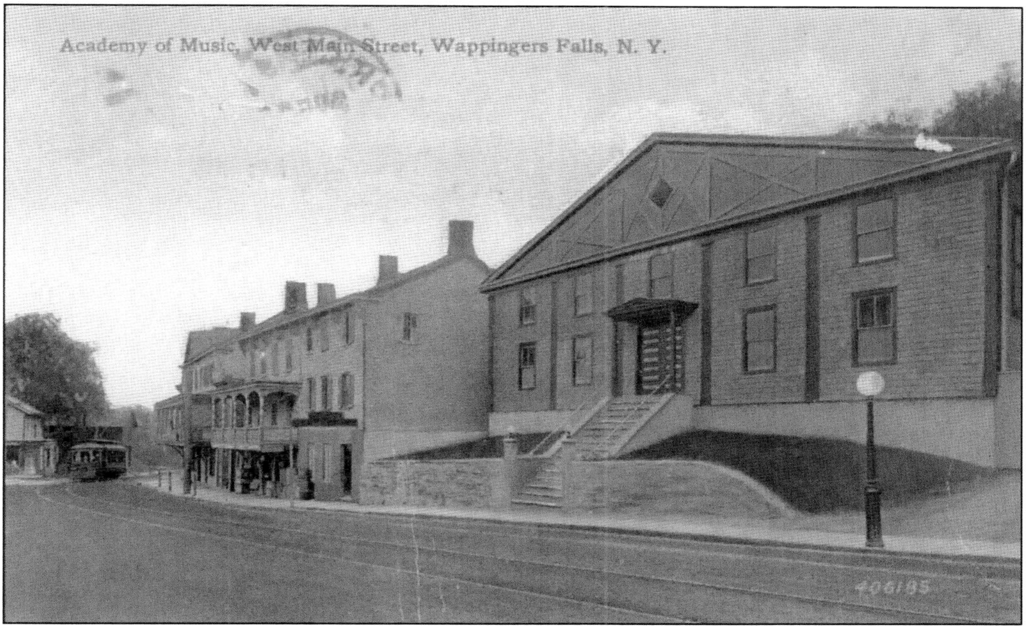

ACADEMY OF MUSIC, 1915. Constructed in 1913 by the O'Rourke family, the building was primarily used as a dance hall and basketball court. In the late 1920s, the academy was converted into a movie theatre that was run by Philip Eisenberg. After a 1930 fire, the front steps were removed and a brick facade was added. (Courtesy of the Wappingers Historical Society.)

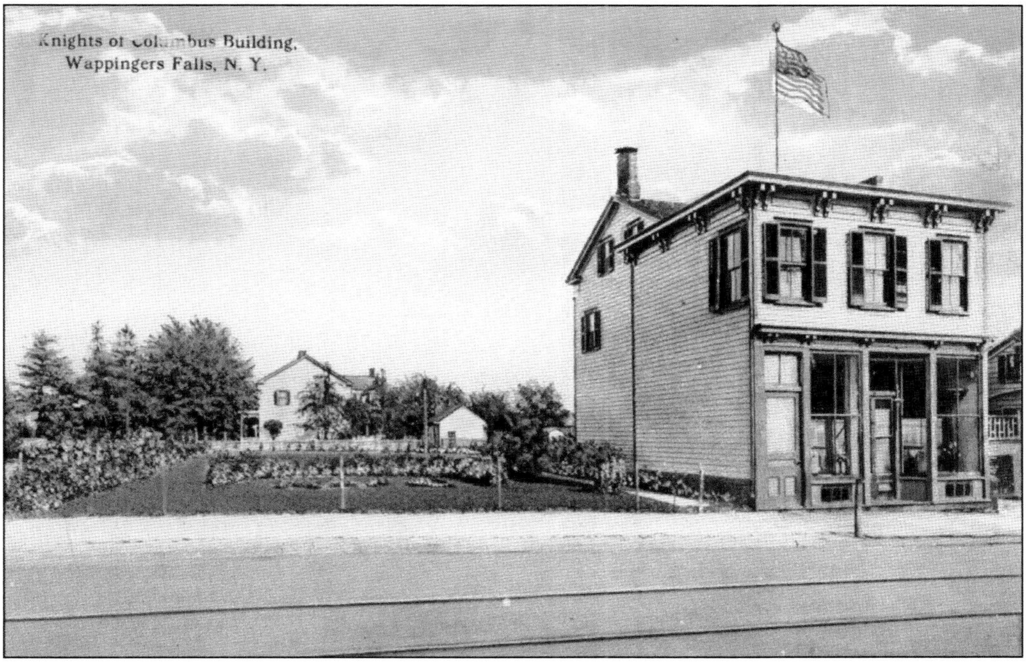

KNIGHTS OF COLUMBUS BUILDING, 1912. In 1912, several prominent citizens organized a Knights of Columbus Lodge for the village. For many years, the society held their meetings in this small building near the corner of West Main and School Streets. The lodge headquarters were upstairs while an open recreation space was on the first floor. The club used this building until the 1960s, when it moved to the old Central Hudson Building on East Main near the stone bridge.

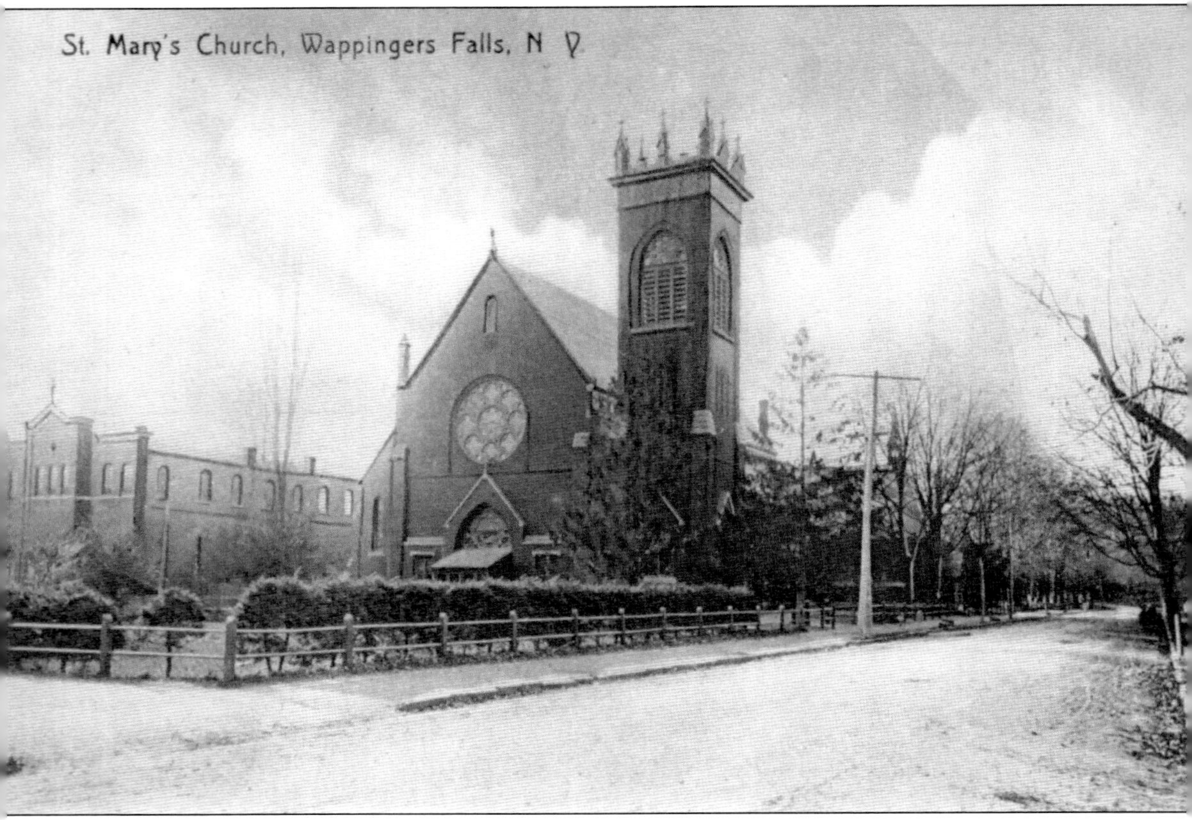

ST. MARY'S CATHOLIC CHURCH, C. 1908. Founded in 1850, the current large brick church was constructed in 1877. The only church on the west side of the creek, St. Mary's was constructed for the predominately Irish Catholic residents that lived along the side streets on West Main Street. In 1894, the church's steeple was struck by lightning, causing a small fire that destroyed the upper portion of the tower. When the spire was reconstructed, the church added a masonry crown and a new set of bells to call parishioners to service. Today, the building remains the village's largest church with a capacity of over 1,000 people. A school was constructed next door in 1956.

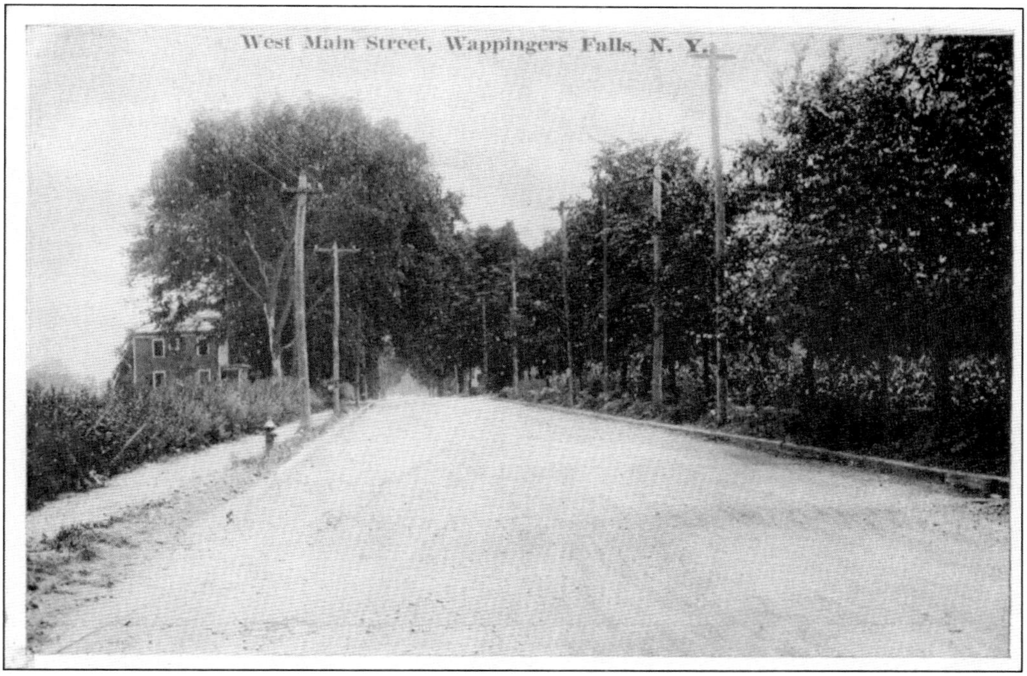

WEST MAIN STREET NORTH, C. 1895. As one continued north, West Main Street became a rural country road. Connecting to the old Kings Highway, present-day Route 9, West Main Street winded its way north towards Poughkeepsie. Much of the land along the route was surrounded by corn and wheat fields, a common sight for the predominantly agricultural towns. (Courtesy of the Wappingers Historical Society.)

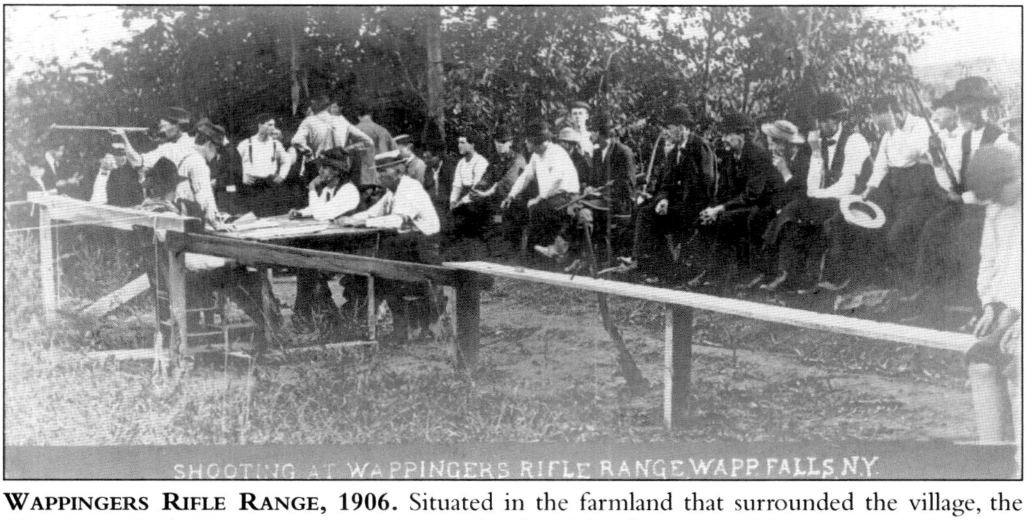

WAPPINGERS RIFLE RANGE, 1906. Situated in the farmland that surrounded the village, the Wappingers Rifle Range was a popular weekend activity for many of the community's factory workers. Shown here, a man takes aim at a distant target while a group of seated judges rank his performance.

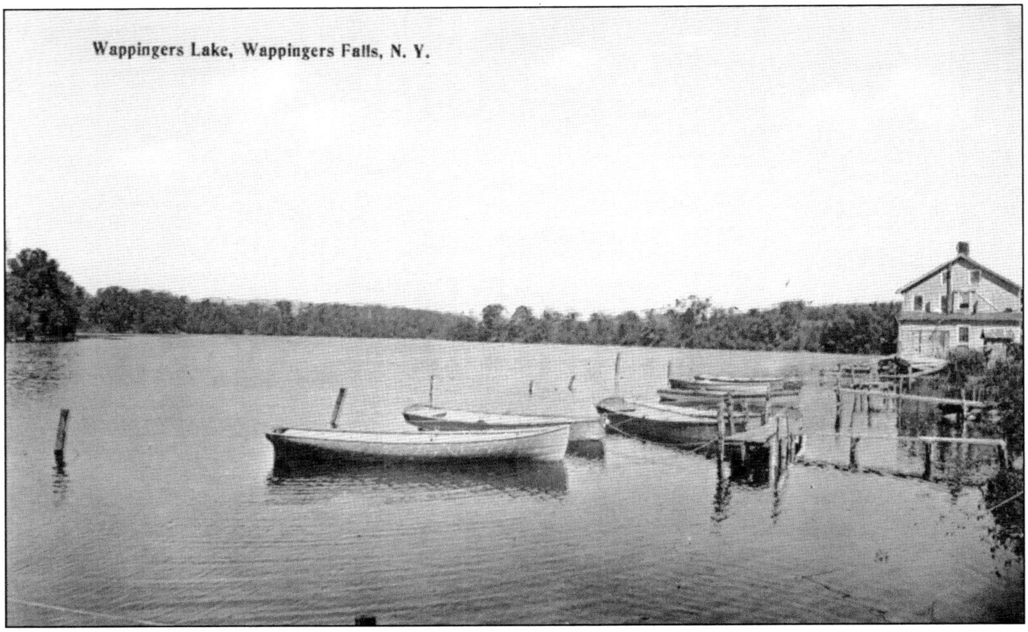

MILL STREET DOCK AT WAPPINGERS LAKE, C. 1918. Although not natural, Wappingers Lake proved crucial to the village's development. Seen here from the Mill Street dock, the lake was created in 1840, when Benjamin Clapp constructed a dam just upstream from the lower falls. The large reservoir was necessary to provide adequate water for the mills downstream during the summer drought.

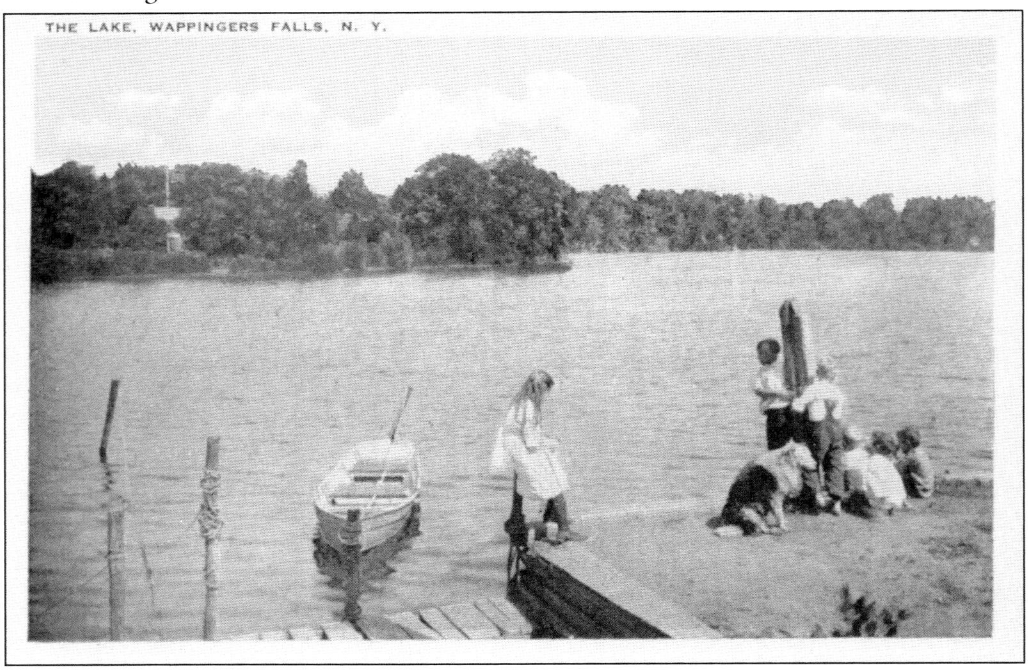

RECREATION ON WAPPINGERS LAKE, C. 1912. The main dock for the village was at the end of Mill Street. Here, rowboats could be rented for fishing or going to the many swimming and diving spots along the shores. It was common for young couples to take a rowboat trip to Lovers Lane, a small path on the north side of the lake where one can find a bit of privacy.

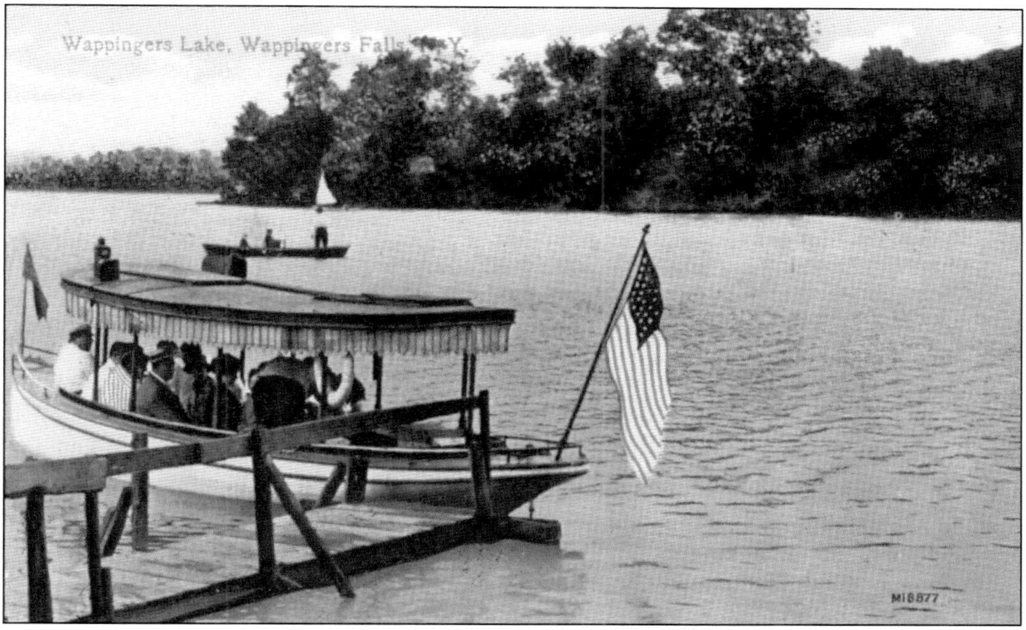

Upper Falls, 1910. In 1908, Albert Brower, the owner of a grocery store on Market Street, operated this small steamboat from the Mill Street dock. Guests would be ferried two miles upstream to the Upper Little Falls Park. There, visitors were able to rent bathhouses for swimming or just relax and eat at the refreshment stands.

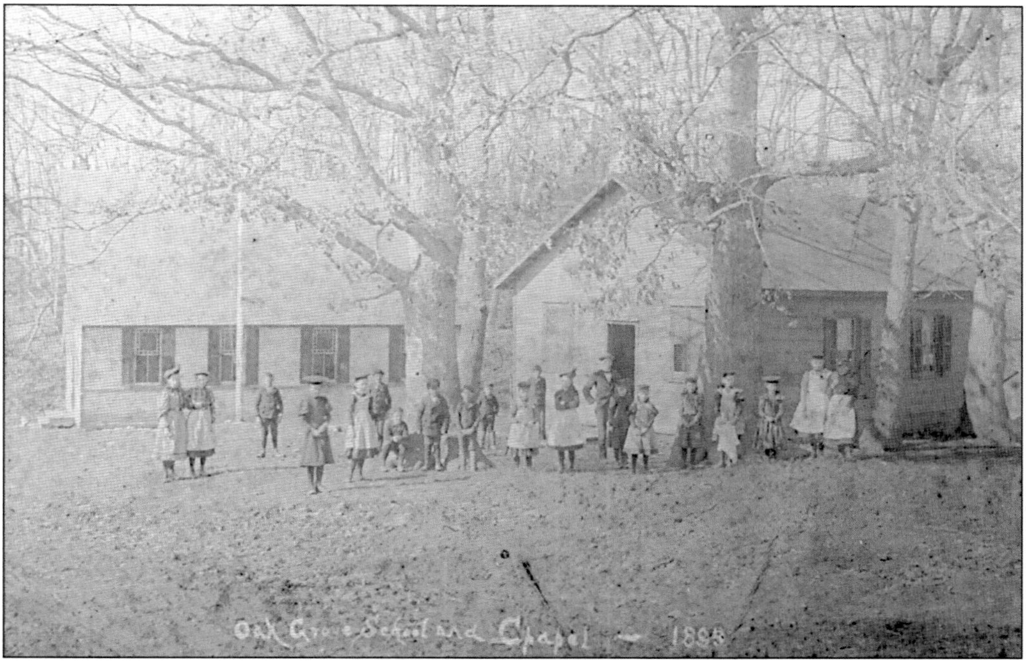

Oak Grove School and Chapel, 1888. Situated on Spring Road near the northern edge of Sheafe Road, Oak Grove was a small farming community of roughly a dozen homes. The schoolhouse functioned as the only school for the village of Wappingers Falls prior to 1830. The more than four mile distance was seen as too much for village resident Benjamin Clapp, who constructed the first school in the village in 1835.

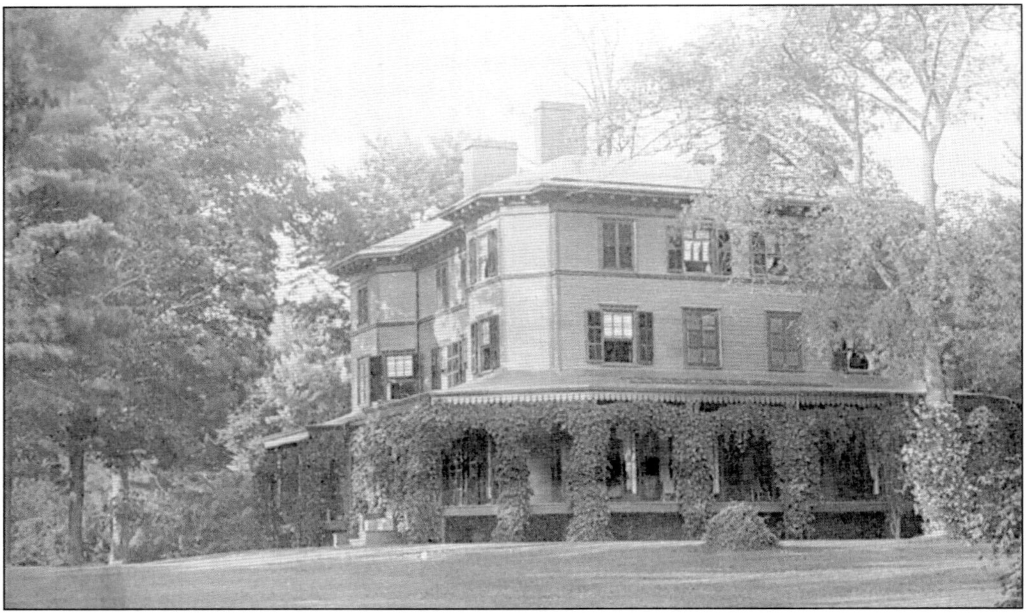

IRVING GRINNELL MANSION, C. 1880. In 1839, Irving Grinnell was born to a wealthy New York City family. His wife, Joanna, was a member of the prominent Howland family who lived in a large mansion just south of Beacon, New York. Grinnell retired early in life and moved to this estate on Sheafe Road in 1864. He was best known as a philanthropist in town, establishing the library in 1888, and donating generously to the Zion Episcopal Church. (Courtesy of the Wappingers Historical Society.)

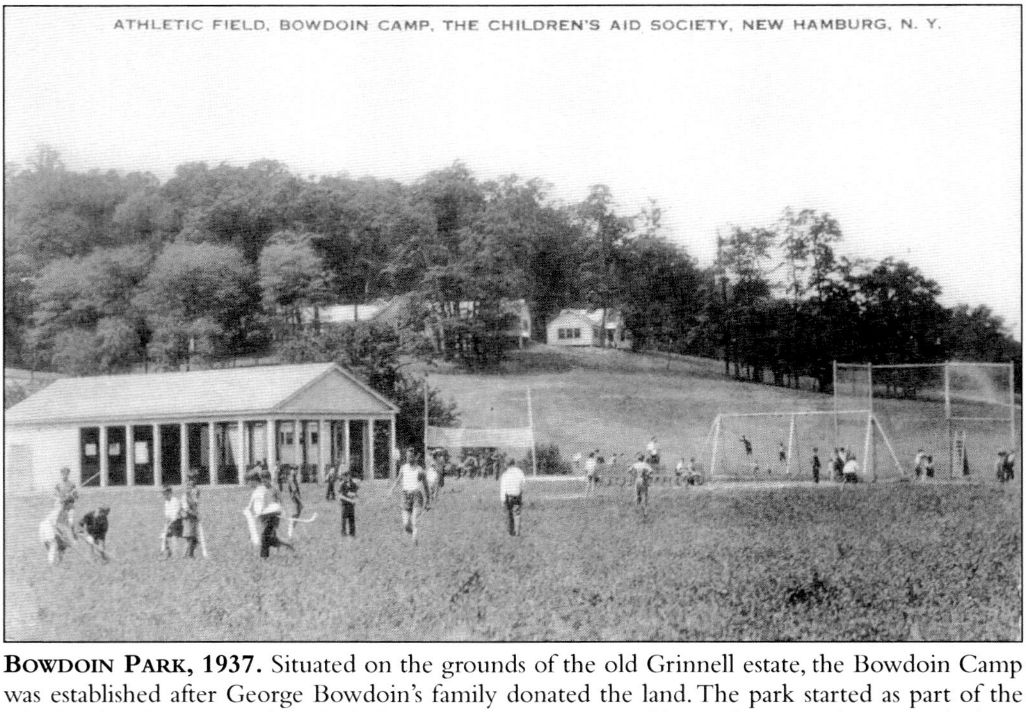

BOWDOIN PARK, 1937. Situated on the grounds of the old Grinnell estate, the Bowdoin Camp was established after George Bowdoin's family donated the land. The park started as part of the Children's Aid Society where kids from New York City would spend two weeks in the fresh air of the Hudson Valley.

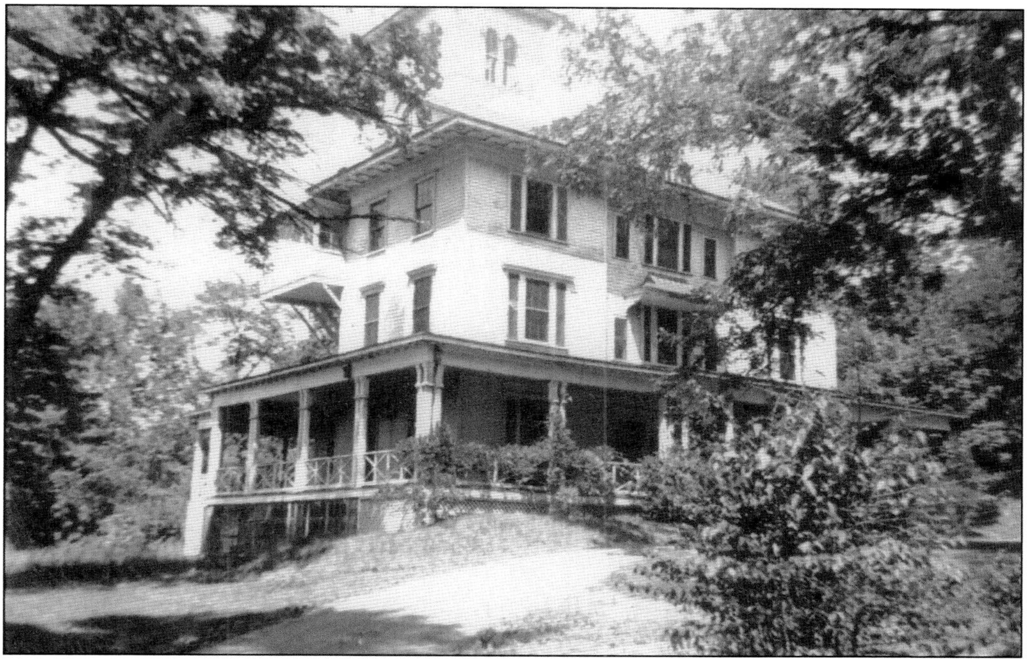

Sheafe Road Mansion, c. 1920. Sheafe Road, which ran north along the Hudson River, had some of the largest homes in the area. This house, once owned by the Banks family, stood near the intersection of DeLavergne Avenue until it burned in the summer of 1937. (Courtesy of the Wappingers Historical Society.)

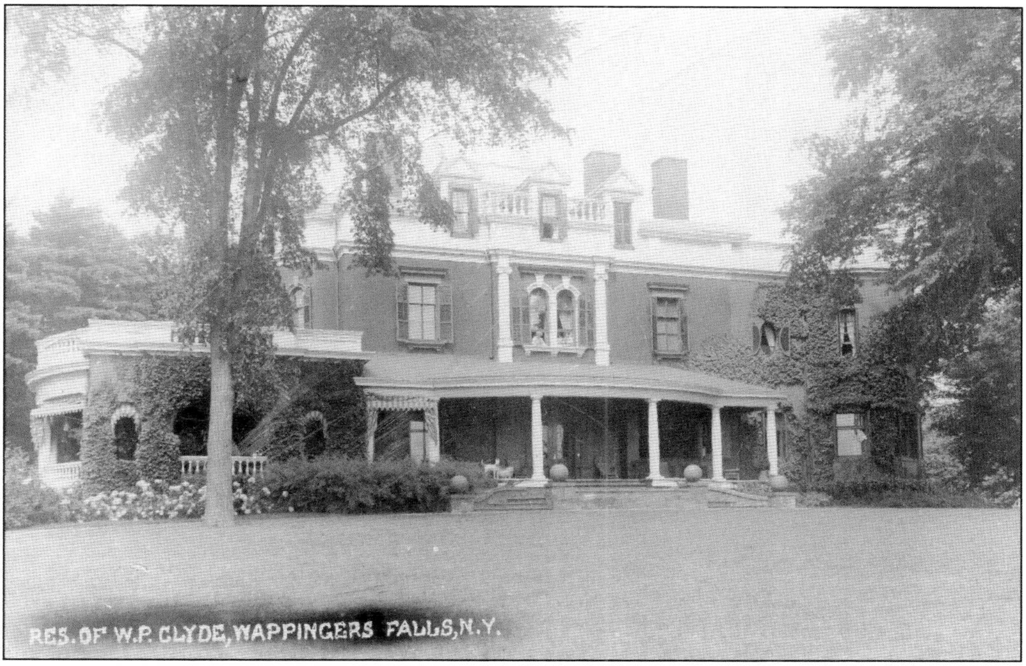

Residence of W.P. Clyde, c. 1910. Sitting on a hill overlooking the Hudson River and the entire village, the home of W.P. Clyde was one of the largest in the area. Purchased by the Catholic Church, the house was removed and replaced with Mount Alvernia Seminary, which still stands today on Delavergne Avenue. (Courtesy of the Wappingers Historical Society.)

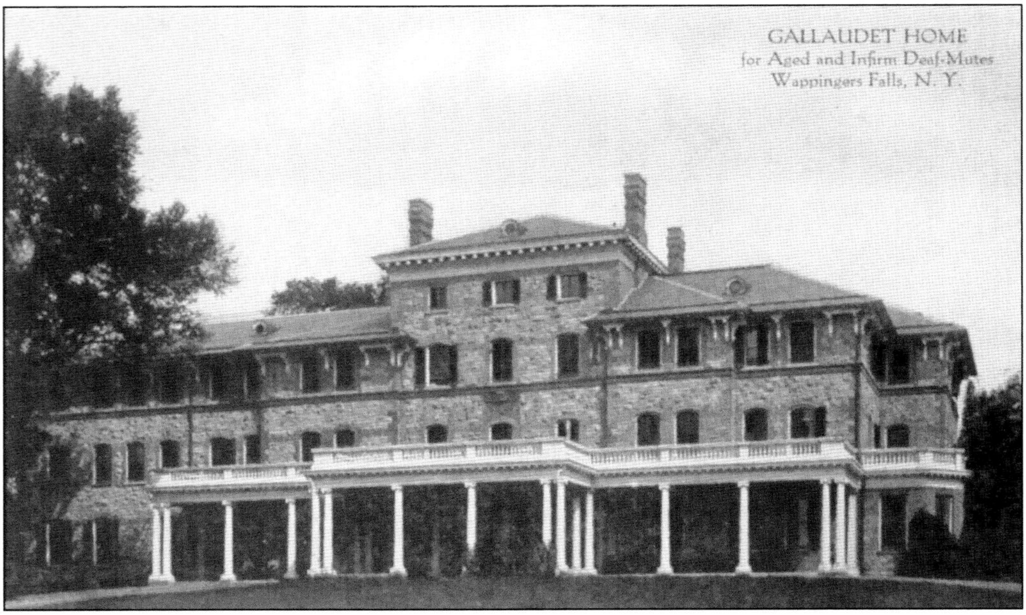

GALLAUDET HOME ON SHEAFE ROAD, 1910. Built in 1903, this large Italianate building was constructed on the ruins of a once ornate mansion that burned a few years before this photograph. Founded by Thomas Gallaudet, the home was established for the education of deaf and mute adults. Thomas's father, Thomas Hopkins Gallaudet, was instrumental in bringing sign language to the United States. The house and the 106-acre estate were sold to the New York Trap Rock Company in 1946. As the large open pit mine expanded, the company tore down the house and mined most of the earth that comprised the vast property.

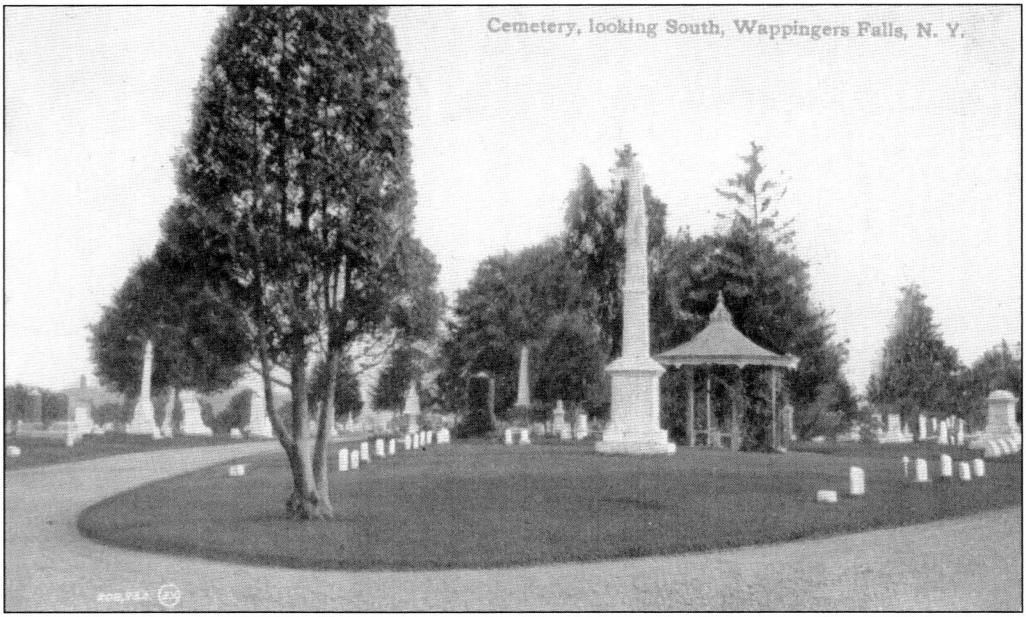

WAPPINGERS RURAL CEMETERY, C. 1910. On September 27, 1849, a large tract of empty land was purchased on the northern edge of West Main Street. Named the Wappingers Rural Cemetery, the grounds extended down to Wappingers Lake with winding gravel paths for families to stroll and visit now passed loved ones.

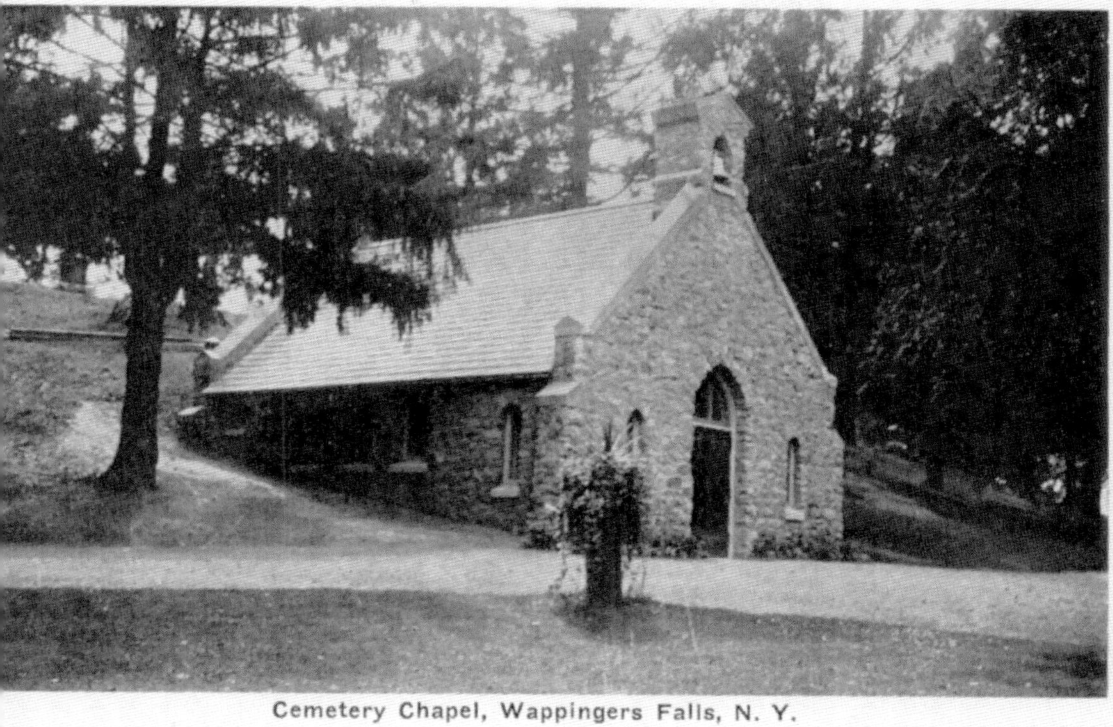

WAPPINGERS RURAL CEMETERY CHAPEL, C. 1930. In 1924, a small chapel was constructed at the entrance of the cemetery under the direction of Lennox Banks. Its main purpose was for those who did not wish to have a funeral at the churches in the village. The more private venue was mostly used for those who lived outside the village. Today, the chapel still stands on West Main Street, now surrounded by towering pine trees. (Courtesy of the Wappinger Historical Society.)